£1.00

The Cairn Terrier

POPULAR DOGS' BREED SERIES

BASSET HOUND	*George Johnston*
BEAGLE	*Thelma Gray*
BOXER	*Elizabeth Somerfield*
CAIRN TERRIER	*J.W.H. Beynon, Alex Fisher, Peggy Wilson and Doreen Proudlock*
CAVALIER KING CHARLES SPANIEL	*Mary Forwood*
CHIHUAHUA	*Thelma Gray*
COCKER SPANIEL	*Veronica Lucas-Lucas*
COLLIE	*Margaret Osborne and Aileen Speding*
DACHSHUND	*E. Fitch Daglish, Amyas Biss and Jeff Crawford*
DALMATIAN	*Eleanor Frankling, Betty Clay and Marjorie Cooper*
DOBERMANN	*Fred Curnow and Jean Faulks*
FOX TERRIER	*Elsie Williams*
GERMAN SHEPHERD DOG	*J. Schwabacher, Thelma Gray and Madeleine Pickup*
GOLDEN RETRIEVER	*Joan Tudor*
GREAT DANE	*Jean Lanning*
IRISH SETTER	*Janice Roberts*
LABRADOR RETRIEVER	*Lorna, Countess Howe and Geoffrey Waring*
MONGREL	*Angela Patmore*
OLD ENGLISH SHEEPDOG	*Ann Davis*
POODLE	*Clara Bowring, Alida Monro and Shirley Walne*
PUG	*Susan Graham Weall*
ROTTWEILER	*Judy and Larry Elsden*
SCOTTISH TERRIER	*Dorothy Caspersz and Elizabeth Meyer*
SHETLAND SHEEPDOG	*Margaret Osborne*
SHIH TZU	*Audrey Dadds*
SPRINGER SPANIEL	*Dorothy Moorland Hooper and Ian B. Hampton*
STAFFORDSHIRE BULL TERRIER	*John F. Gordon*
WELSH CORGI	*Charles Lister-Kaye and Dickie Albin*
WEST HIGHLAND WHITE TERRIER	*D. Mary and Catherine Owen*
YORKSHIRE TERRIER	*Ethel and Vera Munday*

THE
CAIRN TERRIER

J. W. H. BEYNON
&
ALEX FISHER
M.B.E.

Revised by Peggy Wilson & Doreen Proudlock

POPULAR DOGS
London   Melbourne   Auckland   Johannesburg

Popular Dogs Publishing Co. Ltd

An imprint of Century Hutchinson Ltd

Brookmount House, 62–65 Chandos Place,
Covent Garden, London WC2N 4NW

Century Hutchinson Australia (Pty) Ltd
PO Box 496, 16–22 Church Street, Hawthorn, Melbourne,
Victoria 3122

Century Hutchinson New Zealand Limited
191 Archers Road, PO Box 40–086, Glenfield, Auckland 10

Century Hutchinson South Africa (Pty) Ltd
PO Box 337, Bergvlei 2012, South Africa

First published (as *The Popular Cairn Terrier*) 1929
Revised editions 1950, 1961
Revised editions (as *The Cairn Terrier*) 1969, 1974, 1977, 1988

Set in Baskerville by BookEns, Saffron Walden, Essex

Printed and bound in Great Britain by
Anchor Brendon Ltd, Tiptree, Essex

ISBN 0 09 158150 8

Dedicated to the pioneers of the breed, and particularly to the memory of Mrs Alastair Campbell, without whose early efforts it is not unlikely that the Cairn would have remained neglected outside his Highland home

CONTENTS

	Author's Introduction	12
	Revisers' Introductions	14
1	Origin and Early History	19
2	Cairn History since 1912	33
3	Breeding	50
4	Lines and Families	55
5	Influential Dogs	64
6	Starting a Kennel	79
7	The Brood Bitch and the Stud Dog	83
8	Feeding	98
9	General Management and Training	102
10	Accommodation	111
11	Preparation for Shows	114
12	Points and Character	120
13	Judging	136
14	Breed Clubs and the Kennel Club	141
15	Minor Illnesses	150
	Appendix A: Pedigree of Ch. Splinters of Twobees	154
	Appendix B: Champions	156
	Appendix C: Influential Stud Dogs and Brood Bitches	195
	Appendix D: American Breed Standard	199
	Addendum to Fourth Edition	201
	Addenda to Fifth and Sixth Editions	202
	Addendum to Seventh Edition	209
	Index	213

ILLUSTRATIONS

Between pages 48 and 49

Ch. Splinters of Twobees
Bred and owned by Miss Bengough and Mrs Butterworth

Ch. Brindie of Twobees
Bred by Mrs G. Vickers
Owned by Mrs I. V. Bengough

Wasp
Bred and owned by Mrs Alastair Campbell

Flora
Bred and owned by Mrs Alastair Campbell

Granite
Bred and owned by Mrs Alastair Campbell

Brocaire Raonuill
Bred and owned by Mrs Alastair Campbell

Mrs Alastair Campbell in 1909 with Macleod of Macleod, Roy Mhor and Doran Bhan

MacLeod of MacLeod
Bred and owned by Mrs Alastair Campbell

Ch. Brocaire Siteach
Bred and owned by Mrs Alastair Campbell

Ch. Brocaire Speireag
Bred by Hon. Mary Hawke
Owned by Mrs Alastair Campbell

Ch. Gesto and Ch. Brocaire Speireag
Gesto bred by M. McKinnon
Speireag bred by Hon. Mary Hawke
Owned by Mrs Alastair Campbell

Mrs Alastair Campbell in 1946

Roy Mhor
Bred and owned by Mrs Alastair Campbell

Ch. Fimor Katrine
Bred and owned by A. Fisher

Between pages 80 and 81

Ch. Lofthouse Larkspur
Bred and owned by Mrs H. L. Manley

Ch. Merrymeet Tathwell Therese
Bred by Mrs Hawdon
Owned by Mrs Leverton

Mrs Parker-Tucker

Ch. Uniquecottage Sir Frolic
Bred and owned by Mrs Parker-Tucker

Ch. Uniquecottage Brer Fox
Bred and owned by Mrs Parker-Tucker

Uniquecottage Kurt
Bred and owned by Mrs Parker-Tucker

Miss C. H. Dixon

Ch. Ronaldshay of Rossarden
Bred and owned by Miss Dixon

Ch. Rossarden Eyecatcher
Bred and owned by Miss Dixon

Ch. Rossarden Drambuie
Bred and owned by Miss Dixon

Mrs Shuttleworth

Ch. Monary Saucy Kristina
Bred and owned by Mrs Shuttleworth

Ch. Monary Susanella
Bred and owned by Mrs Shuttleworth

Between pages 112 and 113

Madge and Dorothy Hall

Peggy Wilson

Ch. Felshott Bryany

Ch. Felshott Honey Dancer
Ch. Felshott Taste of Honey
Bred and owned by Madge and Dorothy Hall

Ch. Felshott Wine Taster
Bred and owned by Madge and Dorothy Hall

Mrs Diana Hamilton

Ch. Oudenarde Queen of Light
Bred and owned by Mrs Hamilton

Group of Oudenarde Cairns
Bred and owned by Mrs Hamilton

Mrs Drummond

Ch. Blencathra Sandpiper
Bred and owned by Mrs Drummond

Ch. Blencathra Milord and Blencathra Rudolph
Bred and owned by Mrs Drummond

Walter Bradshaw

Ch. Redletter Moonstruck
Bred and owned by Walter Bradshaw

Ch. Redletter McBryan
Bred and owned by Walter Bradshaw

Between pages 144 and 145

Mrs Hazel Small

Avenelhouse Golden Phesant
Bred and owned by Mrs Small

Ch. Avenelhouse Golden Oriole
Bred and owned by Mrs Small

Mrs Sally Ogle

Ch. Pinetop Priscilla
Bred and owned by Mrs Ogle

Ch. Pinetop Montana
Bred and owned by Mrs Ogle

Misses Chrissie Clark and Doris Howes

Ch. Robinson Crusoe of Courtrai
Bred and owned by Misses Clark and Howes

Ch. Courtrai John Julius
Bred and owned by Misses Clark and Howes

Mrs Bunty Proudlock

Seltirk Cairns
Bred and owned by Mrs Proudlock

Baby and Seltirk Cairn puppy

Seltirk Burnt Sugar
Bred and owned by Mrs Proudlock

IN THE TEXT

Figure

1	Whelping box	87
2	Correct type	130
3	Wrong type	130
4	A 'weed'	131
5	Correct front	132
6	Bad and weak front	132
7	Correct ears	132
8	Scottie ears	132
9	Bat ears	132
10	Correct tail	133
11	Gay tail	133
12	Hound tail	133
13	Good hindquarters	134
14	Incorrect hindquarters	134
14	Thin pad	134
16	Weak pastern	134
17	Correct foot	134
18	Feet and pads	135

AUTHOR'S INTRODUCTION TO THE
SECOND EDITION

This revised edition of *The Popular Cairn Terrier* does not differ materially from the first edition. The main facts and points remain the same and include a short history of the breed compiled from authentic records, to which Mr A. Fisher, M.B.E., has contributed much valuable information on the pedigrees and influence of some famous Cairn Terriers.

Some of my observations may not be in perfect accord with the views of many, but that divergence of opinion is bound to exist, as it is this difference of opinion and ideas which add zest and incentive to breeding and exhibiting.

It cannot for a moment be admitted that the Cairn Terrier has reached perfection. Although there is still a divergence of type it is not so marked as it was twenty years ago, and in fact the general standard now appearing at shows is higher than at that time. Progress has definitely been made, all in the right direction. Many of the faults prevalent in the earlier years have now become almost eradicated by careful and discriminate breeding.

The 'Scottie' type is still with us, winning one day, and the pure Cairn the next, sometimes under the same judge. Many of these dogs are good *Terriers*, but *not good Cairn Terriers*, and no stretch of imagination can make them so.

I have endeavoured in this book to illustrate the conflicting types and various prevalent faults as a guide to the novice and rising generation of breeders who will form the backbone of the Cairn Terrier exhibitors in the years to come, and to whom we must look to continue the splendid work which the pioneers of the Cairn Terrier commenced more than fifty years ago.

J. W. H. B.

Castleton
Rochdale
1950

AUTHOR'S INTRODUCTION TO THE THIRD EDITION

The first edition of *The Popular Cairn Terrier* was the sole labour of my old friend Mr J. W. H. Beynon who had very close associations with the pioneer Mrs Alastair Campbell. When he was preparing the second edition he approached me to supply pedigree details and these were presented in a manner which, I hope, proved interesting and informative to breeders but which, I am afraid, were somewhat heavy going to others.

When the present edition was contemplated Mr Beynon was again asked if he would undertake the work, but his advanced years compelled him to refuse and he was kind enough to nominate me as a fitting person to revise and rewrite his and our previous efforts.

There is little to be added to the general comments on the breed, made in the last introduction, though there are two points on which some modification may be made.

I have approached pedigrees and influences from an angle which, I hope, will make more interesting reading than did the details in the 1950 edition.

Condemnation of the 'Scottie' type (by this I mean resemblance to the modern Scottish Terrier) is not so much called for today as it was ten years ago, but there remains a tendency for some Cairns to carry heads too 'blocky' and heavy to be typical of the breed.

A.F.

New Malden
Surrey
1961

REVISER'S INTRODUCTION TO THE FOURTH EDITION

There have been few changes to the subject matter of the Third Edition except those due to the passage of time and the activities of the spirit with the scythe to which we must all fall victim sooner or later. Among the notables who are no longer with us are Lady Burton, Mrs Mirrlees, Miss Morgan, Mrs Payne Gallwey, Mrs Prichard, Miss Reoch, Mr Hunter, Mr Moyes and Lt-Col. Whitehead, all of whom contributed to the spread of the cult of the Cairn.

As for the Cairn itself it can safely be asserted that, so far as can be judged from the specimens which appear at shows, the quality is higher than it has ever been. The chief weakness lies in front action and this, I think, could be improved if the dogs had more steady exercise on hard roads on the lead.

While those of us who can throw our memories back for nearly half a century to recall some of the outstanding Cairns of early years must, in honesty, confess that excellent as they were they had an easier task than have their peers of today. Mouths are far better and while the weak front action of today is due, in my opinion, to slack muscles the same fault in the 1920s was due to wrong bone structure.

However, we can be thankful that there has been no deterioration of the character and personality which are, to my mind, the great attraction of the breed.

Details of Cairns which have achieved the title of champion during the years 1961 to 1968 will be found on pages 167 to 174. These are followed by an addendum dealing with these and with other notable Cairns of the period.

A.F.

Chislehurst
Kent
1969

REVISER'S INTRODUCTION TO THE
FIFTH EDITION

In May 1970 Mr Alex Fisher, M.B.E., handed over all his Cairn Terrier records to the Hon. Secretary of the Southern Cairn Terrier Club, with instructions that they were to be considered the joint property of the three clubs of the breed.

These records are completely comprehensive: every detail has been researched and recorded. The late Alex Fisher must have dedicated all his leisure hours to the breed, yet his knowledge and experience were such that he was able to condense into one volume all the relevant facts for practical everyday use by the successful breeder.

This is not a book merely to be read and half-remembered. It contains the answer to virtually any question likely to be asked about the Cairn Terrier, and is the true breeders' reference book for constant use.

With the aid of the Fisher records, this fifth edition has been revised to the end of 1973 by adding to Appendix B and introducing a new Appendix C which amplifies Chapters 4 and 5. Thus the original text has been disturbed as little as possible.

M.D.W.

Felshott,
Felton,
Northumberland
1974

REVISER'S INTRODUCTION TO THE SIXTH EDITION

It is, perhaps, an indication of the world-wide interest in the Cairn, and the acceptance of *The Cairn Terrier* as the authoritative work on the breed, that this sixth edition is necessary only three years after the fifth edition.

I think that it can be claimed that the unversal popularity of the Cairn has far exceeded the wildest dreams of the founders of the breed. That being so, I would suggest that now, more than ever before, Chapters 12 and 13 assume an ever greater importance. Provided that Mr Fisher's classic interpretation of the Standard is understood and accepted by breeders, exhibitors and judges in every part of the world, then the essential true type and character of the Cairn will be safe.

For this sixth edition I have updated Appendices B and C to the end of 1976, and added a further Addendum which traces the current trends. The main text remains undisturbed except for amendments to indicate the new Kennel Club procedures, and changes relating to Cairn Clubs.

M.D.W.

Felshott,
Felton,
Northumberland
1977

REVISER'S INTRODUCTION TO THE
SEVENTH EDITION

The chapters on the origin and early history, Cairn history since 1912, breeding, lines and families, influential dogs and preparation for a show were written by Mr Beynon and later revised in collaboration with Mr Fisher who added to the chapters on lines and families and influential dogs in the third and fourth editions; these chapters are sacrosanct.

The chapters on starting a kennel, brood bitch and the stud dog, feeding, general management and training and accommodation had not been revised since the early editions, and had become very out of date. The Publishers' have permitted me to revise them and I have endeavoured in these chapters to give practical guidelines which I hope will prove helpful to the novice breeder. The remaining chapters have been amended. Appendices A, B, C are updated to December 1986.

We are indeed lucky in having Mrs Ruth Wadman Taylor who is not only a Cairn breeder with the Ascand prefix, but also a championship show judge of Cairns and a veterinary surgeon. The chapter on minor ailments had become almost archaic and so Mrs Wadman Taylor has re-written this chapter giving sound practical advice which all breeders will find helpful.

In the addendum I have given information on the new families and Cairn achievements during the past ten years. It has also been my privilege to pay tribute to the late Peggy Wilson who previously revised this book, to Mrs Mabel Drummond with her Blencathra strain, Walter Bradshaw and his famous Redletter Cairns, Mrs Diana Hamilton with her well known Oudenardes, Madge Hall of the Felshotts, Mrs Bessie Shea and Alick Hogg.

Doreen (Bunty) Proudlock

Edinburgh
1987

1

Origin and Early History

Writing in the second edition of *The Popular Cairn Terrier* John Beynon penned these words:

No one yet has succeeded in discovering where the first Cairn Terrier had its being. I commence just as far back as I can find a fair record, but it is an indisputable fact that the Cairn Terrier is one of the oldest, if not the oldest, pure British Terrier. It is perhaps open to argument as to whether the first Cairn or Skye Terriers, as they were called in the dim and distant past, came from the mainland of Scotland or from the Isle of Skye and Western Hebrides. From all records I have searched I am inclined to the belief that the original stock hailed from the 'Misty Isle'.

Way back in the sixteenth century there are records by old historians of the 'Earth dogs' from Argyllshire. Turberville and Dr Caius in their writings refer to the Terriers of the North as early as the Elizabethan days, and John Leslie, another writer, makes note of 'a small breed of Terriers used for hunting foxes and badgers in Scotland' a century earlier. Of course this is no conclusive proof that these Terriers were Cairns, but it leaves little room for doubt that they were the progenitors of the present-day Cairns just as it is an indisputable fact that the modern Scottish Terrier has been evolved from the older Cairn.

(It can be interpolated here that there is evidence that towards the end of his reign James the Sixth of Scotland and First of England sent instructions to Edinburgh for half a dozen 'earth dogs or terrieres' to be sent carefully to France as a present, and he directed that they were to be obtained from Argyll, and sent over on two or more ships lest they should come to harm on the way. As James died in 1625 this would seem to indicate that small dogs of a terrier variety were to be found in the west of Scotland over 300 years ago, and that they were considered sufficiently useful to be exported as presents.)

Mr Beynon went on:

We do not want for proof that in those ancient days every chieftain had his pack of hounds and terriers, the latter being used to bolt the foxes, badgers, and smaller fur-bearing vermin which abounded in the Highland fastnesses to a much greater extent than in these days. It is also evident that some of these chiefs took more than a passing interest in their terriers, for several of the old Scottish families have records of the dogs owned by their ancestors going back 200 years, and of these the best known is that of the Macdonalds of Waternish, and the Drynoch strains of the MacLeods, both in the Island of Skye. In the former kennel the favoured colours were dark greys and brindles, and in the latter silver greys predominated.

Another Skye kennel which also played no unimportant part was that of Mackinnon of Kilbride, where the colours varied through all shades from cream to nearly black. It is practically on these three strains that the modern Show Cairn Terrier has been founded. I do not mean to infer that the Cairn Terrier was at this period confined to the Island of Skye, for there were other kennels in Argyllshire, Ross-shire, and so far north as Cape Wrath, also in the Island of Mull and in Harris.

As far as I can learn, the oldest known strain of Cairns is that founded by the late Captain MacLeod of Drynoch, Isle of Skye, which goes back well over 150 years. Mr John MacDonald, who for over forty years was gamekeeper to the MacLeod of MacLeod, Denvegan Castle, kept this strain alive for over seventy years, and I think it can safely be said that the principal present-day strains and winners are largely descended from this and the old Waternish Cairns of the Macdonalds and Nicholsons.

Supporting Mr Beynon's references to early kennels in the Island of Skye there exists a copy of a somewhat acrimonious letter from A. Macdonald of Waternish, addressed to Mr Porritt, then Secretary of the Skye Terrier Club, during the discussions which followed Crufts show of 1910. It is not proposed to quote any of the more scathing remarks about another breed but the following extracts are of interest in relation to the history of the Cairn. Mr Macdonald describes himself as:

a breeder of the Original Short-haired Skye Terriers whose breed has been in my family for upwards of eighty years to my own knowledge, and kept entirely for sporting purposes. These terriers were bred for their sporting instincts and gameness regardless of looks.

My late uncle, Captain Macdonald of Waternish, who was born in Skye in 1823, took more interest in, and knew more about, the terriers of his native Island than anyone living. And he maintained that the short-haired breed was the purest and real Skye Terrier . . . .

Either in the 'sixties or early 'seventies Captain Macdonald was asked to exhibit some of his Terriers at a Dog Show at Inverness; he did so, but was so disgusted at the judges awarding the prize to a Long-haired Terrier (which he described as a white-wash brush) that he ever afterwards refused to exhibit his Terriers. One of the Waternish Terriers shown at Inverness was one of the best of working Skyes. This dog was upwards of twenty years of age, if not more, when his existence was put an end to thirty years ago . . . . When at the Inverness Show the Captain was asked if he would sell this Terrier he replied that money couldn't buy him.

If you or those interested in the matter want further proof of these Terriers in the past, I can procure photos taken upwards of 50 years ago of the Captain and his pack of Terriers in my Grandfather's time.

Another keen sportsman in Skye was Captain Martin MacLeod (of the Drynoch family) who emigrated to Canada in 1845. He was also an enthusiastic otter hunter and kept a fine pack of silver grey short-haired Skye Terriers. He and his terriers are still well remembered by an old man living here whose father used to go about with Captain MacLeod hunting otters.

Another kennel of good short-haired Skyes was that belonging to the Mackinnons of Kilbride. These Terriers were descended from an old breed owned by one Farquhar Kelly who lived in Drumfearn, Skye, in the seventeenth century.

The terriers of these other kennels in Skye were related. Mrs Campbell's Terriers I believe are descended from the Drynoch breed.

Though this letter is undated, it is obvious that it was written early in 1910 and thus indicates that the Short-haired Skye Terrier now known as the Cairn Terrier was well known in the Island of Skye over 100 years ago.

None of the passing references to these early canine inhabitants of the wilds of Scotland contains a satisfactory description, but later references, when linked up with the earlier ones, seem to justify the conclusion that from these animals are descended the three main Scottish breeds, of which, at the moment, the Cairn is, at least from the show point of view, the most popular.

While there are supporters of all three breeds who will assert that theirs is the pure article, there is little doubt that if it were possible to make a complete investigation into their antecedents none would emerge like Caesar's wife.

The date of the emergence of the terriers of Scotland, except the Dandie Dinmont and the Skye, is clearly fixed by Mr D. J. Thomson Gray (he is most frequently referred to as 'Whinstone') of Dundee, who in *The Dogs of Scotland* (published 1891) stated:

Before 1874, therefore, we have no authoritative particulars regarding any of the terriers of Scotland, except the Dandie Dinmont and the Skye, and for ten years previous to this date classes were given at our shows for those two breeds alone.

Later in the same book Mr Thomson Gray wrote:

Previous to 1879 the type of terrier now recognized as the Scotch Terrier was comparatively unknown. This is not surprising when we recollect that they were in the hands of sportsmen, foxhunters, gamekeepers and crofters living in the remote parts of the Highlands and Islands of Scotland, far removed from the influence of dog shows, and having little communication with the world.

To the initiated the whole matter was clear. The dog which the Scottish writers were trying to get established as the Scottish Terrier was the Highland or Cairn Terrier, known in some parts as the short-haired Skye. For years previous to the commencement of the dispute we had these terriers from Mr McDonald, Dunvegan, Skye, and formed a high opinion of them.

Again he stated:

The Terrier we now recognize as the Scottish Terrier is the Hard-haired Highland or Cairn Terrier, known in Skye as the pure Skye Terrier.

Referring to a show held at Dundee the same author wrote:

In 1879 the committee of the Dundee show, on our recommen-
dation, gave a class for these ('hard-haired Scotch Terriers') which
was won by a dog belonging to Mr P. C. Thomson, Milncraig,
Glenisla. This dog we brought from the Island of Skye some years
previous, and it was termed there a 'real, pure, unadulterated
Skye Terrier'.

We are fortunately in a position to get a fairly clear idea of
the type of Scottish Terrier being shown at that time by quoting an extract from *The Complete Book of the Dog* by Mr Robert
Leighton, published by Cassell & Co. in 1922. In his article on
Scottish Terriers the author wrote:

I remember many years ago visiting the late Sir Paynton Pigott at
his home in Norwich. In the course of a conversation about dogs,
my host produced for my examination the well-mounted head and
neck of his long dead terrier, Granite. The dog's coat was light brindle,
the shape of the head was foxy, with a fine short muzzle, tiny prick
ears, and a rather small skull. I identified Granite as a Cairn Terrier.
Sir Paynton acquiesced; but proceeded to inform me that in actuality
Granite had the distinction of being the first 'Scottish Terrier' ever
entered in a Kennel Club show. He was the individual forerunner of
the modern Scottish Terrier and lineal ancestor of Ch. Heyworth
Rascal . . . and yet Sir Paynton Pigott explained that the dog's
pedigree went back to a strain of Highland Cairn Terriers bred in the
neighbourhood of Dunvegan, in the Isle of Skye. I believe it was in
the year 1878 that Granite was first exhibited in a variety class.

An illustration of Granite appears between pages 48 and
49.

Another view of the former situation was expressed by
Baillie Flett in the introductory remarks to his report on the
breed at a show which he judged in 1928. He wrote:

In East Aberdeenshire quite a great number of Cairns were to be
seen and my father bred them in the 60's, but they were then known
as Scotch Terriers, and in 1876 to 1883 I possessed one which was
the mascot of our local cricket team. He was a light brindle with the
true Cairn head, great jaw power, dense hard coat, good bone with
beautiful small ears and dark eye, and weighed 14 lb. There were
quite a number in Aberdeenshire, and they undoubtedly were the
origin of the present-day Scottish Terrier; Roger Rough, Bon
Accord, and Splinter II, undoubtedly hailing from Aberdeen, these
being crossed with terriers from the West of Scotland, a much bigger

and longer dog, lower in leg and with big round-pointed ears, but the Aberdeenshire Terriers had sharp-pointed small ears and bred true to type, and were very similar to the best of our present show Cairns, but with harsher and denser coats.

Baillie Flett's reference to the position in the east of Scotland in the early days is supported by the writings of a terrier enthusiast of my native county. Many years ago he wrote:

Early in the 'fifties I was initiated into the love of a Scotch Terrier Dog – I mean the old-fashioned 'sandy'. These terriers were all small – say about twelve pounds. They were principally of a wheaten or sandy colour, of the smartest possible contour. Several were not 'hard-haired', but that was of minor importance when rodent killing was their special purpose.

While my memories of the canine inhabitants of the County of 'Kingdom' of Fife do not reach back as far as the 'fifties of last century I can recall, during the 'nineties, many small terriers of a wide range of colours which were variously called just 'terrier', 'Scotch Terrier', 'rough terrier', and 'broken-haired terrier', some of which ran about with little attention from their owners.

The close approximation of the measurements of the early representatives of the Short-haired Skye and Scottish Terriers to those of the modern Cairn may be appreciated by a perusal of the table on page 140. After making all due allowance for different methods of measurement there can be little doubt that the Scottish Terrier of early show days bore a striking resemblance to the Cairn of today.

While the relationship of the Scottish Terrier to the common ancestors of all three of the main Scottish breeds may be, to a great extent, inferential, there can be no doubt about the very close association of the West Highland White Terrier. There has always been a strain of very light-coloured dogs running through both Cairns and Scottish Terriers and, no doubt, these light-coloured terriers appealed to the Malcolms of Poltalloch who concentrated on such colours and finally evolved the Poltalloch Terrier now known as the West Highland White Terrier. The consanguinity of the Cairn and the West Highlander was not only accepted by the Kennel

Club but, in the early days, interbreeding was encouraged by the ruling body.

Early in 1916 some of the owners and breeders of certain gundogs in which interbreeding was permitted petitioned the Kennel Club to take 'immediate and effective action to deal with the question to preserve, as far as possible, purity in the breeding of the several varieties of Retrievers'.

As a result of this petition Mr E. W. Jaquet, the then Secretary of the Kennel Club, addressed, to the secretaries of the clubs whose breeds were involved in interbreeding, a circular asking them 'to obtain the views of your club on this matter as it affects the breed in which it is interested, and to transmit it to my Committee'.

The circular letter went on:

The Committee think it advisable to point out the reason why the Kennel Club originally recognized that the interbreeding of different varieties of certain breeds should be allowed and sanctioned by their Regulations.

In 1905, representations were made to my Committee that to pre-vent the evil consequence of inbreeding – such as loss of fecundity and immunity from or resistance to disease – in certain breeds which had then become apparent, it was necessary that fresh blood should be introduced, and after the matter had been very carefully gone into it was recognized that for the good of the said breeds, some such legislation was necessary. It was also well known that in many breeds interbreeding of their several varieties was already resorted to, and it was decided that it would be better that this should appear on the Register form than that such facts should be suppressed. As you are no doubt aware, the following interbreeding was allowed . . .

There follows a list of thirteen groups of associated breeds of which the only one of interest to supporters of Cairns was:

| Highland Terriers | West Highland White Terriers
Cairn Terriers |

The letter then went on to invite the views of any club or per-son who might think that the time had come for some modification.

As the interbreeding of the two breeds was carried on until the end of 1924 it is to be assumed that the clubs were in favour of its continuance.

By the kindness of Mr C. A. Binney, Secretary of the Kennel Club, the catalogues of Crufts and the Kennel Club's shows during the years of the emergence of the Cairn have been examined; particulars extracted from these catalogues are given in pages 146, 147 and 148.

Having disposed of certain aspects of the early history we are now able to turn our attention to what might be termed the officially recorded story of the breed.

While there were frequent references to Short-coated Skye Terriers, and while entries at shows were made under that name, the early registrations were listed by the Kennel Club in the *Kennel Gazette* under Prick-eared Skye Terriers, that breed being, in the early years of this century, treated as having two varieties.

The first entry recognizable as a Cairn is that of Calla-mhor which appears in the June 1907 issue of the *Kennel Gazette*, the details being: 'Calla-mhor, b, Mrs I. A. Campbell's by Mr N. Nicholson's Fearg – his Speraig, April '94.' (The year is obviously a mistake for 1904.) In the same issue appears the notification of the registration of Cuillean Bhan, also in the name of Mrs Campbell, out of the same bitch but sired by Mr Harris's Brassy and born in March 1905. The only other registration in 1907 is that of Roy Mhor, which appears in the November issue in the name of Mrs Campbell and of which she is given as the owner of both sire and dam, Morghan and Calla-mhor respectively. In 1908 there were but two registrations, both in the name of the lady who can justly be described as the founder of the breed as an exhibition animal – Mrs Alastair Campbell. In 1909 the number of registrations rose to fourteen and there appeared the names of two animals which, in their different ways, are worthy of note. The first is that of Bruin, the first Cairn registered in the name of the Hon. M. C. Hawke, who was the sister of the famous cricketer Lord Hawke. The interest in Bruin lies in the fact that in him we have the most remote, in age, of all terriers accepted as Cairns, his birth being given as in October 1897. The fact that Bruin was not registered until 1909 might raise doubts as to the correct date of birth were it not that there exist illustrations which confirm the point. The second name of interest is that of Aberdeen Beauty, whose particulars are contained in the far from illuminating phrase: 'pedigree and date of birth unknown'; this statement, in itself, was not unusual at that early date but it would seem that there existed, at about the same time, a Scottish Terrier of the same name whose dam was Aberdeen Lassie and who is shown to be a member of Scottish Terrier Family No. I stemming from Splinter II.

In the June 1910 issue of the *Kennel Gazette* Cairn registrations were removed from those of Prick-eared Skye Terriers and appeared under the heading 'Any other breed or variety'. During this year 35 were registered.

The breed was given a separate register in 1912, during which year 134 were registered; in this year, also, championship status was granted, the first certificates being on offer at the Richmond show when Mrs Alastair Campbell judged.

However, the path of the Cairn to the exalted position of championship status had not been free from struggle and strife. Only as a matter of interest need we, at this late date, refer to the argument of the late 1870s on the question of Long- and Short-coated Skyes, except to reproduce, between pages 48 and 49, a drawing of Flora quoted as belonging to the working type of Skye; Flora's measurements are given in the table of comparative measurements on page 140.

The use of the phrase 'Short-coated Skyes', in relation to Cairns in the early years, soon led to objections by the owners and exhibitors of Skye Terriers. The story of the Cairn's first appearance at Crufts can best be told in the words of the judge – Mr Robert Leighton – as set out by him in *The Complete Book of the Dog* published in 1922. He wrote:

In the spring of 1909 at Crufts show I happened to be appointed judge of Skye Terriers. I had got through my work, as I thought, when I discovered that there were additional classes to be judged under the unrecognized breed name of 'Short-haired Skyes'. The ring stewards and one or two exhibitors objected to my paying any attention to these unfamiliar dogs, on the plea that there was no such breed, and that 'mongrels' ought not to have been admitted to the show. But, as the numbers were entered in my judging book, I, of course, resolved to do my duty.

A goodly team was emptied into the ring – lively, energetic little animals, superficially different one from another, but having a general similarity in type, which stamped them as a distinct and genuine breed. Happily – fortunately – I was not a stranger to such dogs. I had known and even possessed terriers such as these in my boyhood in Argyll, and I recognized them at once as the original, unspoiled working terriers of the Highlands.

I learned, afterwards, that their guardian was Mrs Alastair Campbell, who had brought them all the way from Ardrishaig, on Loch Fyne; and that the terriers to whom I had awarded first, second, and third prizes were named Doran Bhan (a light-red dog with dark muzzle and ears), Roy Mhor (a red brindle), and Cuilean Bhan (wheaten with black points). I have no record of the others, but these three chosen ones became famous. But the ring stewards were vexed.

In 1910 Mrs Campbell had entered Doran Bhan, Roy Mhor, and McLeod of McLeod, and Miss Hawke had entered Bride in the Skye Terrier classes. The consequences can best be set out by repeating the statement kindly supplied by the Kennel Club.

Although there were two classes scheduled for 'Cairn or Short-haired Terriers' at Crufts in 1910, Mrs Campbell and Miss Hawke entered their dogs in the Skye Terrier classes. Miss A. K. Clifton, the judge, in her report on the Skye Terrier classes said: 'By an unfortunate mistake a breed now generally known as Cairn Terriers was entered in these classes, and as I was judging by the Skye and Clydesdale Terrier Club Standard, and failed to find one point in these dogs that in any way approached the Club's description of the Skye Terrier, I could take no other course than to mark them "Wrong Class".' As a result of the action of these pioneers the Skye Terrier Club sent a deputation to the Committee of the Kennel Club on 6 April, 1910, and the following is an extract from the *Kennel Gazette*:

The Committee considered the question of the registration of Skye Terriers.
The Secretary stated that at their last meeting a letter was read

from Sir Claud Alexander in which he asked the Committee to receive a deputation upon the subject under discussion.

On the 12 March, he (the Secretary) received the following letter and enclosure from her Excellency the Countess of Aberdeen:

> Vice Regal Lodge,
> Dublin.
> 11 March, 1910

Dear Mr Jaquet, – With reference to the question of the short-haired Skyes about which we have corresponded, I beg to forward copy of a letter which I am sending to Mr Porritt to be read at the annual meeting of the Skye Terrier Club of England.

I hope that it may be possible to hold such a conference as I have suggested, and I would like to know whether the term Cairn Terriers of Skye might not be a solution.

> Believe me,
> Yours sincerely,
> ISHBEL ABERDEEN

(Copy)

> 11 March, 1910

Dear Sir – I have to thank you for your letter of the 9th with Agenda for Annual General Meeting.

I beg to convey my best thanks to the members of the Skye Terrier Club of England for their kindness in re-electing me as president. I am not sure, however, that I should have accepted this nomination, as probably my views regarding the little short-haired terriers from Skye are divergent from those of the majority of the club. If this proves to be the case, I trust that the club will allow me to resign in order that they may elect a president who would more truly represent their views.

As, however, you ask me to give an expression of my own opinion on the subject to lay before the meeting on the 16th, I would like to say that I think some sort of conference should be held between the representatives of the Skye Terrier Clubs of England and Scotland with those who represent the small breed, which it is now desired to register under a definite name. It is clear that both breeds have been recognized for many years in Skye, and that both therefore have a right to have the word 'Skye' included in their official designation. It is however also a fact that for many years the Skye Terrier has been recognized by the Kennel Club and by dog fanciers as meaning the long-bodied and long-haired dog; and I personally think that the term, 'Short-haired Skye', would create confusion, as people would look for a long-bodied dog with short hair.

On the other hand, it seems to me that the members of the Skye Terrier Clubs should not dispute the right of the smaller breed to indicate the place of their origin. I would therefore advocate the adoption of some such name as 'Cairn Skye Terrier' or 'Cairn Terriers of Skye'.

I trust that some such conference may be held as I have ventured to suggest.

I remain,
Yours very faithfully
ISHBEL ABERDEEN

James Porritt, Esq.

The following gentlemen formed the deputation:

Sir Claud Alexander, Bart. Mr Robert Leighton, Mr James Porritt, and Mr E. R. Sandwith.

Sir Claud Alexander, in introducing the deputation, informed the Committee that Skye Terrier breeders and exhibitors were much perturbed at the introduction to shows of so-called 'Short-haired Skyes'. These dogs differed materially from the accepted type of Skye Terrier, but they were accepted for registration in the Skye Terrier Register.

Sir Claud further informed the Committee that it had been suggested by an exhibitor of the so-called 'Short-haired Skyes' that they should be called Cairn Terriers, and with that suggestion the deputation was entirely in accord.

After some further discussion and inspection of photographs the deputation retired.

The Committee decided:

That the breed (hitherto described as 'Short-haired Skye Terriers') shall only be registered as Cairn Terriers in the register for British, Colonial, and Foreign Dogs, which have no separate classification on the register.

It was further decided that Cairn Terriers already registered as Skye Terriers will be transferred to the new register free of cost until 1 July, 1910.

In 1911 four classes were scheduled and drew an average entry of eight, with Mr Ferrier of Dundee judging; in the following year Mr G. J. Ross judged the six classes which had a total entry of 44, and in 1914, with challenge certificates for the first time at Crufts, Mr R. Leighton again judged an entry of 64 in seven classes with Gesto and Tighru Fiona winning the certificates.

The Kennel Club show did not schedule the breed until after championship status had been granted. In October 1912 Miss Hawke judged the 48 entries in the six classes with Gesto and Tibbie of Harris winning the certificates; in 1913 Mr C. McNeill was the judge of the seven classes with 66 entries, the certificate winners being Firring Frolic and Sheila of Harris.

At a meeting of the Committee held 29 May, 1912, Cairn Terriers were given a separate register.

After 1912 the increasing popularity of the breed is reflected in the steady rise in the number of registrations which continued until early in 1917 when the Kennel Club ceased to license shows as a contribution to the war effort. That club also decreed that no dog would be registered for competition unless it was the progeny of certain parents in respect of which, in the interest of later breeding, special breeding licences were issued.

There were but four championship shows in the years 1917, 1918, and 1919 (two in 1917 and two in 1919), but in 1920 shows were back to normal, and the Cairn continued to make progress to the position he holds today as the most popular of all terriers, not only on the show bench but in the eyes of the general public.

During 1924, there arose a clash of opinions when the Kennel Club in this country decided to follow the example of the American Kennel Club and cease to accept for registration the progeny of Cairn and West Highland White Terrier crosses. Earlier, white pups of such a mating had been accepted as West Highland Terriers, while darker members of the same litter were accepted as Cairns.

There was considerable correspondence in the papers devoted to canine affairs but, unlike much earlier correspondence on doggy affairs, it was conducted with restraint. Some of the correspondents were for the suggested new ruling and some were strongly against it. Indeed, it ended in an application being addressed to the Kennel Club that the existing conditions be continued; this application was considered by the Committee at a meeting held on 18 November, 1924, when the following resolution was passed: 'The Committee considered the question of interbreeding between Cairn Terriers and West Highland White Terriers, and decided that the application be refused.'

The registration of the progeny of such interbreeding ceased as from 31 December, 1924.

No doubt there are still some diehards who regret the ruling but, whatever could be said for such interbreeding in the early days, there is little to be said for it today when the types of the two terriers are so divergent, and its revival would do a great deal of damage to both breeds.

There was no further disturbance in the steady advance of the Cairn until the outbreak of war in 1939, during which the breed, in common with all others, declined in quality but from which it has now recovered, until it would be true to assert that at no previous date in its show history has the average quality of the Cairn been higher than it is today.

2

Cairn History Since 1912

However great may be the appeal of any breed to the general public, its progress lies mainly in the hands of the enthusiasts who, either as a hobby or as a profession, breed and exhibit the dogs. The influence of any breeder or kennel will, of course, depend on the extent of the breeder's activities and the number and quality of the inmates of the kennel.

After both world wars there was a great increase in the interest taken in well-bred dogs, but whereas, after 1919, a number of very large kennels developed, since 1946 development, even in the larger kennels, has been on a smaller scale.

The earliest of the prominent kennels, the Firring kennel, is dealt with in another place (*see* pages 65 and 66).

In those early days Mr Simon MacLeod was breeding Cairns of more than ordinary merit whose place of birth was indicated by their names: Ch. Skye Crofter and Skye Cottar. Also, there was Maid of the Mist, while, a year or so later, he owned Glasein for a short time. Residing in Skye at a time when transport was not too easy, Mr McLeod had little chance of attending shows but Crofter, Maid of the Mist, and Glasein each won two certificates while in his hands.

The Harris kennel, owned by Lady Sophie Scott, had the honour of housing the first Cairn champion, Ch. Tibbie of Harris, which won her third certificate on 23 January, 1913, after having won the same award at the two previous championship shows; Tibbie won six certificates in all. She and her full sister (later litter), Ch. Maisie of Harris, had a pedigree of extreme brevity, the sire being 'pedigree unknown' and the dam unregistered. Of the first nine champions of the breed four carried the Harris affix, and all reports indicate that the inmates of the kennel were good specimens, but they are now of no more than historical interest as their influence has long ceased.

Another early starter in the Cairn world was the kennel of the Hon. Miss M. Hawke, who can be said to hold for England the same pioneering position that Mrs Campbell did for Great Britain. Miss Hawke never lost her interest in the breed, but her kennel made no great impression till towards the end of her life. This lack of influence may have been due to the fact that she was little interested in Cairns of any colour other than light red, and her obsession for this colour sometimes blinded her to faults.

In 1935 she bred two dogs, both sired by Ch. Splinters of Twobees but from different dams; one was light red and was retained in the home kennel to become Ch. Lockyers Ian, the winner of eight challenge certificates; the other was grey and was sold to Mrs Fleming, to become Ch. Silver Hawk Out of the West, the winner of fifteen certificates.

To many present-day devotees of the Cairn, the prefix Mercia may lead them to think that the late Miss Viccars's interest in the breed does not date back very far, and it may surprise them to learn that it goes back to 1913 when, in partnership with Colonel Young, she became the owner of Skye Crofter, already the winner of two challenge certificates, and soon increased to the necessary qualifying three. Further comment will be limited to that period when the prefix was carried by dogs in the sole ownership of Miss Viccars; eleven of them won certificates and three – Ch. Rogue of Mercia, Ch. Miss Rogue of Mercia, and Ch. Nuzzle of Mercia – became champions. The predominating influences were Hyver, Harviestoun, Carngowan, and Frimley, and the general result was an effective association of head and body properties characterizing the true Cairn.

In the 1930s Miss Viccars, Miss Crossman (later Mrs Rudland), and Miss Ward formed a triumvirate, which showed as a partnership as well as individually.

In earlier times Miss Viccars had a strong kennel of West Highland White Terriers under the prefix Childwick. She was one of the strongest opponents of the Kennel Club's decision of 1924 that interbreeding of Cairns and West Highlanders should cease.

Major Ewing, the owner of the prefix Nisbet, though unknown to the majority of present-day supporters of the breed, had at one time a considerable kennel. He registered his first Cairn in 1912, and therefore can, with Mr Donald Hunter of Oban, be described as one of the very few remaining representatives of the early pioneers. Unlike many of the early kennels, there was a complete absence of West Highland blood in his Cairns. It is many years since any product of the kennel appeared in the show ring. Major Ewing was, for a number of years, Hon. Secretary of the Cairn Terrier Club.

The Ardsheal kennel of Mr Donald Hunter, the only other male pre-1914 supporter of the breed, was at a disadvantage owing to its geographical siting, for at that time transport was very different from what it is today. However, despite this handicap, his Cairns had much influence in the period prior to 1939, when the owner was frequently seen in the ring both as exhibitor and judge.

The Cloughton kennel of Miss Lockwood, another of the early enthusiasts, is noteworthy as that in which Cloughton Kyle first saw the light of day. Later Kyle was acquired by Mrs Fleming and as Kyley Out of the West was the dam of many of the outstanding inmates of the Out of the West kennel. From the show point of view Ch. Cloughton Drumochter, Cloughton Bunty, and her daughter Cloughton Lorna (which both won certificates) were the most prominent members. The influence of the kennel has long since ceased.

Miss Lockwood was a well-known animal artist who specialized in the portrayal of horses.

Any kennel which won its first certificate in 1914 and its last (to date) in 1958 must be credited with having had more than a little influence on the breed. These dates include the long history of the Dochfour kennel owned by the Baroness Burton. The first champion was Rona, a daughter of Firring Fling, which takes us right back to the earliest championship-show days.

The kennel has, through the years, housed 21 certificate

winners (one, bearing the prefix, won a certificate after leaving the kennel), of which eleven became champions.

Three Cairns, Castlehill Tang, Ch. Rona, and Ch. Ross-shire Warrior, were the three certificate winners which did not carry the kennel prefix.

Of the eleven champions that have been housed in the kennel, perhaps the two most notable were Ch. Dochfour Vennach and her daughter Ch. Dochfour Vuiach Vorchad which, between 1922 and 1926, won twenty-one challenge certificates, the former winning ten and the latter eleven. When they were alive there was considerable difference of opinion as to which was the better, and it is possible that today there would be the same divided opinion. On one point, however, there could be no discussion: their ability to hold their own against present-day Cairns.

The great desire of the owner of the kennel had been to maintain and continue the 'Brocaire' type, and of the four champions which have reached that rank since 1946 three carry a goodly proportion of Brocaire influence.

The only time a member of the British Royal Family ever showed a Cairn was at the Caledonian Canine Society's championship show of 1 January, 1924, when the Prince of Wales (later Duke of Windsor) entered Dochfour Molly, which won the reserve bitch certificate.

In addition to her various activities in the Ladies' Kennel Association, Lady Burton was for many years President of the Cairn Terrier Club.

The Inverness kennel of Mr Charles Thompson, while of considerable size, has never exercised any great influence; only one inmate, Inverness Doran, reached any prominence; he won two challenge certificates in 1916. Another, Inverness Glenorlie, won a certificate in 1924, but by that time it was not owned by Mr Thompson and only remotely was it of Inverness blood.

Like many of the early breeders, Mr Thompson owned both Cairns and West Highland White Terriers, and there was evidence of considerable interbreeding, the results of which contributed to Cairns bearing the Glenmhor and Harviestoun prefixes.

It was this kennel that supplied the basis from which the very potent Family No. 59 is descended.

Although the word 'Eyes' was not registered as a prefix or affix, it was by no means inappropriate for the breed, and Mr Caspersz used it more or less as such, qualifying it with 'Charming', 'Wistful', 'Mystic', and 'Laughing'.

Mr Caspersz's interest in the breed was first stirred when, while serving in the Navy in the First World War, he was stationed on the west coast of Scotland. His first champion was Laughing Eyes, which won its title in 1922; she was a descendant of Ch. Gesto, Cairn Reich, and Ch. Skye Crofter, as well as others of the early stalwarts. Other prominent members of the kennel were Turfield Smiling Eyes (one certificate) and Ch. Turfield Mystic Eyes, the former the pup and the latter a tail female descendant of Ch. Laughing Eyes.

Mr Caspersz was the first Hon. Secretary of the Cairn Terrier Association and, with Mrs Caspersz, analysed early Cairn pedigrees and applied the Bruce Lowe line and family system to them.

The Knipton kennel of Mrs Payne Gallwey had been in the show ring for a long time. For a brief period the famous Ch. Gillie of Hyver bore the name of Knipton Gillie, but, on the whole, the kennel has been self-contained and was, perhaps, at its height in the late 1920s and early 1930s, when it held two champions, Knipton Bundle and Knipton Tibbie, and a certificate winner, Knipton Careless. Since 1946 the most prominent product has been Knipton Buntylow, the winner of two certificates: she was a great-grand-daughter of Ch. Knipton Tibbie. The main influences in the kennel have been Harviestoun and Hyver, a mixture which has proved successful elsewhere.

Although Mrs Prichard was better known to the majority of the breed supporters as the late Hon. Secretary and Hon. President of the Southern Cairn Terrier Club, there was a time when her prefix 'Donnington' figured frequently and successfully in the show ring.

Early in the 1920s Mrs Prichard acquired from Mr McLennan a pup named Carngowan Manus, which won its first certificate at ten months and went on to become a champion. It thus

follows that there was a good deal of the influence of the
Firring and Carngowan breeding in the early inmates. In
addition to Manus, the kennel has housed two home-bred
champions, Ch. Donnington Cheeky and Ch. Donnington
Badger, as well as five other certificate winners. The tragedy of
the kennel was Donnington Surprise, which won two
challenge certificates and no fewer than six reserve challenge
certificates, but did not win the coveted third certificate.

In addition to the influences already mentioned there had
been a judicious mixture of Harviestoun and Hyver blood in
the inmates of the kennel, few of which have been seen in the
ring in post-war years.

Mrs Prichard devoted much of her time to the affairs of the
club of which she was Hon. Secretary from 1932 until
1957.

The 'Ross-shire' kennel of Mrs Forbes was another of the
remote kennels whose activities were, no doubt, restricted by
its position. Like most of the very early breeders, Mrs Forbes
did a considerable amount of interbreeding between the two
then permitted breeds, there being little doubt that the dam of
the only champion bred there was a West Highlander. The
champion in question, Ch. Ross-shire Warrior, was a light
silver, and won his title in 1922. His sire, Ross-shire Glenara, a
dark-red brindle, won one certificate.

Another very light-coloured Cairn, bearing the name Ross-
shire Old Gold, had a great deal of influence in the Otford
Kennel of Mrs Saunders.

The Guynach kennel, owned by Lieutenant-Colonel
Whitehead, D.S.O., had, so far as the English Kennel Club
activities go, produced two champions. The first, Ch.
Guynach Eachunn, was bred by Mrs Whitehead while her
husband was serving in the Army, and the other, Ch.
Prestbury Silverfyord, was bred by the Colonel in 1925.
Eachunn had considerable influence in Ireland, where he was
at stud for some time.

Colonel Whitehead, except for a brief interval, had been in
control of the affairs of the Cairn Terrier Club since 1926.

The early inmates of the Frimley kennel owned by Mrs
Basset, like all other contemporary kennels, had quite an

admixture of West Highland Terrier blood. The prefix was borne by thirteen winners of challenge certificates, of which five became champions. The earliest certificate was won in 1916 and the last in 1934. The first champion of the kennel, Ch. Ian of Frimley, as well as four certificate winners of the early years, were all descendants of Ch. Firring Frolic. Of the four later champions, Ch. Lottie of Frimley, Ch. Lady Gay of Frimley, and Ch. McRob of Frimley were all derived from the same stock, but Ch. Callum of Frimley was mainly of Ross-shire extraction.

From the breeding point of view, perhaps, Offley Brimon, by Ch. Harviestoun Brigand out of Canna of Frimley, was the most impressive, as he sired many big winners though he was himself no great success on the show bench.

The great importance of Mrs Stephens's Hyver kennel is dealt with elsewhere (*see* pages 71 and 72), and here it is only necessary to remark that the inmates of the kennel were all good specimens of the breed, the uniform excellence of the head being very noticeable.

It is no exaggeration to assert that the main influence in the Gunthorpe kennel of Mrs Dixon was derived from Harviestoun blood. Mrs Dixon purchased Harviestoun Forgie, and his name, and those of Harviestoun Raider and Ch. Harviestoun Brigand, appear with great frequency in Gunthorpe pedigrees.

Between the wars the kennel was one of the largest in this country, and the affix was borne by seventeen certificate winners, of which fifteen were home-bred, and, of the seven champions, six were home-bred. In addition to Cairns bearing her affix, Mrs Dixon won certificates with Ch. Geum Woffington, which was also of pure Harviestoun breeding.

An examination of the pedigrees of all the better-known inmates of the kennel discloses how complete was the reliance on Harviestoun blood. In none of them do the names of Harviestoun Raider or Harviestoun Forgie lie very far back, and where they are a little more remote the nearer ancestry is all derived from these two.

Despite the relatively large number of its products the kennel had no great influence outside its own inmates. Although the inmates retained several of the qualities derived from their ancestors, there was a loss of leg-length and, in some, a heaviness of body which deprived them of the active appearance usually looked for in the breed.

While the influence in this country was limited, and is mostly in evidence in Family No. 17, there is little doubt that exports to the United States had considerable effect.

The now defunct Harviestoun kennel of Mr J. E. Kerr has been dealt with elsewhere (pages 75 and 76).

The Moccasin kennel of Mr Alex McKenzie of Inverness was another which at one time carried both Cairns and West Highlands, and the first Cairn inmates were a mixture of the blood of both breeds. Although there was a fair number of inmates throughout the years, few reached the top level, and then not in the ownership of the breeder; this was no doubt due to distance, and the owner being engaged in his own private business. Chs. Moccasin Linda and Moccasin Betsy were the only two which achieved the title, and Moccasin Mercy won one certificate. In this kennel, also, the Harviestoun influence was much in evidence. Little was seen of the owner, or his dogs, in the show ring after 1939.

Mrs Mirrlees, the owner of the Shinnel prefix, continued her interest in the breed until the time of her death. The kennel first came into prominence in the early 1920's when Ch. Shinnel Simon started his successful career. In the following decade the inmates included four more certificate winners, of which the last to appear, Ch. Shinnel Wistful, was the only one to qualify for the title in this country, though one or two of the others may have reached that position abroad.

The main foundation was Out of the West, with which there was a judicious mixture of Harviestoun and Dochfour.

It is doubtful if any kennel ever started under more auspicious circumstances than did the Bogton, owned by Mr Moyes. Towards the end of 1923 Mr Moyes purchased from Mr Munro the bitch Minx of D'Ornum in whelp to Brogach Out of the West, one of the offspring of numerous Doughall Out of the West and Kyley Out of the West matings. One of the resulting pups was Ch. Bogton Brindie who won five certificates in all, and of which Lady Burton thought so highly that she awarded him three of them. Later the kennel was adorned by Ch. Bogton Balloch, Ch. Bogton Breda, and five others which, though they won one or two certificates, never attained the title. In consequence of its origin the kennel inmates always carried the influence of the Out of the West blood, though in the later members, Dochfour, Guynach, Ross-shire, Harviestoun, and Valiant were introduced.

The prefix Beechacre, of the kennel owned by Miss Irving, was carried by sixteen certificate winners, of which seven won the title of champion; in addition to those Cairns with her own prefix, Miss Irving also owned Ch. Glencairn Gillian and Glencairn Kirstie. The basis of the breeding was to a very great extent Harviestoun, though there were touches of Moccasin, Brocaire, and Dochfour blood, and in later members of the kennel the influence of Hyver and Donnington appears.

One of the Cairns bred in the kennel, Valiant Leaflet of Beechacre, was the youngest of the breed ever to win a challenge certificate; she was born on 20 October, 1938, and, having passed into the hand of Miss Reoch, won the certificate at the Great Joint Terrier show of 9 May, 1939, when Mrs Gardiner judged.

The inmates of the Beechacre kennel had all the physical properties of the Harviestouns, and while little fault could be found with the conformation of the head, the expression was not always so pleasing, the eyes being rather small and hard.

The Treblig prefix, originally in the name of Mr B. Gilbert, and later owned by Mrs Gilbert, came into prominence soon after the end of the First World War, and between then and the cessation of show activities in 1939 had a great deal of success. The first was with Cionas, a bitch which did not carry the prefix, and was followed by nine other certificate winners which did carry it; of this total of ten, five became champions. The inmates carried a deal of Harviestoun blood, sometimes direct and at others through the Gunthorpes; there was also a mixture of Brocaire, Dochfour, Out of the West, and Frimley strains.

Undoubtedly the two most important products of the kennel were Ch. Gillie of Hyver and Ch. Treblig Janet. It would be difficult to assess the importance on the male side that Gillie has had on the breed, and, in view of the limited opportunities of bitches to exert influence, it cannot be denied that Janet has been of equal importance. While the influence of Gillie has been mainly on the males, that of Janet seems to have been greater in her own sex.

Mr Errington Ross, the owner of the Glenmhor prefix, was interested in the Highland Terrier, both Cairn and West Highland. All the Cairns bearing his prefix carried a very large proportion of the blood of their white relations. The result was that they were usually endowed with a head of stronger proportions than many of his early contemporaries considered correct. He was much more successful with his West Highlanders, several of which became champions, than he was with his Cairns. However, the stock of a number of very successful kennels can be traced back to the mixed Cairn and West Highland Terrier breeding of the Glenmhors.

Glenmhor Rascal, which, being by Harviestoun Raider, was pure Glenmhor on the male side, was the only Cairn bearing the prefix to win a certificate, and this was not until 1927, after which little was seen of Mr Ross in the show ring.

Mr Ross was one of the founders of the Cairn Terrier Club.

The Keycol kennel, whose prefix was in the name of Mrs Johnson but whose breeding activities were carried out by Mr Johnson, was founded on Ch. Dochfour Kyle, which was purchased from Lady Burton. This bitch naturally had considerable influence on the development of the kennel, but the dominating blood was Out of the West, though there were careful admixtures of Brocaire and Ross-shire. The kennel produced a number of very typical Cairns of which Bruin of Keycol, Sammy of Keycol, and Una of Keycol became champions. The kennel ceased in this country when the owners emigrated to Canada in the 1930s.

Miss Bunbury's 'of the Shieling' kennel has never been large, but it has always produced very typical specimens of the breed. Its earliest success was with Ch. Beansith Dhu of the Shieling, which became a champion in 1928. This Cairn was the result of a blending of Brocaire, Dochfour, and Frimley blood. The kennel did not again touch the highlights until

1939, when, just before the outbreak of war, Ch. Ruffie of the Shieling won his third certificate. His breeding was very different from that of his precursor, being a mixture of Out of the West, Wealden, Harviestoun, Dochfour, and Ross-shire.

The surprising thing about the Otford kennel, whose prefix was in the name of Mrs Saunders, was that it never housed a champion though it held an excellent type of Cairn of which seven won challenge certificates and numerous other high awards. The stock was built up on an association of Ross-shire, Harviestoun, Dochfour, Frimley, and Out of the West blood. Quite a number of the Cairns bred in this kennel went to the United States and elsewhere. None has been shown in this country since before the last war.

The Fair City kennel was formerly in the names of the two Misses Bell but is now in that of the sole survivor. The breeding of the kennel was based to a very great extent on Harviestoun, but the influences of Brocaire and Dochfour were also present, and the result is a pleasing association of the best qualities of such a mixture. The kennel produced five certificate winners, of which Corrie-Ba of Fair City and Puithar of Fair City became champions. After an absence of some years from the show ring, the inmates have recently reappeared.

The Trashurst kennel had a very successful run between 1929 and the middle 1930s; it was owned by Miss Crossman, later Mrs Rudland. The earlier Cairns of this kennel derive from Frimley and Hyver blood, those later mainly from Harviestoun and Hyver crosses, a mixture that has shown itself to be very effective. Of the nine certificate winners carrying the prefix, two achieved the title, Ch. Trashurst Chip and Ch. Trashurst Fan; the former is noteworthy as having been the sire of Ch. Splinters of Twobees.

Major Townley's Carysfort kennel was a relatively latecomer to the pre-war show ring, making its first prominent appearance at Crufts in 1930, when Fearnought took the first step to the title which he reached three months later. The five champions and the five certificate winners which the kennel owned were founded on a mixture of Hyver, Out of the West, Carngowan, Harviestoun, Guynach, and Firring ancestry, the Hyver influence being the most prominent. Ch. Fear Nil of

Carysfort, by Ch. Fearnought of Carysfort ex-Ch. Fifinella of
Carysfort, won more challenge certificates than any other
bitch in the history of the breed – 24; some judges considered
her rather masculine, and thought her dam the better
Cairn.

Major Townley was an excellent handler and always got the
last ounce out of his exhibits. He was for some years Hon.
Secretary of the Cairn Terrier Association and carried that
body through a very difficult period.

The Warberry kennel of Mrs Hoyle is another which
suffered the handicap of remoteness from the centres of
championship-show activities, but despite this the owner
exhibited with great regularity and won certificates with five
Cairns, one of which, Ch. Warberry Frederick of Dalry, has
reached the highest rank. In the early days the influences were
Firring, Harviestoun, Out of the West, and Mercia, but recently
the basis has been Twobees, Blencathra, Redletter, and
Rossarden, with that of home-kennel products. Mrs Hoyle
also ran a kennel of West Highland White Terriers.

Miss Reoch, the owner of the Valiant kennel, was originally
interested in Bulldogs and West Highland White Terriers, but
she soon transferred her activities to, and concentrated on,
Cairns, though she also, at one time, owned a Gordon Setter
or two. The Cairn inmates were, in the main, based on an
admixture of Harviestoun and Hyver blood, which achieved
an association of the best head properties of both, with the
good physical properties of the former. Seven certificate
winners bore the prefix and two of them were record holders;
Valiant Leaflet of Beechacre (bred by Miss Irving) won a certificate when only six and a half months old, while Ch. Valiant
Rob Roy of Rhosbridge (bred by Miss Moody) was the first
Cairn to become a champion when championship shows were
revived in 1946; there were only four shows with certificates
that year, and Rob Roy won that for dogs at all four; his final
total was eight.

For many years Miss Reoch was Hon. Vice-President of the
Cairn Terrier Club and Hon. President of the Southern Cairn
Terrier Club.

Lady Gooch's kennel of Drungewicks has now ceased its

activities so far as Cairns are concerned, but at one time it held a very strong hand, and in a short period housed three champions – Ch. Drungewick Junk, Ch. Drungewick Jeanetta, and Ch. Drungewick Jacob – while earlier it had a winner of one certificate in Drungewick Jade. Junk, having been sired by Ch. Trashurst Chip, was a half-brother to Ch. Splinters of Twobees, while his dam was a mixture of Hyver, Harviestoun, and Out of the West blood. Jacob was a son of Junk out of a bitch of Brocaire and Hyver blood. Jeanetta was not bred by Lady Gooch, and was of pure Harviestoun ancestry.

The Thistleclose prefix, formerly in the name of Mrs Leigh and later in that of her husband, is that of the kennel in which the powerful Family 59 was developed (*see* pages 62 and 63).

The Twobees kennel, formerly owned jointly by Miss Bengough and Mrs Butterworth but now in the name of the former, is another which has had to be dealt with elsewhere because of its great influence on the breed, mainly through Ch. Splinters of Twobees.

The o' the Braes kennel of Mrs Rhodes was established midway between the wars, but it was not until 1946 that it came prominently to the fore. It has housed four champions and two certificate winners, all of them carrying a great deal of the influence of Splinters of Twobees in association with Brocaire and Thistleclose blood, though one, Ch. Cinders o' the Braes, was the successful mixture of Harviestoun and Hyver. The other champions were Brilliant, Broc and Uiseag, all o' the Braes.

The Haywood kennel of the late Misses Gray-Buchanan is mentioned as being the only one on record as having won two certificates with a Cairn about which nothing was known; the bitch was Haywood Dilly, and the records state that her breeder, date of birth, sire and dam were all unknown. She was an excellent cream Cairn, perhaps a shade low to ground.

Miss Morgan's Woodthorpe kennel had been winning the highest honours for over twenty years, during which time eight inmates have won challenge certificates, and two have achieved the title of champion – Ch. Woodthorpe Madcap

before the war, and Ch. Woodthorpe Clansman since. The
kennel has been built up on mixtures from Cairns from other
kennels, most prominent of which are Hyver, Harviestoun,
Treblig, Out of the West, and Twobees.

Mrs Drummond's kennel of Blencathra Cairns in the early
days was based largely on a judicious mixture of Hyver,
Harvieston, Brocaire, Donnington and Twobees influences.
Blencathra Crackerlad was winner of two challenge certificates
prior to 1939; but it was not until after the war that the
Blencathras came into their own, making up twenty-five
champions from 1949–71. The Blencathras were renowned
for their outstanding heads.

On and after this point the kennels dealt with are those
which have asserted their influence since the resumption of
shows in 1946. Some of them may have been showing prior to
that year but had made little or no impression worthy of
note.

The Rhu kennel formerly carried on by Mr J. Keay, and now
in the name of his daughter-in-law Mrs Keay, had been breeding in quiet seclusion for some time until it was discovered by
Colonel Whitehead, who induced the owner to enter the show
ring. The earliest prominent exhibit was Ch. Rufus of Rhu,
whose main fault was a rooted objection to the show ring.
Through him, and others not so well known, the kennel has
had considerable influence on later generations.

The Oudenarde kennel owned by Mesdames Hamilton and
Temple has assumed front rank in the past thirteen years, and
has housed sixteen champions and eleven certificate winners.
The strength of this kennel obviously lies with the bitches: of
the winners of the seventy-seven certificates bitches out-
number dogs.

In addition to Cairns the kennel has had notable successes
with Dalmatians and Irish Terriers.

On the death of her partners, Mrs Diana Hamilton carried
on the Oudenardes adding more champions to their records.
For twenty-five years Mrs Hamilton was secretary to the Cairn
Terrier Association. On the death of her mother the Oudenardes
passed into the very capable hands of her daughter Miss
Ferelith Hamilton (Mrs Somerfield).

During the whole of the fifty-six years of championship-show history of the Cairn Terrier, only the Out of the West kennel of Mrs Fleming has approached the success which has attended that of Mr Bradshaw's Redletter. Although the owner had been interested in Flatcoated Retrievers for some years prior to 1939, it was not until 1946 that he entered Cairn circles. Since that year the kennel has housed thirty-two winners of challenge certificates of which twenty-nine have become champions. In addition to having won the greatest number of certificates ever won by a kennel of Cairns, 199, it had in Ch. Redletter McMurran the Cairn winning the highest number of certificates. In addition to siring McMurran, Ch. Redletter McJoe sired eight other champions, while McMurran sired six. A number of cairns from this kennel have been exported to both Canada and the U.S.A., it is therefore expected that they have had considerable influence on the breed in these countries. The Redletter Kennels were one of the leading and influential kennels until Walter Bradshaw's death in 1982. The Redletters held a number of records some of which still stand today.

The Hillston kennel of Mrs Garbutt is another of the kennels which emerged after 1946. The various successful Cairns that have appeared under this prefix were bred from a mixture of Hyver, Blencathra, Woodthorpe, Beechacre, and Out of the West blood with, latterly, a touch of Redletter. Eight certificate winners have borne the prefix and four have become champions. Mrs Garbutt's activities were interrupted for a few years while she was in Kenya, but since her return she has again taken up the breed.

Miss Nichols, whose kennel is in Devon, has, as a rule, to face considerable journeys to reach the majority of championship shows, but despite the handicap of distance she has handled three champions and four other certificate winners since 1946. The pedigrees all show the influence of Hyver and Twobees through Ch. Splinters of Twobees, and of Thistleclose from Ch. Treblig Janet, with touches of Out of the West and Blencathra. Michelcombe Fearless, the winner of one certificate, has had considerable influence, being the sire of two champions and one certificate winner, and the grand-sire of another certificate winner, all carrying the prefix.

The kennel of Mrs Yeend, of which the name Yeendsdale is

sometimes used as a prefix and sometimes as an affix, to date has produced seven certificates winners, of which six have become champions. These are the result of an admixture of Woodthorpe, Frimley, Treblig, Carysfort, and Out of the West influences, which are, in later products, linked with Redletter and Twobees.

The Pledwick kennel of Mrs Summers has produced two champions and two certificate winners in recent years. On the female side there is a predominance of Woodthorpe blood, with Thistleclose and Hillston, while on the male side Twobees is very much to the fore.

It is quite a few years since Mrs Leverton was, with Miss Foster (now Mrs Henderson), joint owner of the Crantock prefix, and it is as the owner of the Merrymeet prefix that most current exhibitors will recognize her. So far, the title is carried by six of the inmates, and every one that has won a certificate has achieved the title. While a great deal of the present breeding is being carried out with home-bred bitches, the influences of Blencathra, Twobees, Donnington, and Thistleclose can be seen by examining the extended pedigrees.

The Rossarden kennels were founded by the two sisters Betty and Charlotte Dixon. This was another kennel reaching prominence during these years. Their first champion was Ch. Rogie of Rossarden, their first CC (challenge certificate) winner was his litter sister Rhoda of Rossarden; this was followed by Ch. Whinyon of Rossarden, and her litter brother Riskin of Rossarden was a certificate winner. Ch. Rufus of Rhu has had a great influence in this kennel in association with home-bred bitches founded on Hyver and Mercia. Since the untimely death of Betty Dixon in 1968, Charlotte (Charlie) has carried on the Rossarden strain with continuing success up to the present day.

The Fincairn kennel of Mrs Finlay, also a newcomer, has made quite an impression. In the birth of Ch. Fincairn Gillian, in 1949, there appeared a bitch which has done much better than most; in one litter she produced Ch. Redletter Fincairn Frolic and Ch. Redletter Marjose, and later she followed this by whelping Ch. Lynwil Lady MacIan, to say nothing of the certificate winner Fincairn Silver Charm.

Ch. Splinters of Twobees, b. 1933

Ch. Brindie of Twobees, b. 1949 *(Thomas Fall)*

Wasp. From an engraving of Rosa Bonheur's painting of *Le Chien Favori*, *1856*

Flora, the old working type of Skye Terrier, from *The Illustrated Book of the Dog*, by Vero Shaw, published *c*. 1880

Sir Paynton Pigott's Granite – the first Scottish Terrier entered at a Kennel Club Show (in 1878). (From *The New Book of the Dog*, by Robert Leighton)

Left: Brocaire Raonuill, b. May 1916
This photograph was specially taken on his twelfth birthday for the first edition of this book

Below: Mrs Alastair Campbell in 1909
MacLeod of MacLeod in her arms, Roy Mhor on her right, and Doran Bhan on her left

MacLeod of MacLeod, b. *c.* 1908

Ch. Brocaire Siteach, b. 1915

Above left: Ch. Brocaire Speireag, b. 1911

Above: Ch. Gesto, b. 1909, and Ch. Brocaire Speireag, b. 1911

Below: Roy Mhor, b. *c.* 1907

Above: Mrs Alastair Campbell at the Cairn Terrier Club Championship Show on 29 May 1946, a few weeks before her death

Right: Ch. Fimor Katrine, b. 1950

The Uniquecottage kennels were owned by Misses Long-more and Marshall. Jollee was Miss Longmore's prefix for her Cairns and West Highland White Terriers. When the partnership was formed the Cairns were registered under the Uniquecottage prefix, Jollee being retained for the West Highland White Terriers. The Uniquecottage Cairns, particularly on the female side, were based largely on the Jollee Cairns formerly in Miss Longmore's name only.

Jollee Gay Memory and her sister Jollee Gay Sprite figure prominently in the pedigrees of the majority of the most successful of the inmates. Of the four champions bearing the prefix, two own Gay Memory as dam, and two have her as grand-dam; her certificate-winning daughter, Uniquecottage Goldigger, being the only bitch in the history of the breed which has whelped three champions in one litter. These are: Ch. Uniquecottage Sir Frolic, Ch. Uniquecottage Blackgold, and Ch. Redletter Miss Muffet, a trio which between them have won twenty-nine challenge certificates.

On Miss Longmore's marraige the partnership was dis-solved and she started the Avenelhouse kennels in partnership with her husband Major Small. The Uniquecottage kennel remained in Miss Marshall's name until her marriage and is still run by her but under her married name, Parker-Tucker.

While the Rhosbridge kennel of Miss Moody has made no home-bred champion, Miss Moody had the satisfaction of breeding the first post-1946 champion in Ch. Valiant Rob Roy of Rhosbridge, as well as another early champion of the same period, Ch. Valiant Rab.

It is suggested that the reader follows up this chapter by turning to Appendix B and C where the post-war CC winners and champions and influential stud dogs and brood bitches are recorded.

3

Breeding

Throughout the years there have been many theories on the subject of the reproduction of animal life, ranging from the idea that the female parent was just a form of animated incubator which nurtured and developed an embryo that was the sole product of the male, to the suggestion that the male was responsible for certain attributes while the female was responsible for others. During the latter half of the nineteenth century nearly all the accepted theories became suspect, and inquisitive minds tried to find sounder reasons for the various standards presented by the wide range of quality visible in the animal kingdom.

In the 1890s a Mr Bruce Lowe set about investigating the breeding of racehorses. He traced the pedigrees of a large number of winning racehorses to the roots, and demonstrated that many of the most successful winners could be traced back to very few stallions and to a limited, though larger, number of mares. This statement referred only to the top line of stallions and the bottom line of mares, because he assumed, for the sake of his system, that the middle part of the pedigree cancelled itself out. Thus:

$$
A
\begin{cases}
B \\
\\
C
\end{cases}
\qquad
\begin{cases}
D \\
\\
E
\end{cases}
\begin{cases}
F \\
\\
G
\end{cases}
\qquad
\begin{cases}
H \\
J
\end{cases}
\begin{cases}
K \\
L
\end{cases}
\begin{cases}
M \\
N
\end{cases}
\begin{cases}
O \\
P
\end{cases}
$$

the line is B, D, H while the family is C, G, P. Assuming that H is the earliest traceable male on the top line of the pedigree, and P the earliest traceable female in the bottom line of the pedigree, an animal is said to belong to the line of which H is the founder and to the family of which P is the founder. In order to avoid confusion the line is indicated by the initial letter of the name of the 'founder' (in this case H) while the family is indicated by a number (in this case, say 2). Assuming A to be a male, he and B, and D, belong to line H, while he and females C, G, and P belong to Family No. 2.

This system has been applied to many breeds of dogs. It was first applied to Cairns by Mr and Mrs Caspersz, and was set out in full in *Cairn Terrier Records*, published in 1932 and followed by a revised edition about a year later.

In applying the system to dogs, the qualification for the most remote dog or bitch to be treated as the founder of a line or family is that one or more champions can be traced back to that remote ancestor, as shown in the example.

It must be made clear that this system has no scientific basis. It can be of use only when regarded as a series of finger-posts indicating the manner in which certain results have been achieved; the great flaw in the original idea lies in the assumption that the animals in the central part of the pedigree have no influence.

Although there are many breeders who scoff at the Bruce Lowe system, there are just as many who laugh at the idea of breeding being based on scientific knowledge.

All attempts at scientific breeding, whatever may be the subject, are today based on what is known as 'Mendelism'. While Bruce Lowe was pursuing his analysis of racehorse pedigrees, there lay buried and forgotten in Austria the records of experiments on which all present-day knowledge of inheritance is based.

Since the rediscovery of the papers describing Mendel's experiments, the secrets of heredity have gradually been revealed by scientists who, during the past fifty-odd years, have made extraordinary progress in the study of what is known as genetics.

Let it be stated at once that the whole subject of genetics is so vast and so intricate as to be of little use to Cairn breeders, but no one can breed any animal intelligently without some knowledge of the workings of what have been called the laws of heredity.

While we all glibly say that such-and-such a dog or bitch transmits his or her special feature, the dog or bitch in question does not, in fact, do so. What he or she does is to transmit an influence or factor which, in the absence of any modifying factor, will lead to the pup or pups developing a strong resemblance to the sire or dam in that particular feature. These factors or influences are believed to be contained in extremely minute particles called genes, which appear under the microscope in the form of thin thread-like substances called chromosomes. (It must be understood that even the chromosomes, which are formed of an unknown number of genes, are so small that they are clearly visible under the microscope only after they have been dyed.)

As is well known, conception takes place by the fertilization of the ovum by the sperm. The sex cells of the dog (ovum and sperm) each contain thirty-nine chromosomes; thus, when they combine, the resulting cell, from which all other cells develop by division, contains seventy-eight chromosomes. Every breed of dog so far investigated has seventy-eight chromosomes; the number in other animals, including man, varies according to the species. While the number of chromosomes are known, the number of genes in each remains a mystery.

When fertilization takes place, it is accepted that the chromosomes containing similar factors or influences assume juxtapositions. Then, when the first cell divides into two cells, the chromosomes split longitudinally, so that the two resulting cells each receive the same factors or influences which were contained in the first; this process continues until maturity is reached. Geneticists, in the main, accept the close association of similar chromosomes and their constituent genes, while some maintain that the genes influence not only their opposite numbers but that also there is a good deal of cross-influence.

When one gene in, say, the ovum amalgamates with its partner in the sperm, the influences each one contains may associate happily when each carries the same attribute, or one or other may dominate its partner, whose influence is not thereby extinguished but only suppressed; the feature carried by the influence which is suppressed will not show in the resulting pup, but may be transmitted to and appear in future generations.

There is one exception to the rule of the association of similar chromosomes, and this is the sex chromosomes. It may be a shock to extreme feminists to know that all mammalian females can transmit through the ova only the factor for femaleness, while the sperms contain the factors for femaleness and maleness in equal proportions. Thus, the sex of the pup depends on whether the ovum is fertilized by a sperm carrying the male factor, or one carrying the female factor. To balance this it should be explained that the sire has nothing to do with the number of puppies in a litter; it seems to be a law of nature that there shall be a much greater number of sperms than of ova, otherwise the practice of artificial insemination would not have reached the proportions it has in some breeds of animals.

Enough has been written to show that the science of genetics is far too complicated to be of much use to breeders of Cairn Terriers in which the standard of the individual depends entirely on the presence or absence, in varying degree, of certain physical properties which are due to the conflicting influences inherited from their ancestors. But, it is hoped, what has been written may show how essential it is to be certain, as far as is humanly possible, that the influences which are associated as the result of a mating are such as to ensure that there is no violent conflict, but rather a firm association of those influences that will ensure the dominance of desirable features. This can best be achieved by mating the bitch to a stud dog which should, from its breeding, and judged by its progeny, carry a large number of the influences likely to produce the good points visible in the bitch.

As the object of any serious breeder, apart from the wish to produce a 'flyer', should be to improve the general level of the animals in which he or she is interested, it is possible that by associating the principles of inheritance, as explained by scientists, with the 'fingerposts' set out in the Bruce Lowe system, some considerable control may be exercised on the gamble of breeding.

Whatever may be said against the acceptance of the 'Line and Family' system it cannot be denied that, when a certain series of matings produces a higher proportion of champions than other series of matings, the former has something which the latter seems to lack. In other words, fortuitously or otherwise, there has been built up an association of influences which has resulted in the appearance of a number of animals of outstanding quality. Thus, it should be the policy of every breeder to try to get into his Cairns, throughout the whole body of the pedigree, as many of these successful influences as possible. This will involve the careful study of the pedigrees not only of his own bitches but also of those of the stud dogs he is considering as suitable mates.

4

Lines and Families

When Mr and Mrs Caspersz completed their analysis of the pedigrees of all Cairn Terrier champions which had achieved the title prior to 31 December, 1933, they had, working on the line and family system, established that there were eleven male lines and fifty families, which, on the Bruce Lowe scheme of tracing the sire back to his original male ancestor and the dam back to her original female ancestor, so far as these could be ascertained, had produced at least one champion Cairn. Since that time no further male lines have emerged; in fact, the influence of a number of the original eleven lines has terminated, and others have become very attenuated. Quite a number of the original fifty families have ceased to have any influence, but in this case there has been a considerable increase in the number of new families which have produced champions.

An examination of the pedigrees of champions created since 1946 shows that of the original eleven lines four have added further champions to their total, some to a much greater extent than others, and of the original fifty families thirty-four have disappeared, and ten have added not more than two names. During the period 1934 to 1939 there was an addition of ten new families and of these seven have added no more than two to their individual scores since 1946. One of these ten is, however, an outstanding family and will be referred to later. Since 1946 the number of families has been increased by nineteen, of which only three have so far produced more than two champions.

It can, of course, be argued, quite justifiably, that the line and family system can have no scientific foundation as it is

wrong to assign to any one succession of ancestors any more
influence than that of any other line of predecessors. This is
quite true, but when an investigator analyses any collection of
facts and discovers that a certain sequence emerges time after
time, such evidence cannot be entirely ignored.

When, for instance, the pedigrees of the 132 champions
which have achieved the rank since 1946 are broken down,
and it is found that no fewer than seventy-two belong to a
certain male line, it is difficult to assert that the line in question
has not, somehow, built up some transmittable quality which
has a beneficial effect on succeeding generations. Again, of
these champions no fewer than forty-seven are members of
four families which have scores of seven, eight, twelve, and
twenty respectively. It so happens that the blood of the most
potent line, that with the seventy-two champions, is frequently
associated with that of the family with the twenty champions.
As the object of all breeding is, or should be, to improve the
stock in which the breeder is interested, it is difficult to
understand why any 'fingerpost' should be derided. It must
always be remembered that the male has many more opportunities to stamp his influence and inheritable factors on a
breed than has the female.

Again, it is well to bear in mind that every animal is descended
from a large number of ancestors; for instance, a six-
generation pedigree contains no fewer than 126 names, of
which sixty-four are those of great-great-great-great-grand-
parents, and the number is doubled by each generation
further back. Thus, a pedigree could contain a widely conflicting blend of influences if there were not some inbreeding or
line-breeding. While a detailed study of an extended pedigree
can be interesting and, in some cases, informative, it is doubtful if, in most cases, a pedigree going beyond five generations
is of effective use unless the potent factors are recognized.
Although five generations involves a period of from fifteen to
twenty years, it is proposed to examine the influences which
have been at work over a longer period and to deal with the
post-1946 Cairns, but to refer only to the earlier animals that
can be said to have transmitted effective influence.

In 1933 it was obvious that there were four main male lines

of influence, and that three of these were concentrated in three separate kennels. The three lines were identified by the initials D, G, and SD, the first two being the initial letters of the names of the most remote male ancestor traced, and the last the initial of the remote ancestor linked to that of the most important descendant.

The D line came from Ch. Firring Frolic through the Carngowan kennel, an inmate of which, Ch. Carngowan Murran, sired the dog which, in the hands of Mrs Stephen, became famous as Ch. Gillie of Hyver and proved to be one of immense influence through the Hyver, Donnington, Carysfort, Trashurst, Treblig, and many other kennels, particularly the Twobees and Redletter kennels of today. From the year 1912 to the present time 380 Cairn Terriers have become champions. Of that number 184 have been members of this line, and, of the 184, 140 have been bred since 1946, which would indicate that the influence of the line is increasing.

Mr and Mrs Caspersz set out the D line with three branches: DR being used to indicate all direct descendants of the originator Duan through Raeburn Conas; DF for all direct descendants through Firring Fling; DG for all direct descendants through Ch. Gillie of Hyver. Later, DGS was added to indicate all descendants of Ch. Splinters of Twobees.

The G line which could, quite correctly, be referred to as the Glenmhor-Harviestoun line, also had wide ramifications, but it was most in evidence in the Beechacre, Gunthorpe, and Valiant kennels, and, when it was associated with the Brocaire and Hyver bloods, produced some very good specimens of the breed. The G line has, during the years, produced eighty-five champions of which thirty-two have been bred since 1946, but through the termination of the three kennels which were founded mainly on this line its influence can be expected to decline.

The G line was also subdivided into GB, GC, GF, and GR branches, which indicated direct descendants of Ch. Harviestoun Brigand, Ch. Harviestoun Chieftain, Harviestoun Forgie, and Harviestoun Raider respectively.

It can quite truthfully be asserted that the SD line owes its position to that extraordinary sire Doughall Out of the West, which was responsible for a large number of big winners and back to which all the descendants that have made the line famous can be traced. The influence of the line was obvious in the home kennel, and in the Bogton, Keycol, and Shinnel kennels. It has given the breed thirty-three champions, of which only nine have emerged since 1946.

The only other male line to be represented by additional champions since 1946 is the I line, which was brought into prominence by Ross-shire Glenara and his son Ch. Ross-shire Warrior. The influence of this line was more widely distributed than the others and, being less concentrated, has declined more rapidly. Of the fourteen champions in the line prior to 1934, twelve of them bore different prefixes. Since that time it has produced thirty-two champions of which thirty-one are post-war.

In the case of the I line, the subdivision indicated by IG (the G standing for Ross-shire Glenara) proved the most influential.

The four lines and the branches which have added champions to their totals since 1946 are:

Line D		1946–1960	1961–1968
	Branch DG	15 champions	—
	Branch DGS	57 champions	60 champions
	Branch DR	7 champions	1 champion
Line G			
	Branch GB	27 champions	4 champions
	Branch GR	5 champions	—
Line I		12 champions	19 champions
Line SD		9 champions	—

The allocation of importance on the family, or female, side of a pedigree is a much more difficult problem than in the line or male side. There can be no comparison between the relative opportunities of even the most successful bitch, whether viewed from her wins on the show bench or from that of the excellent quality of her pups, with those of the equally successful dog. If a bitch gives birth to as many as forty pups in her lifetime she has done more than her fair share of maintaining the Cairn population, particularly if she has had an exacting show career. A prominent show and stud dog, on the other hand, can be the sire of the same number of pups in a fraction of a Cairn's life.

The position is made more difficult in Cairns by the fact that, working on the Bruce Lowe system, such a large number of families producing one or two champions has been traced; the number of such families now exceeds the century mark, and though the effective total is being reduced by the failure of established families to continue the production of more champions, these reductions are being balanced by the emergence of other families.

Bearing in mind the restricted area from which the Cairn emerged about fifty years ago it is possible that this multiplicity of families is due to the absence of knowledge of the very early breeding; it is not unlikely that if we had reliable information for a few more generations further back we would find that many of the families would link up and be found to be descended from one bitch.

Since 1946 only six of the original fifty families have added substantially to their original totals. In some of these six families it is possible to ascribe to certain bitches an important part of the continued potency, but this is not so obvious as in the male lines.

It is hardly necessary at this date to indicate any of the bitches that may have carried on the good work prior to 1939, as twenty years in canine genealogy may mean anything from five to ten generations.

The first of the early families to increase the number of its champions to any appreciable extent was Family No. 2, which was founded on an unregistered bitch named Spuch. Three of the four additions are dogs, so that its continuance as a family from those sources is impossible, and as the kennel which houses the bitch is at present in abeyance it would seem that this family may, in future, fall out, unless there are other branches which have so far failed to make an impression.

Of the four additions since 1946, Ch. Valiant Rob Roy of Rhosbridge, Ch. Valiant Rab, and Ch. Brilliant o' the Braes all trace back to the original through several generations of the inmates of the Shinnel kennel, owned by Mrs Mirrlees, which is now inactive. This family has produced sixteen champions in all.

Family No. 3, which descended from the pedigree-unknown Raitts Rannaich, has been much more prolific since 1946, having added 12 champions to its previous total of seven. In this family it is easily possible to pinpoint a bitch which has been responsible for a part of its development. The bitch Jollee Gay Memory, formerly owned by Miss Longmore (now Mrs Small), was the dam of two champions, Ch. Uniquecottage McAilenmor and Ch. Uniquecottage Maningrey, and her daughter, Uniquecottage Goldigger (a winner of one certificate), was the dam of three, Ch. Uniquecottage Sir Frolic, Ch. Uniquecottage Black Gold, and Ch. Redletter Miss Muffit. Ch. Bonfire of Twobees, one of the earliest post-war champions, is also a member of this family, his dam Mitsie of Zellah being an ancestress of Jollee Gay Memory. Three other members, Ch. Oudenarde Duskie Belle, Ch. Oudenarde Souvenir, and Ch. Oudenarde Live Spirit, all have a common ancestress in Cora of Weston-on-the-Green. Two other members, Ch. Altbeck Clever Girl and Ch. Hillston Madcap Madame, have nothing in common either with each other or with the other members, except in very remote stages. The remaining champion, Ch. Redletter McRufus, is a son of Ch. Redletter Miss Muffit.

There is a complete absence of any concentration in Family No. 4, which was traced back to Banshee Donan. This family has augmented its pre-1939 score of eleven champions by the addition of five more since 1946. Of the original eleven champions only three had anything in common and even this association was three and four generations back. The five recent champions, Ch. Clenmacrobin Five Finches, Ch. Brackendene Brig of Cona Lynn, Ch. Redletter Miss Splinters, Ch. Redletter McBrigand, and Ch. Redletter McBryan, are, so far as earlier parts of their pedigrees are concerned, but very loosely related, but McBrigand and McBryan are litter brothers owning Miss Splinters as dam; as Ch. Redletter Miss Splinters is now in Canada, her personal powers of transmission are no longer in this country.

Family No. 5, with six champions prior to 1939, has produced five more since 1946. This family emerged from a bitch named Tibbie whose pup Bride was born in 1906 and registered by the late Hon. Mary Hawke in November 1909, as was Bride's pup Brigit, born in March 1909. These three generations had considerable influence in the early days of the Lockyers kennel. Of the five recent champions in the family no fewer than four appear to have been derived from Irish stock, as the extended pedigrees of Ch. Redletter Penny of the Blarneystone, Ch. Daleacre Jerogi, Ch. Redstacks Kerry Dancer, and Ch. Redstacks Demoiselle disclose a number of well-known Irish animals, of which Shanganagh Sunshine is common to all four. The fifth member, Ch. Broc o' the Braes, is related to the earlier Ch. Lockyers Ian through the remote Jill of Blackpark.

In Family No. 6, which had four pre-1939 champions and has produced six more since 1946, the continuity of influence is much more obvious. The family was founded on Ceoach, one of whose early descendants was Ch. Corrie Ba of Fair City which, with her daughter Ch. Puithar of Fair City, achieved the title before 1939. Not only do five of the six recent champions stem back to Corrie Ba but one of them, Ch. Fincairn Gillian, is the dam of three of the others, Ch. Redletter Marjose, Ch. Redletter Fincairn Frolic, and Ch. Lynwil Lady MacIan; the fifth, Ch. Michelcombe Mr Chips, has slightly different immediate ancestry derived from the same source. The pedigree of the sixth, Ch. Cairntop Nicholas, also leads back to the Fair City kennel.

With Family No. 17, which was graced with six champions before 1939, and which has increased that number by seven since then, we arrive at what, to some, will be an unpalatable truth. There is no doubt that the foundations of this family were based, in the main, on Scottish Terriers. Smallburn Daisy, the bitch on which Mr and Mrs Caspersz based the family, was a Scottish Terrier – at least the majority of her ancestors were Scotties. It must, however, be repeated that the Scottish Terriers of those early days bore little resemblance to the Scottish Terriers of today. The family can be considered the feminine equivalent of the G line and its branches: in its earlier stages it was mostly to be found in the Harviestoun and

Gunthorpe kennels and in the produce of those kennels, and
six of the champions which have been whelped since 1946
carry Gunthorpe blood; the other goes direct back to Harviestoun. Five of the recent champions have been bred in the
Yeendsdale kennel, Ch. Rob of Yeendsdale, Ch. Joyous of
Yeendsdale, and Ch. Merrymen of Yeendsdale having Jean of
Yeendsdale as dam, while Ch. Yeendsdale Masterpiece is a
grandson of Jean, and Ch. Yeendsdale Inspiration is a great-
grandson. The other two champions, Ch. McEan of Ellandee
and Ch. Merrymeet Tathwell Therese, go back to the original
source by different ancestry.

In dealing with Family No. 59, which produced one champion prior to 1939 and which has now raised its total to twenty,
we have the most successful family of all time. When I took
over and developed, in respect of later years, the work done by
Mr and Mrs Caspersz for the period up to the end of 1933, I
found that Ch. Treblig Janet had created a new family to
which No. 59 was assigned. When the pedigree was being
traced to the foundations the name of a bitch Culaig was
reached. A perusal of copies of the personal records of the
owner of the kennel which had bred Culaig disclosed the
details of at least two bitches bearing this unregistered name,
and as the pedigrees differed I decided to accept Culaig as
the founder.

After Ch. Treblig Janet, the family produced nothing
further until 1946, since when there has been something of a
spate. This family, more than any other, has produced a
limited number of bitches, from which have stemmed the
majority of the champions that have adorned it.

There can be little doubt that the success of the Thistleclose
kennel since 1946 is due, to a very great extent, to the acquisition
of Mrs Leigh, from Mr Gilbert, of Treblig Janet, and to the
intelligent use of her descendants, the crowning feature of
which proved to be Thistleclose Rosette, whose name appears
in the family lineage of Champions Thistleclose Fling,
Thistleclose Posy, Thistleclose Rosada, Thistleclose Marigold,
and Thistleclose MacGregor; the name of Rosette also appears
in the same positions in the pedigrees of Ch. Michelcombe
Fay, Ch. Redletter Matelot, and Ch. Uiseag o' the Braes. Ch.

Thistleclose Pennyroyal, the sixth champion bearing this prefix, did not own Rosette as an ancestress. It is rather surprising
that of the eight champions which have descended from Ch.
Treblig Janet seven have been female and only one male.

Thistleclose Rosette was not the only bitch from this family
which has had a great influence in the production of a number
of high-class specimens. Foundation Sylvia has been the dam
of Ch. Brindie of Twobees, Ch. Redletter Elford Mhorag, Ch.
Blencathra Elford Chiefton, and Ch. Elford Shantry, and the
grand-dam of Ch. Redletter Midas. Ch. Glenmacdhui
Marylin and Ch. Glenmacdhui Mohra, which are full sisters,
are decended from a half-sister of Foundation Sylvia. The
other two champions of this family, Ch. Blencathra Clive-
green Timothy and Ch. Redletter McMurran, while distantly
related, are not closely connected with the other eighteen
recent champions.

The extraordinary manner in which the female members of
this family seem to produce of their best when mated to males
of the DGS branch of the D line is demonstrated when it is
noted that of the twenty recent champions thirteen are members of that branch, one a member of branch DR, two of
branch line GB, and four of line I.

Family No. 80 is the only one emerging since 1946 that has
produced any considerable number of champions, its score
being eight. The foundation was an unregistered bitch named
Dinkie, from which a number of the Sinclairtown and Rhu
inmates are decended.

The two sisters, Brown Owl of Barassie and Bubbles of
Barassie, are the animals which have had most recent influence,
the former being the dam of Ch. Blencathra Galgate Lady
Piper and Ch. Blencathra Pipit, and the grand-dam of Ch.
Blencathra Redstart, Ch. Dochfour Bean-Mormhair, and Ch.
Blencathra Milord. Bubbles of Barassie was the dam of
Greetavale Golden Girl which, in turn, was the dam of Ch.
Redletter Mac E Boy and Ch. Lofthouse Golden. The remain-
ing champion, Lady Jane of Cyrisorene, has no recent
relationship to the other seven.

5

Influential Dogs

In the pedigree history of Cairns, as in that of all other animals, many matings have been the result of careful thought and calculation, but some, though made on an opportunist basis, have resulted in the birth of one or more specimens which have had a great influence on a section of the breed and, in some cases, a very large proportion of the breed at a given time; also, in a more limited number of cases, this influence has continued through many generations and in an ever-widening stream.

The measure of the personal quality of any animal rests entirely on his or her physical appearance, and the final assessment of that appearance can be gauged by its success in the show ring when contrasted with that of its contemporaries. But the measure of its quality as the transmitter of those properties for which the 'fancier', or indeed the utility breeder, looks can be measured only by the quality of its offspring. A prominent continental geneticist, adversely commenting on the high price of young stud animals of a certain utility breed assessed solely on the strength of the pedigree, expressed the opinion that the natural wish to obtain stock from a prominent winner, simply and solely because of his show record, was not always to the benefit of the breed.

The breeding history of the Cairn provides a number of examples of well-known winners producing excellent specimens, while others, equally successful, have failed to reproduce their equal, and still a third group, much less successful on the show bench, which have been responsible for outstanding specimens.

Going right back to the beginning we find that on 4 January,

1911, before the Cairn had received general show recognition, Mr J. McDonald bred a litter, by Doran out of Stratag, two pups of which became known to the show ring as Firring Fling and Ch. Firring Frolic; these two brothers had a very great influence, not only in those early days but also ever since, for, if anything, it has widened and increased until it is the dominating influence today.

Although they were bred by Mr McDonald, they soon passed into the hands of Messrs Ross and Markland, then the owners of the Firring prefix. None of their ancestors, of which three generations are known, was registered, and it is to be presumed that the mating was made either, and more likely, just to get a few more working dogs or to meet the growing popular interest in the breed.

It can be assumed that the demand for the services of a champion, until it is clear that he is not transmitting his qualities, will always be greater than that for a non-champion, yet these two in the first generation were very closely balanced: Fling sired three winners of challenge certificates, of which Ch. Rona (winner of six certificates) and Ch. Sporran (winner of five certificates) became champions; Frolic sired four winners of certificates but none became a champion.

Fling was described as a light brindle, and an illustration shows him to have been a sturdy well-built dog, rather heavy in ear, and strong in foreface; from a photograph of Frolic it would seem that his red brindle coat was more profuse than that of his brother, and that he stood higher on the leg.

Fling had the honour of winning the first certificate ever offered for the breed, but he never repeated the success; Frolic, on the other hand, won eleven in all; his appeal, as a show animal, to two of the original founders of the breed in that sphere is shown by the fact that Mrs Alastair Campbell awarded him three of his certificates, and Lady Sophie Scott two.

The initial letter of the name of Duan, the grandsire of Doran, was taken by Mr and Mrs Caspersz as the distinguishing symbol for the line which was first created by Ch. Firring Frolic, and whose branches have been indicated by DR, DF, DG, and DGS.

There are few outstanding Cairns today which have not, somewhere in their pedigree, the names of one or more ancestors belonging to this influential line.

In contrast to the extraordinary influence the line has always had on the breed, the Family (No. 20) to which Fling and Frolic belonged has been responsible for no other champion than the founder – Ch. Firring Frolic.

The kennel which flourished under the Firring prefix, originally in the joint hands of Messrs Ross and Markland, soon passed into the sole ownership of the former as, by the end of the First World War, all registrations appear in his name alone.

On the day when Fling won his first challenge certificate his kennel-mate Firring Flora won the first bitch certificate. Flora was bred by Mrs Alastair Campbell, and though she won another certificate she never became a champion. The prefix was carried by seven certificate winners, of which three became champions; these three were Frolic, Ch. Firring Fox, and Ch. Firring Fionn. Fox must have been given the prefix in transit through the kennel, as he was bred by Mr J. McDonald and won his three certificates in the hands of Mrs L. Hean Gaydon in three successive shows in the summer of 1914, in the thirteen days between 25 June and 7 July – surely one of the shortest periods in Cairn history.

Fionn was a later product of the kennel, being born in August 1923, and winning the first of her seven certificates in February 1925; she was heavily inbred to Frolic on her dam's side. She was bred by Mr Ross and was the last product of the kennel carrying the prefix to make a big impression. Mrs Ross was for many years the Cairn Terrier correspondent to *Our Dogs*, and was the author of the first book dealing with the breed.

In the April 1910 issue of the *Kennel Gazette* there appeared the announcement of the registration of Gesto in the name of Mr S. McLeod; Gesto was whelped on 22 March 1909, and was by Sgithanach Bhan out of Torvaig; the breeder was Mr M. McKinnon. Sgithanach Bhan was either a white Cairn or a West Highland White Terrier; the names of the other ancestors of Gesto are of no importance as they could easily have been used, and no doubt were used, as are Spot, Prince, etc., today.

As he was born early in 1909 it is obvious that the mating which produced Gesto was not made with an eye on the show ring. However, that was his destination; sometime before the end of 1910 he was acquired by Mrs Alastair Campbell.

Gesto first made his presence felt south of the Border in October 1912, when the Hon Mary Hawke awarded him the first of his five challenge certificates at the Kennel Club show.

He was a grey brindle, and from the reports of some of the judges of the period he appears to have been rather straight in stifle but otherwise to have deserved his wins.

As Mrs Campbell was, at that time, resident at Ardrishaig in Argyllshire, it is not surprising that Gesto's influence was confined mainly to her own kennel and to the locality where, as he ran more or less wild, it was no doubt considerable. He sired six certificate winners, of which Brocaire Spiereag, Brocaire Siteach, and Langley Tiggy became champions.

Unfortunately, Gesto cannot be said to have any influence today as both the line B, and Family No. 21 to which he belonged, have produced nothing since the resumption of activities in 1946.

As Ch. Gesto, though not bred by Mrs Campbell, was the first champion owned by her, this seems a good point at which to introduce some particulars of this pioneer.

The prefix of the kennel, Brocaire, and the name of its original owner, are two names which should always be remembered by lovers of the breed. Mrs Alastair Campbell must be given credit for being the earliest and most consistent pioneer the breed had. The first seven dogs registered as Prick-eared Skye Terriers (later transferred by the Kennel Club to the Cairn Terrier register) in the years 1907 to 1909 were in the name of Mrs Campbell; she showed four of these at Crufts in 1909, and three at the same show in 1910; she became the first Hon. Secretary of the Cairn Terrier Club; she judged the first show at which championship status was granted to the breed;

she bred the bitch (Firring Flora) to win the first bitch challenge certificate, and she owned the first dog champion, Ch. Gesto.

Ch. Gesto won the first certificate for his owner in October 1912, and Mrs Campbell won her last certificate in April 1939. During these years the kennel housed, at one time or another, seven champions and three other certificate winners.

While the physical properties of the Brocaires were not always what they could have been, the head properties left nothing to be desired and were, indeed, a healthy corrective to the heavier and harder type due to crossing with West Highland White Terriers, also, if the truth must be written, with Scottish Terriers.

We know that Mrs Campbell was at Crufts in 1909, and as her last appearance was at the Cairn Terrier Club's show of 29 May, 1946, she can be said to have given unstinted support to the breed in one way or another for forty years. It is a pleasure to state that the Cairn which she showed at her last show carried the same type as did those of her earlier successes, and the judge was justified in the award of a first prize. Mrs Campbell died within a fortnight of that show.

The first champion owned by Mrs Campbell, though sired by Ch. Gesto, was bred by Miss Mary Hawke; this was Ch. Brocaire Speireag; she was followed by five other champions, all home-bred. Two other products of the kennel won one certificate each. The three earlier certificate winners, Ch. Speireag, Iteag, and Ch. Siteach, were all sired by Gesto. The happy association of Harviestoun and Brocaire blood was demonstrated by the appearance of Ch. Brocaire Donan of Gesto and Brocaire Dhorhan from separate litters, both by Harviestoun Raider ex-Brocaire Daffodil, and the litter brother and sister Ch. Brocaire Hamish of Gesto and Ch. Brocaire Jura by Raider ex-Brocaire Jonquil.

The last champion carrying this prefix was Ch. Brocaire MacRose of Carse, which was born in 1935 and won his title in 1939. His pedigree was wholly Brocaire, and in the background carried the names of the stalwarts on which the earlier fame of the kennel was founded.

It is unnecessary to enter into any detailed description of the inmates, particularly the early inmates, of this kennel except to remark that judges' reports frequently included such phrases as 'very typical', 'very good', 'beautiful', 'impossible to fault', though there were occasionally qualifications as to lack of size, and the Cairns were not always put down in the best possible condition.

The later successful specimens from this kennel were members of branch GR and Family No. 15, both having some recent influence, the branch line having produced five champions and the family two champions since 1946.

While Ch. Brocaire Donan of Gesto was bred by Mrs Campbell, he did all his winning in the hands of Mrs Stanton. The last time he was seen in the ring was in May 1928, when, at the age of seven years, he was awarded the reserve certificate in very hot younger competition.

Another dog that had considerable influence in the early days was Ch. Skye Crofter, one of the products of Mr Simon McLeod of Skye. Crofter was sired by the Countess of Aberdeen's Ferracher, whose parents bore the not too enlightening names of Jack and Nancy; his dam was Morag, whose sole claim to notice is that she was a daughter of Ch. Gesto.

Crofter won his first two certificates at successive shows while still in the hands of his breeder in 1912; by the time he won his qualifying certificate he was in the possession of Miss Viccars and Colonel Young.

Opinions as to his quality seem to have been sharply divided, one judge writing: 'Perhaps a little lacking in size, as good a Cairn as we have seen,' while another asserted: 'I do not care for the dog's type of coat or his outlook, to my mind he is short of Cairn character.'

Whatever he was like is of no more than historical interest today as neither the line J, nor the Family No. 22, to which he belonged, has any influence.

A kennel which had considerable influence in the earlier years was that owned by Mr D. McLennan. It would seem that he originally used the prefix Raeburn, but later registered that of Carngowan, and it was bearing the latter that his most successful exhibits appeared. Mr McLennan started his

certificate-winning career with Cuag, which won one certificate and must not be confused with Ch. Carngowan Cuag, a
later inmate of the kennel. The first champion bred and
owned by the kennel was Ch. Sporran, litter brother of Cuag,
which was described as a light brindle. All the reports of
judges indicate him to have been a sound terrier, though one
commented unfavourably on his coat. Sporran was sired by
Firring Fling and was thus a member of the branch DF of the
line D; his dam, Raeburn Morag, was a member of Family No.
26. Neither the branch nor the Family has produced a champion since 1946.

Ch. Sporran's most noteworthy pup was Ch. MacSporran,
whose dam was Lugate Lively, which had as grand-sires Ch.
Gesto and Ch. Skye Crofter. MacSporran, himself the winner
of five challenge certificates, mated to Ch. Carngowan
Ailsaveg (winner of four certificates), produced Ch.
Carngowan Canach (five certificates) and Ch. Carngowan
Cuag (six certificates) in one litter, and Carngowan Peter in a
later litter. MacSporran was also the sire of Ch. Carngowan
Manus (four certificates).

The two reports on MacSporran that are available are somewhat conflicting; the first, after remarking 'a really beautiful
dog', ends 'might be a bit smaller in ear and perhaps a shade
harder in coat'; the second reads 'splendid hard double coat',
and refers to his large ears.

He was described as a silver grey.

Ch. Carngowan Manus, described as a light red, was further
evidence of the breeder's ability in the use of inbreeding and
line-breeding. Not only were his sire (Ch. MacSporran) and
his dam (Carngowan Feorag) pups of the same bitch (Lugate
Lively), but his grand-sires Ch. Sporran and Raeburn Conas
were by the brothers Firring Fling and Ch. Firring Frolic,
respectively, out of the same bitch (Raeburn Morag).

Manus passed into the hands of Mrs Prichard as a pup and
won his four challenge certificates under her guidance, his
first when he was about ten months old. Naturally he had a big
influence on the Donnington kennel, though his sole personal
contribution to winners of certificates in that kennel was
Donnington Nibs, which won one certificate.

Perhaps the most influential of the many Cairns bearing the Carngowan prefix was Ch. Carngowan Murran, whose sire was Raeburn Conas and his dam Lugate Lively. Murran was the sire of Ch. Gillie of Hyver and his name is, therefore, to be found in the pedigrees of many Cairns today.

Quite obviously any kennel that, during the period 1915 to 1939, produced or owned nine champions and nine other challenge-certificate winners cannot be passed over without some comment on the breeding methods followed by the owner. A scrutiny of many of the pedigrees indicates a careful and intelligent use of both inbreeding and line-breeding. A number of the Cairns bred in this kennel had only five grandparents instead of the usual eight, and in some instances these grandparents were closely related. As there has never been a perfect Cairn it cannot be said that the Carngowans were faultless, but all were well-built specimens with little indication of the fearful results so often predicted by the opponents of inbreeding, so we are entitled to assume that in this kennel the inbreeding was conducted in a manner which excluded such risks.

The last champion made up by Mr McLennan was Ch. Carngowan Clarice, which reached that position by winning the last challenge certificate for Cairns at the last championship show to be held prior to the outbreak of the Second World War; the show was at Harrogate, the date 2 September, 1939.

Ch. Gillie of Hyver. In Gillie of Hyver we have one of the three great sires which dominated the breed during the decade between 1920 and 1930. Gillie was bred by Mr Gilbert but ultimately passed into the hands of Mrs Stephens, with whom he won eight certificates, whose kennel owed a great deal to his influence. He sired three champions and four certificate winners, and by his won efforts and those of his numerous sons had a great influence in many other kennels throughout the breed.

He was whelped on 7 April, 1921, and, as already stated, was by Ch. Carngowan Murran; his dam was Gillassie of Ninfield whose dam, the pedigree-unknown Raitts Rannaich, was at one time owned by Mr Brester MacPherson, an early

supporter of the breed and a founder of the Cairn Terrier
Club.

In view of his influence Mr and Mrs Caspersz used the G of
Gillie's name as the symbol of the DG branch of the D line:
this branch is undoubtedly the most potent influence in Cairn
breeding today. Of the 132 champions which have reached
that title since 1946 no fewer than seventy-two are direct
descendants in the male line from Ch. Gillie of Hyver.

Gillie was a red brindle, and as he won his certificates under
both specialists and well-known all-rounders, it can be
assumed that he deserved the good opinion of those judges
who reported on him.

There is little doubt that the strength of the Hyver prefix
and the kennel of Mrs Stephens, the owner, can quite
truthfully be ascribed to her acquisition of Gillie. Mrs
Stephens either deliberately or by force of circumstances
appears to have concentrated on males. Of the twelve Cairns,
bearing the Hyver trademark, which won one or more
challenge certificates, only one, Ch. Bussels of Hyver, was a
bitch. But with the passing of generations the influence is now
equally distributed between the sexes, since, of the seventy-
two champions belonging to the DG and DGS branches
produced by the descendants of this kennel since the last war,
thirty-five are dogs and thirty-seven bitches.

In her early days in Cairns, Mrs Stephens was also interested
in breeding cats, and in those days, when money had some
value, she sold one for £100.

At the Out of the West kennel though Mrs Fleming had
been an early supporter of the breed, having won her first
certificate, in May 1914, with Loch Scolter Out of the West,
which was bred by Mr C. McNeill, an early authority on the
breed, and others with Fireboy Out of the West, Sgitheach
Dearg Out of the West, and Cuckoo Out of the West (the last
two being pups of Loch Scolter by different sires), it was not
until after she had acquired the two Cairns best known as
Doughall Out of the West and Kyley Out of the West that the
kennel rose to the eminent position it occupied for so
many years.

Doughall (whelped 1 March 1919) was bred by Mr T. Harper,

and was originally registered under the name of The Digger; he later passed into the hands of Captain R. Carpentier who changed Digger's name to Hispid of Hardings; on becoming the property of Mrs Fleming he was given the name by which he is famous.

Meanwhile Miss L. Lockwood had bred a bitch, born on 26 August, 1919, which she had registered as Cloughton Kyle; when Mrs Fleming saw Cloughton Kyle at a show she decided that Kyle was an ideal 'wife' for Doughall, so she bought her and changed her name to Kyley Out of the West.

Neither Doughall nor Kyley was an outstanding specimen from the show-bench point of view, so the 'hunch' which moved their final owner seems to have been very near to second sight.

These two were mated on a number of occasions and, while it would be tedious to list all their offspring that became prize-winners, those which reached the higher ranks are worthy of mention. The first to start the ball rolling was Ch. Fury Out of the West which won her first certificate in August 1922, and completed her score of sixteen in May 1926; the next mating produced, in November 1921, Ch. Bonfire Out of the West, which won four certificates, and Rime Out of the West, which won one certificate; then, in April 1923, there was born the most successful of all the inmates of this kennel, Ch. Fisherman Out of the West, which won a total of twenty-two certificates, and his litter brother Ch. Spunkie Out of the West, whose winnings were the modest score of three certificates. Finally, there was born in February 1926 Ch. Tam o'Shanter Out of the West, the winner of six certificates.

Any series of matings which produces five champions and one certificate winner with a total score of fifty-two challenge certificates is a remarkable record.

As was usual in this kennel the five champions were all some shade of what is called red – they were described as sandy or cream; Rime was said to be silver.

The reports of the various judges who awarded the challenge certificates to this impressive family all have a some-what monotonous use of such phrases as 'almost perfect', 'hard to fault', 'no flaw', and similar expressions of quality, though one judge described Fury as rather small, and another indicated that Tam o'Shanter was a late developer.

In addition to the six certificate winners which Kyley bore him, Doughall was the sire of five other certificate winners: Ch. Quicksilver Out of the West, whose dam was Shinnel Silver; Dusk of Cleasby ex-Shinnel Storm Cloud; Shiela of Holt ex-Jane of Holt; Shinnel Dosag ex-Dochfour Cailidh, and Treasure Trove Out of the West, a daughter of Ch. Derelict Out of the West. Derelict Out of the West was, so far as pedigree went, a complete departure from the usual inmates of the kennel, being of pure Harviestoun blood.

During the twenty-five years between winning the first and last certificate the affix of this kennel was borne by twenty-four winners of certificates, of which twelve became champions; the champions not already mentioned were: Ch. Dulse, Ch. Lassie, Ch. Quicksand, Ch. Seaworthy, and Ch. Silver Hawk – all Out of the West. The total number of certificates won during the quarter of a century by Cairns bearing the suffix was 102.

The influence of the line SD to which the Doughall-Kyley offspring belong is still with us, nine champions having been added since 1946. The Family No. 16 has, however, added nothing.

While Ch. Fisherman Out of the West was the most successful male Cairn in the show ring he was not an outstanding sire; it can safely be assumed that his great success on the show bench led to many calls for his services, but he sired only one champion, Ch. Scenic Lassie, none other even winning a certificate. The same situation appears to hold regarding Doughall's and Kyley's bitch pups; there is little evidence that they transmitted the properties inherited from their parents.

In addition to her ability to pick suitable mates on very little evidence, the owner of the kennel can be described as the finest handler of a Cairn the breed has ever seen; there seemed to be some strange association between handler and exhibit, compelling the Cairn to give of his or her best.

Later in the same year (1919) which saw the birth of Doughall Out of the West there was whelped the third of the

great stud forces of the 1920's. This was Harviestoun
Raider.

Early in the 1914–18 war Mr Errington Ross had disposed
of his Glenmhor kennel of Cairns and West Highland White
Terriers, lock, stock, and barrel, to Mr Kerr of Harviestoun in
Clackmannanshire, so that he, Mr Ross, could devote his full
energies to the agricultural pursuits in which he was chiefly
engaged. It was to this foundation that the many successful
inmates of the Harviestoun kennel owe their origin.

The extraordinary influence of Raider, and his sons, is
difficult to explain as there is very little doubt that his ancestry
was a mixture of Cairn, Scottish, and West Highland White
Terrier blood.

(When attention is drawn to the presence of Scottish
Terriers in pedigrees of the early days it should be remembered that fifty or sixty years ago the disparity between the
appearances of the Cairn and Scottish was not so pronounced
as it is today.)

Like his contemporary Doughall, Raider was no great
success on the show bench, but his influence was more wide-
spread, as very few kennels of the period did not try to get
some of his blood into their Cairns.

Raider sired eleven champions and five certificate winners;
of the eleven champions Ch. Harviestoun Brigand and Ch.
Harviestoun Chieftain (dam Harviestoun Jet) were litter
brothers; Ch. Brocaire Hamish of Gesto and Ch. Brocaire Jura
(dam Brocaire Jonquil) were litter brother and sister, and Ch.
Derelict Out of the West and Ch. Geum Woffington (dam
Woffington Peggy) were litter sisters. In all, Raider's pups won
forty-eight challenge certificates.

Ch. Harviestoun Brigand was the most outstanding of
Raider's sons; in the first place he did quite a lot of winning,
and was also a sire of successful stock; he sired five champions
and four certificate winners which won twenty-four certificates
in all.

The second champion to carry the prefix of the home kennel,
Ch. Harviestoun Chieftain, did nothing to augment the
record, only one of his pups winning a certificate.

Another of Raider's pups to make an impression on the breed while carrying the original prefix was Harviestoun Forgie. Forgie was acquired by Mrs Dixon, in whose Gunthorpe kennel he sired one champion and three certificate winners carrying the Gunthorpe label, and one other in another kennel. While Forgie won his way on to the Stud Book on several occasions he never achieved the higher ranks.

The home kennel also housed at one time or another Ch. Harviestoun Aristocrat, and the certificate winners Charmer, Ina, and Lavinia, all bred on much the same lines as the more prominent inmates.

As has been said already, full use was made of the inmates of this kennel by other breeders, so that its influence soon spread throughout the breed, not always, it must be confessed, with the happiest results. However, there seems to have been an affinity between Harviestoun and Brocaire lines, and Hyver and Harviestoun lines, which produced some very pleasing specimens.

The influence of the blood from this kennel was continued most potently in the Valiant, Beechacre, and Gunthorpe kennels; in the Valiant kennel of Miss Reoch it was associated with Hyver influences, while the Beechacre animals were, in the main, pure Harviestoun.

Raider was a sound, well-built Cairn, dark-red brindle in colour, but one not blessed with the most pleasing of heads and expressions; his head was rather coarse and his expression hard. However, those judges who expressed an opinion on his kennel offspring always spoke highly of the head properties and used such expressions as 'perfect head', 'a grand terrier', 'a beautiful dog all over', and 'a top-hole little bitch', but sometimes referred to a lack of substance.

Harviestoun Raider was, of course, the root from which the G line based on Glenmhor Pride (a West Highland White Terrier), the branches GR, GC, GB, and GF, sprang, and its universality can be measured from the fact that the thirty-two champions belonging to this line when Mr and Mrs Caspersz completed their analysis were derived from no fewer than twenty families.

Since 1946 the GB branch has produced thirty-one champions, and the GR branch five champions, but while this line is the only one approaching the D line it is likely to lose its influence as the three kennels, Beechacre, Gunthorpe, and Valiant, which contained its main descendants, have now ceased to function.

Since 1912 many reports have been written and published on the numerous Cairns that have appeared in the show ring, but it is doubtful if there has ever been such unanimity as in those about Ch. Splinters of Twobees. Those of us who had the pleasure of seeing him and handling him will not be prepared to unsay one word of the eulogies written about him. A few quotations from judges' reports will give some idea of his quality: 'a great dog', 'a grand dog', 'a very lovely dog, with a really beautiful expression, a real pleasure to handle', 'a most gorgeous head – never puts a foot wrong', and 'a happy medium in all things and with that look of an outdoor dog that makes his expression so true'. All these quotations are from seasoned judges not given to the use of extravagant language in their descriptions.

Splinters was bred by Miss Bengough and Mrs Butterworth, and was born in January 1933. He started life as a red brindle but, like so many other Cairns of that colour, finished life as a dark grey brindle. During his career as a show dog he won eight challenge certificates.

Great as was his success on the show bench, it was as a sire and as an influence on the breed that he is most worthy of note. Five of his pups, four born in 1935, became champions in this country, winning a total of 36 challenge certificates, and two others won one certificate each. How many of his pups became champions overseas is not known to the writer.

It was not solely through the reproductive efforts of his outstanding prize-winning sons and daughters that Splinters transmitted his qualities, since even his less successful off-spring also carried the ability to produce Cairns of outstanding merit, as has been demonstrated by the fact that of the 216 champions which have adorned the breed since 1946 no fewer than 117 are his direct descendants in the male line. In addition to this impressive total of direct descendants there are very few Cairns both on and off the bench today which have not somewhere in their pedigree the name of this outstanding Cairn. His pre-war champion pups were Ch. Stanhurst Splinters of Boydon, Ch. Lockyers Ian, Ch. Silver Hawk Out of the West, and Ch. Binkgo of Twobees; in addition, Rufus of Coila and Titania of Hearn each won one certificate. Since 1946 he has been responsible for one more champion, Ch. Bonfire of Twobees.

As well as Bonfire, the kennel has housed four other champions since 1946: Ch. McJoe, Ch. Simon, and Ch. Brindie, all of Twobees, and Ch. Elford Shanty. Although the last named has no recent Twobees blood in his ancestry his pedigree is liberally sprinkled with the name of Splinters. In view of the great influence on the breed of Ch. Splinters of Twobees his extended pedigree is given in Appendix A.

In contrast to the great influence of the line it is a strange fact that the Family No. 8, of which Splinters was a member, has made no addition to its list of champions since his birth in 1933. Appendix C lists influential stud dogs and brood bitches from 1946 to the present day.

6

Starting a Kennel

The novice has a number of things to consider carefully before launching into starting a kennel.

First, have you got the time and if so are you willing to devote it to the many and varied jobs involved with looking after dogs: exercising dogs both in fair weather and foul; cleaning up excreta left in the runs every day; scrubbing out kennels and dog boxes; sitting up all night (after a hard day's work) whelping a bitch; spending many hours of loving care nursing a sick dog. If these chores are irksome to you dog breeding is not for you.

Having made the decision to start a kennel the beginner must then consider accommodation: there must be a large area either surrounded by a wall or a dog escape-proof fence. A pocket handkerchief of a garden or a backyard are not suitable. A check should be made with the local authorities as to whether planning permission would be required to erect a kennel. Also thought must be given to the possibility of upsetting the neighbours, particularly in a built-up area. Finally there should be a room in the house which can be converted into a whelping room where a bitch can whelp and nurse her puppies in peace and warmth yet at the same time under supervision.

When dealing with the subject which is the heading of this chapter, John Beynon, in a previous edition of this book, wrote:

In starting a kennel, the beginner cannot be too careful. There are all sorts of pitfalls and traps into which, in his or her sublime innocence or ignorance, he or she may stumble headlong, with disastrous results to pocket and ambition, for usually the beginner is an

out-and-out optimist and counts his first prizes before the first
puppy is born, which of course is all very nice, but very foolish. All
ideas of big winners for the first year should be excluded, except as
an incentive and ultimate goal.

The following are a few guide lines for the novice to consider
before embarking on buying stock.

1. Begin with one or two, not more, young bitches.
2. Buy the best your means will permit: better one good bitch than
    a couple of moderate specimens.
3. Don't be in too much of a hurry to buy the first that comes along
    with a long line of champions in her pedigree.
4. A puppy should never be bought solely because the colour
    appeals to you, it is the quality of the dog which is all-
    important.
5. Don't buy a nervous cringing puppy because you are sorry for it,
    heart-breaking though it is to see it. It will not prove to be a
    sound foundation bitch on which to build your kennel.
6. Take a good look round and see other kennels before
    deciding.
7. Always ask to see the dam and if possible the sire and
    grandparents.
8. A warning – don't be taken in by the flashy advertisement in the
    local paper where Cairns along with several other breeds are
    advertised from the same kennel. These are likely to be puppy
    farms where puppies are bought from indiscriminate breeders
    at the tender age of 5 or 6 weeks for a quick re-sale. Pet-shops
    invariably work on the same principle.

I cannot too strongly recommend to beginners to found their kennels with one or two brood bitches which are proved breeders and
reliable mothers, for by long personal experience as a breeder,
exhibitor and judge, I have found the strength of a kennel lies in its
bitches. There are kennels that have built up their reputation upon
the influence of the stud dog, but in my experience these are the
exceptions rather than the rule and, being so, start with a good
young brood bitch. But how am I to know if it is a *good* Cairn? asks
the beginner. Well, there are many well-known kennels in the
country, and be it said to their honour, their owners are always ready
and willing to assist a breeder to make a good start. Go to one of
these, keep your eyes and ears open, and absorb all the knowledge
you can. Above all don't be afraid to display your lack of knowledge
and ask for help and advice; you will not ask in vain.

Ch. Lofthouse Larkspur, b. 1963

Ch. Merrymeet Tathwell Therese, b. 1956, dam of 3 champions
(*Thomas Fall*)

Mrs Parker-Tucker with 2
Uniquecottage Cairns

Ch. Uniquecottage Sir Frolic
(*C. M. Cooke*)

Ch. Uniquecottage Brer Fox

Uniquecottage Kurt (*Thomas Fall*)

Miss Dixon with 2 of the Rossardens
(*John Williams*)

Ch. Ronaldshay of Rossarden
(*B. Thurse*)

Ch. Rossarden Eyecatcher
(*Thomas Fall*)

Ch. Rossarden Drambuie (*Thomas Fall*)

Mrs Shuttleworth with 3 winning Monarys
(*Hinckley Times*)

Ch. Monary Saucy Kristina

Ch. Monary Susanella

While this is sound advice, Peggy Wilson, the previous reviser, is not inclined to give it unqualified support: 'In the first place, most breeders who have retained a bitch until it has had even one litter do so because they have reason to expect that she is likely to produce something good, and the mere fact that they are willing to dispose of her may mean that their hopes have not been fulfilled. It is most unlikely that any breeder would be willing to dispose of a bitch, however unsuccessful as a show specimen, that has produced pups of a good average quality interspersed with a "flyer" or two. No one can imagine the late Mrs Noney Fleming having even contemplated disposing of Kyley Out of the West after she had produced a litter of the high quality of which she was capable.'

Peggy Wilson gives further good advice to anyone contemplating starting on the absorbing hobby or enterprise of breeding and showing Cairns, which would be to visit a good number of shows and note the winners, thus getting a well-balanced idea of what a number of judges consider typical specimens. 'Make a selection of those which appeal, obtain from the owners copies of the pedigrees, and after being satisfied with the breeding, endeavour to obtain one or two bitch pups either from the one kennel or from different kennels. This will as a rule prove cheaper, and will also place in the hands of the purchaser the interest and responsibility of training the youngsters to a routine which will not clash with former activities.'

When you have made the final decision as to which bitch you wish to buy to be the foundation of your kennel, your pride and joy and your entry into the Cairn fraternity, I must emphasize that before the final monetary transactions are completed you must be emphatic that you receive a pedigree signed by the breeder, the Kennel Club Registration Certificate and the Veterinary Record of Vaccinations.

In addition to the two methods of starting a kennel already mentioned there is a third way: by obtaining a mature bitch on 'breeding terms'. These terms may be whatever the original owner of the bitch and the temporary owner may decide, and may be for any period of time or for an agreed number of litters. The agreement can also include a provision that a certain stud dog must be the sire. The 'payment' may consist of the original owner having the choice of a pup or pups from one or more litters; or there might be the payment of a sum of money for the use of the bitch. In addition the expenses in connection with the mating or matings may fall on the temporary owner. Whatever the terms are, they should be clear and succinct and should be registered with the Kennel Club, which will charge a registration fee.

However this method has certain disadvantages. Should there be a single puppy in the litter the breeder will rightfully claim it and you will be left with nothing. If there are several puppies in the litter you may set your heart on one particular puppy; this will most likely be the best in the litter as quality always stands out. When the breeder comes to see the litter to claim her puppy she may very well pick the one which you have fallen for and intended to keep. This can cause a lot of heart-break and ill-feeling between the parties concerned.

7

The Brood Bitch and the Stud Dog

The Brood Bitch

If you start your kennel with an adult bitch, check whether she has had a litter her previous season, if she has, rest her this season. If on the other hand you start with a puppy on no account mate her in her first season, a bitch should be eighteen months to two years before she is bred from. Take into consideration the time of year the puppies will be born and running about, i.e. if you mate your bitch at the very end of August or beginning of September those puppies will be seven or eight weeks old on Christmas day. Puppies should never be sold as Christmas presents. If you mate at this time you must be prepared to run the puppies on into the New Year – again not an ideal time with snow, winter storms and cold winds, for puppies to play outside exercising their limbs. When planning your mating, plan it so that you have spring or summer puppies who can scamper about and enjoy the sunshine.

Having planned to mate your bitch, at least two months before she is due in season do some homework on which stud dog you wish to use. Don't be tempted to use the dog next door or down the road because it is handy unless by good luck he is a championship show winner and an experienced stud dog producing quality puppies. If you have bought your bitch from an experienced breeder who has championship show-winning stock you could seek his or her advice as to which stud dog would suit your bitch.

Alternatively write to the Kennel Club, 1–4 Clarges Street, London W1Y 8AB or if you are resident in Scotland write to the Scottish Kennel Club, 6 Forres Street, Edinburgh EH3. They will give you the dates of the Championship shows in your area which you can visit, see the dogs (which are judged in the morning) and speak to their breeders, who you will find will be helpful and willing to send you a copy pedigree of their stud dogs. When writing to the above you can ask them to give you the name and address of the Secretary of the Cairn Club in your area, who will be able to give you valuable information.

When you get the Stud dog's pedigree study it against your bitch's pedigree to see if there are common ancestors, preferably champions or from the top winning kennels; this is called line breeding. Outcrossing means that there are no identical ancestors.

When you have made the big decision as to which dog you wish to use for your bitch, at least a month before she is due in season contact the owner of the stud dog and book a service. Enquire the cost of the stud fee, which is paid at the time the bitch is served. There are some stud dog owners who will take a puppy in lieu of the stud fee. As mentioned in the previous chapter, this can cause disappointment when they want the puppy you have set your heart on, or if there is only one puppy in the litter. It will have to be handed over to the stud dog's owner as fulfilment of your transaction and you are left with nothing. If you decide to obtain a bitch on 'Breeding Terms' I cannot emphasize too strongly that the terms of the agreement be drawn succinctly and in duplicate, both parties signing the agreement and retaining a copy. It should then be registered with the Kennel Club who will charge a small fee for this service. Verbal agreements can and very often do end up with your friendships being shattered and, at the worst, in court cases.

If the bitch is to be mated at her next season she must be prepared for motherhood: if she is too plump her weight must be reduced so that she is in hard condition; the over-fat flabby bitch can have problems whelping. If her coat is heavy and shaggy she should be tidied up. A check should be made that her vaccination boosters are up to date. It is important that the bitch is wormed before she is mated. The novice often asks 'How do I know when she comes into season?' About three weeks before she is due in season put either a white sheet or towel on her bed, inspect it every morning to see if there is any trace of blood, when you see the first spots of blood tip her up and you will see that the vulva has become swollen. When you have established that she is in season make a note of the date and let the stud dog owner know. During the three weeks while she is in season she must be under observation at all times; it has been known for a bitch to slip out and find her own husband or for an enthusiastic Romeo to leap a garden fence! If the worst happens and she gets caught by a dog from another breed all is not lost, consult your vet immediately and discuss with him whether to have the pregnancy terminated.

This is as good a place as any to suggest to those readers who may have heard of, and be prepared to accept, the idea of what was called 'telegony', to discard it once and for all. 'Telegony' was the word used to describe the theory that a mating to a dog of another breed resulted not only in the ensuing litter being either crossbreeds or even mongrels, but that all subsequent litters, no matter how well bred the sire, would be tainted by the 'foreign' blood. It cannot be too strongly stressed that each litter is entirely and completely self-contained, and influenced solely by the parents involved in its conception.

The bitch is generally ready on the eleventh or twelfth day from the start of her season, but there are exceptions to the rule. During her second week scratch her round the root of the tail, if she starts to swing her tail round on to her hip she is ready to mate. Take a swab from the vulva; the discharge should be almost clear, another sign that she is ready. Let the stud dog owner know, and make arrangements to take the bitch over for mating. The bitch must be mated when she is ready even though this may upset your social engagements. When the bitch has been successfully mated and you have paid the stud fee make sure you have been given the stud dog's pedigree.

The gestation period is normally 63 days, but this can vary four or five days either way. When the puppies have arrived let the stud dog owner know and ask them to send you a Kennel Club Registration form with the details of the dog filled in and their signature confirming the mating – you can then fill in the bitch's details and register the litter with the Kennel Club. If the bitch has failed to have puppies, also let the stud dog owner know. Usually they will give you a free service at her next season; however this is an act of grace, not one which can be demanded.

The mother-to-be should lead a normal life for the first five weeks, taking the same amount of exercise which she has been accustomed to. As the pregnancy progresses she will slow down. Feeding the bitch: she should be kept on the diet she is used to provided this is a balanced diet. If she is fed on one of the proprietary brands check that both vitamins and minerals are incorporated in the diet. If however she is fed on fresh meat and biscuit, add either half a teaspoon of sterilized bone meal and one halibut oil capsule or alternatively one of the Vitamin/Mineral supplements to her food. The bitch should be encouraged to drink milk; should she become loose on cows' milk give her Carnation milk following the dilution instructions on the tin. From the sixth week increase her food gradually until she is getting half as much again of her usual ration, as she increases in size her food should be divided first into two and then three small portions.

Thought must be given to where she is going to whelp, this must be in a quiet corner away from the mainstream of domestic traffic. One suggestion is a walk-in cupboard, the door of which should be temporarily removed and replaced by a half door made of plywood or similar material. Another suggestion is a room which is not in general use; a corner can be barricaded off remembering to roll up the carpet. Whichever place you choose the floor should be washable as there is plenty of mopping up to do with young puppies. The bitch's whelping quarters should be on the ground floor for easy access to the garden, also it is unwise for a bitch heavy in whelp to go up and down stairs.

The whelping box can be either of wood or heavy-duty cardboard; if made of wood it should be varnished with a water repellant varnish for easy cleaning. An ideal size is 28 ins (70 cm) long, 18 ins (45 cm) wide, 18 ins (45 cm) high. In the front panel of the box 3 ins (8 cm) from one end, a 10 ins (25 cm) wide section should be cut out to within 7 ins (18 cm) of the bottom of the box. This allows the bitch freedom to go in and out but also keeps the bedding in and small puppies from escaping. The box should have a hinged lid; this allows the breeder access to attend to the bitch and puppies, and when the lid is closed it helps to keep them warm and out of draughts. The box should be raised off the ground to allow air to circulate and keep the box dry. When the puppies are running around there are plenty of puddles and the urine can seep under the box. Screw either rubber or plastic door stops to each corner of the box, these don't absorb urine and they keep the box clear of the floor. (With a cardboard box glue door stops to the bottom of the 'box' so raising it off the ground.)

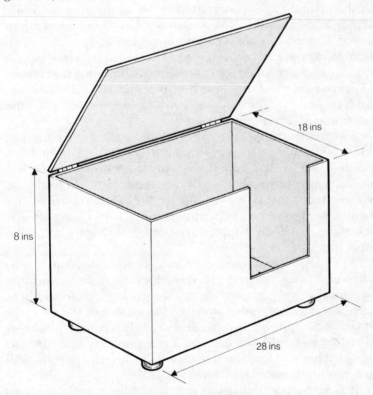

18 ins

8 ins

28 ins

Figure 1 *Whelping box*

The bitch should be introduced to her whelping quarters at least two weeks before her puppies are due so that she is quite at home in her new surroundings.

For bedding, collect clean newspapers from all your friends and relations – you can't have too many, not only to use as bedding but to spread over the floor when the puppies start running about. Place two or three whole newspapers in the bottom of the whelping box; the bitch will enjoy scratching and tearing them up to make a nest for her expected family. When whelping is in progress it is simple to remove soiled wet papers and slip fresh papers under her. Once the puppies have arrived there is a choice of bedding. Assimilated sheepskin pads can be cut to fit the box. These are machine washable and can be purchased at pet shops or at the trade stands at dog shows. Newspaper is easily disposed of when soiled, but straw is not recommended; the sharp ends can go into young puppies' eyes. If you do decide to use straw obtain it from a source where chemical sprays have not been used. Don't put a rug in a whelping box, the bitch will ruck it up into folds, a young puppy may crawl into a fold for warmth and the bitch may inadvertently lie on it.

A word of warning – once the puppies have arrived, friends, neighbours and relations will want to see them. Put the bitch out into the garden, take the visitors to see the puppies, but don't let anyone touch them in case of infection, then take the visitor into another room and let the bitch return to her family. Bitches can get very upset, particularly during the first few days after their puppies are born, if strangers come too near their babies.

Whelping is too complex a subject for inclusion in this chapter. However there are several excellent books dealing specifically with mating-whelping-weaning, some of these have spectacular photographs and diagrams of the different stages of a puppy being born. It is strongly recommended that the novice should not only read but purchase one of these books. They will find it full of invaluable information and will treasure it as a reference book.

It is important that from the age of four weeks puppies should be handled gently and played with so that they become socialized. It is a good idea to have a radio on in their room or kennel so that they get used to different noises before going out into the world and their new homes.

This Breeder's Code has been accepted by the British Cairn Clubs and several have incorporated it in their rules:

Cairn Terrier Breeders' Code

1. Before breeding a litter, equal weight should be given to type, temperament, health and soundness. Nervous or aggressive dogs are not satisfactory pets or breeding stock.
2. No bitch should be required to have an excessive number of litters, and no bitch should be mated at every season without regard to the well-being of the bitch. No bitch should be mated before the age of 12 months, nor after the age of eight years.
3. All breeding should be aimed at the improvement of the breed. Members should do all in their power to discourage breeding from clearly inferior specimens, and those members who own stud dogs should refuse stud service to such specimens.
4. No member should breed a litter unless he has the time and facilities to devote proper care and attention to the rearing of the puppies, and the well-being of the dam, and no member should provide stud service unless he is satisfied that the owner of the bitch has such time and facilities.
5. No member should breed a litter unless he is reasonably sure of finding homes for the puppies. No puppies should leave the breeder before the age of eight weeks.
6. No puppies should be exported beore they are fully inoculated or before the age of three months, unless they are travelling in the personal care of the owner or his known representative.
7. No puppies should be sold to countries where they are

not protected by anti-cruelty laws. (If in doubt consult the Ministry of Agriculture, R.S.P.C.A. or the Kennel Club.)

8. No puppies should be knowingly sold to laboratories, pet shops, or dealers in dogs, or to persons known to sell puppies to any of the above, nor should stud services be provided for such persons. (A dealer is defined as any person who regularly buys puppies in the hope of selling them for profit. A person who buys puppies as an agent for a known individual is not necessarily a dealer.) No puppy should be sold or offered as a prize in a raffle or competition.

9. Prospective buyers of puppies should be screened for suitability and should be advised of the characteristics of the Cairn Terrier as a breed, with the need for grooming and exercise. Puppies should not be sold to homes where they will be on their own all day.

10. No puppy which has any physical defect, or which shows any definite departure from the standard, should be sold without the buyer being made fully aware of such defect or departure from the standard and its possible consequences. Members should sell only animals which, to the best of their knowledge, are in good health at the time of sale.

11. Each purchaser of a Cairn puppy should be provided, at the time of sale, with a pedigree, diet sheet, and information about training, worming and inoculations.

12. No puppy that is of unregistered, or partly unregistered parentage, should be sold without the buyer being made aware that he will be unable to register it on the Kennel Club breed register.

13. It should be impressed on buyers that they should contact the breeder in the event of any problem with the puppy. Breeders should make every effort to be of assistance in these circumstances.

14. Advertising by members should be as factual as possible. Misleading exaggeration or unfounded implications of superiority should not be used. Members should refrain from making unfair or untrue statements about the dogs or practices of others.

15.   Officers or committee members of the Club are always
       ready to do their best to help members with any queries
       or problems.

The Stud Dog

The acquisition of a stud dog or, indeed, the retention of a
male pup as a stud dog, in a small kennel is not advisable. The
objections are many, but the most obvious is the temptation to
use him, sometimes to unsuitable bitches, rather than have
the trouble and cost of sending to kennels where more suitable mates are to be found. Another objection is that, should
he prove just a moderate winner, there will be little demand
for his services, and then not by owners of outstanding
bitches. While in all breeds there have been instances of
excellent specimens being produced by indifferent parents,
these cases are rare when compared with the many occasions
when the mating of outstanding specimens has resulted in
excellent pups. There have, of course, been a number of successful show-bench winners that have proved indifferent sires;
also a number of moderate show-bench specimens that have
sired good pups, but the ideal stud dog, from the owner's
point of view, is the big winner which demonstrates, by the
merit of his progeny, his ability to transmit the qualities that
have led to his own show success.

To be a real success the stud dog must be capable of mating
bitches of all temperaments, from the nervous to the relatively
bad-tempered. The pups he sires must be uniform presentable specimens of the breed, must be free from any tendency
to abnormality or to the repeated appearance of any fault or
faults. In addition to the siring of consistently good average litters, his success will depend to a great extent on the number of
outstanding prize-winners he sires.

It is obvious that a champion will always be in greater
demand that a non-champion, and the champion sire of a
champion or champions will, perhaps understandably, be in
greater demand than another with no prominent progeny. So
often a mediocre bitch is taken to a champion dog and then he
is expected to pass on his points and correct all her outstand-

ing faults in the ensuing litter – this is aptly described in the poem, *Lament of a Stud*, by Rosemary Hubrich.

My job is making puppies and I get two tries at that.
They pat me and tell 'Good Boy', and that's the end of that.
It's half my job to give 'em teeth, toplines, front and others.
Remember, it's only half my job—they also have a mother.

It's *not* my job to carry pups and make 'em grow and nurse 'em,
And feed and clean and make 'em strong, that's for a mother
      and a person.
It's *not* my job to wean and feed calcium and food,
And stack and gait and housebreak and make 'em a showing
      brood.

It's *not* my job to plan the breeding and learn what produces
      well,
To study pedigrees, learn what's there and pick out those to sell.
It's *not* my job to guarantee the Champs, the breeder picks the
      pair
To mate and whelp and feed and show—and hopes a champ is
      there.

It's *not* my job to be on hand when points are given out.
The breeder, owner, dam and friends take credit with a shout.
It's *not* my job to deliver a winner—it's only genes I sell,
But let those puppies turn out bad, and guess who catches
HELL??

If, despite the worries associated with the possession of a stud dog, the kennel owner decides to proceed, there are many things that must be done before he can expect even the minimum call for the dog's services. It is necessary, first, to prove that the dog is capable of siring; this is best done by mating him to one of the owner's own bitches that is already a proven breeder. It is most undesirable that both dog and bitch be initiates. In Cairns, the first mating is best carried out when the dog is between ten and twelve months old. Taken earlier he may not be well enough developed to realize what is required of him, and if left much after twelve months he may need more education. There have been dogs who have been mated for the first time at four and five years of age, and even later, but such are exceptions, and initiation during the latter part of the first year is desirable.

After the dog has had his first experience of stud work it is advisable to leave any further stud work until he is at least 15 months old, and not to call upon him frequently until he is between 18 months and two years old. This may seem a policy of perfection and, in view of competition, not really necessary, but the effective stud life of a dog can be very greatly restricted by over-use in his earlier days.

The number of times and the intervals at which a dog should be used at stud will depend on the demands for his services but, provided he is kept fit, well fed, and properly exercised, no harm will follow an average of two or three matings a fortnight, though it is unlikely that such a demand will be placed on any but the most successful of stud dogs. It goes without saying that the stud dog must be kept in good hard condition, the fat flabby dog seldom proves keen at stud. His coat must be kept in show condition. It does not impress the owner of the bitch to see him looking scruffy when they may not have seen him in all his glory in the show ring.

Assuming the dog fulfils all the requirements of a successful stud dog, certain duties and responsibilities are undertaken by his owner when he accepts visiting bitches, and provision must be made for meeting these responsibilities.

Safe and comfortable accommodation must be provided for the bitch, for it must be remembered that she will be in strange surroundings at a very disturbed period of her life. Whether the bitch is housed indoors or in a kennel will depend on conditions at the stud-owner's premises, together with the circumstances under which the bitch is kept when she is in her own home, an effort being made to duplicate these conditions as far as possible. In whatever manner she is housed, great care must be taken to see that she does not escape. If she is placed in an outside kennel, it should be of such construction that will prevent any athletic male, either from the kennel or from the outside world, paying an unauthorized call. The kennel should be as far distant from that of the home stud dog or dogs as possible, and if the kennel has a run this should be securely surrounded and covered with strong wire netting; the covering is necessary, because height alone will not keep out a determined Cairn, some of which have been known to climb six or eight feet, like cats.

If the bitch is sent by either rail or air ask for her to be sent a couple of days before she is due to be mated, this will allow her time to get used to her new surroundings and to the owner of the stud dog. Ask the owner of the bitch to phone you when she is despatched and you will reciprocate on her safe arrival.

No matter how the bitch is received, she should not be taken out of her box until she is in a place from which she cannot escape; the recipient must bear in mind that he has no knowledge of the bitch's disposition and that in any case the journey may have disturbed what is normally a very equable animal. Before being placed in her temporary home she should be thoroughly examined to verify that there is no evidence of parasites or any signs of contagious skin trouble. If either is noticed, the action to be taken is a matter for the stud-dog owner, but it is better to forgo a stud fee than to risk a condition which may cause a great deal of trouble, and perhaps cost more than the fee. Readers may think reference to such a situation strange, but I was once brought a bitch by a woman, a prominent member of a well-known movement, who was off on a tour of inspection; when she had left my house I found the bitch to be the worst case of lice infection I have ever seen.

Should a bitch fail to have a litter it is usual to give a second mating, free of charge, at the next season, but this is usually a matter for mutual arrangement between the two owners.

It is preferable for the owner to take the bitch to be mated. Her owner can then hold the bitch while she is being mated which will give her confidence. It is always more satisfactory to see the mating take place – should she miss there are no doubts that she wasn't mated properly.

The actual mating should normally be attempted as soon as the bitch is prepared to stand to the dog; this is usually between the ninth and twelfth day after the beginning of oestrum or 'heat'. It is well to give the animals an opportunity of getting to know each other before finding out if the bitch is willing to be mated. In an experienced bitch this is soon demonstrated by her playful attitude, and by the manner in which she curves her tail to one side. The maiden bitch may prove a different matter and will have to be approached with some circumspection. As has been mentioned, the first mating, whether of the dog or the bitch, should be to an experienced member of the opposite sex. In the first mating of a bitch it is well to smear the little finger lightly with Vaseline and insert it very carefully into the vagina to make certain there is no serious stricture; if there is, veterinary assistance should be obtained. Such trouble, however, is by no means common in Cairns, any slight restriction usually collapsing to slight pressure from the finger.

Neither the dog nor the bitch should be fed within two or three hours of the mating, and both should be given opportunities of obeying the calls of nature before any attempt at mating.

When it comes to the act of mating it is advisable to restrain the bitch, especially if she is a maiden, as any violent objection on her part can have a disastrous effect on the dog, and could turn a good stud dog into one which will mate only with the quietest and calmest of bitches; and if he had a succession of obstreperous bitches he might be permanently ruined as a stud dog. With a Cairn, which is a relatively small dog, the restraint is best applied by placing one hand in front of the chest and the other under the chest near the front legs, as in this position there is no obstruction to the dog's efforts.

There are some who advocate the use of a table for mating, but this is not to be recommended; the average Cairn spends very little time in an elevated position and many resent being more than a few inches above ground level; despite the discomfort associated with the devotional attitude essential to assisting at a mating at floor level, this is the most satisfactory and safest position. The animals should be placed on a piece of old carpet which has been firmly secured to the floor so that the dog may have a secure foothold.

Assuming all goes well, and the mating is satisfactorily achieved, there is more need for restraint after the 'tie' than before; the early restraint was with the intention of making the act of union as easy and expeditious as possible, but the restraint afterwards is for the much more necessary purpose of preventing injury to either the dog or bitch, a result which could easily follow the struggles of an inexperienced bitch.

Once the pair are more or less subdued, the handler should assist the dog to place himself alongside the bitch and thereafter carefully lift one or other hind leg over the bitch's back so that they are standing more or less tail to tail; by a little careful manoeuvring the two tails can be placed side by side and held firmly to prevent any movement. The 'tie' can last for any time, from a few minutes to over half an hour or more. After a natural separation has occurred the bitch should be put into her quarters to rest. It is wise to see that she does not urinate for at least thirty to forty minutes after mating. Before returning the dog to his kennel you should check that his penis has fully returned into the sheath.

There are breeders who believe that a 'tie' is necessary for a mating to prove fruitful, but this is not so, although it is advisable to hold the dog in position for some minutes lest, through some abnormality, a 'tie' is not effected. Again, some breeders believe in two matings, which, they allege, ensures bigger litters; this reasoning is without foundation as throughout the mammalian world the number of offspring from any union depends more on the ova produced by the female than on the sperms extruded by the male, the latter being incalculably more than needed to fertilize the relatively few ova of the female.

Another claim sometimes made on behalf of stud dogs is that they sire a higher proportion of male than female pups. There are periods when it would seem that, in the dog kingdom generally, more pups of one sex than the other are being born, but it will be found that over a lengthier period there is near equality. Some years ago the writer carried out a 'Gallup Poll' on the sex of puppies, using the details of births, as given in one of the canine papers, as a basis; the record was kept for a year and it transpired that the proportion of males to females, in that year anyway, was much the same as in humans, approximately 109 to 100 (the figures for humans are 105 to 100).

This seems an appropriate place to make reference to the conditions called cryptorchidism and monorchidism. The former is the term used for a male neither of whose testicles has descended into the scrotum, and the latter for a male where only one testicle has descended into the scrotum. The cryptorchid is unfertile; the monorchid can sire progeny, but the retained testicle can become cancerous. Veterinary advice should be sought.

At the end of the Revised Breed Standard accepted by the Kennel Club in 1982 is a Note – 'Male animals should have two apparently normal testicles fully descended into the scrotum'. At a show it is the responsibility of the judge when the dog is on the table to assess whether he is entire and make his awards accordingly. One must always keep in mind that it is the objective of the Kennel Club and the various Cairn breed clubs to promote the breeding of sound healthy dogs free from anatomical faults.

8
Feeding

Rearing Puppies

A day or two after the pups are born they should be examined for dew claws, that is, claws bearing some resemblance to the human thumb, situated on the inside of the leg a little distance above the foot. Most pups have such claws only on the front legs, but in some they are to be found on the back legs also. They should be removed early in life, and this is best effected on the third or fourth day; the removal can be done with a pair of sharp scissors, care being taken not to cut too deeply or to leave any gristle of the claw, otherwise the claw will grow again. (Some breeders leave the dew claws on the forelegs, but this is not wise because, being subjected to no wear, they continue to grow, become incurved, and require frequent attention to prevent them causing trouble.) Each small wound can be touched with an antiseptic that is not too objectionable, after which the dam's tongue will soon assist complete healing.

It must be stressed that the bitch must not be shut in the whelping box as puppies can be very demanding; at the same time she must have easy access to the box so that she can go in and out to feed and clean them when she wishes to. From the second week the puppies' nails should be trimmed and checked every week as long as they are feeding from the mother; the nails are very sharp and if left unattended will lacerate the bitch's tummy when they pummel with their front feet while they are suckling.

It is most important to worm the puppies starting at three weeks, it would be wise for the novice to seek advice from the vet who will give instructions on the dose and the necessary pills. The bitch should be wormed at the same time as the puppies are wormed.

Weaning should start at three to four weeks, this depends largely on the size of the litter, a bitch with six puppies will need help feeding her puppies earlier than a bitch with two puppies. The weaning process should be gradual. Make up a mixture to the consistency of thick cream from one of the cereal baby foods, alternatively a tin of creamed rice put through the liquidizer comes out at the right consistency. Half fill a small shallow dish or saucer and put a towel on the table, this stops the puppy slipping and catches any food which is spilt. Take each puppy out individually, place it on the table holding it gently but firmly, hold the dish under the puppy's chin and gently push its head into the dish so that it realizes there is food there; then the puppy will start lapping. It is a good idea to have a sponge or small piece of towel to wipe the puppy's face and feet as this first stage is very messy; but they get the hang of lapping very quickly. For three or four days continue giving the puppy one meal per day then increase it to two meals per day. The next step is to introduce the puppy to more solid foods, e.g. minced beef, poached fish (check there are no bones) or scrambled egg. These should be mixed with either brown bread crumbs, crushed Weetabix or soaked puppy meal moistened with either milk or warm water. A good way to start introducing the puppy to the higher protein diet is to feed each puppy individually. Take a small quantity of mince, roll it into a ball and hold it between your finger and thumb. Allow the puppy to eat small quantities of meat from your fingers which they will do with relish. By the time the puppy is six weeks old it should be having three meals per day plus a drink of milk. The bitch's milk will have almost dried up by the time the puppies are six weeks old. Take the bitch away from the puppies for 24 hours then allow her back for a short period so that they can suckle her. Remember the puppies have teeth by now so she won't tolerate them for long. The next step is to keep her away from the puppies for 48 hours, allowing her back for a short time and they will drain off the last of her milk.

If you feed your adult dogs on tinned or fresh meat, or tripe and biscuit, the puppy can be introduced to this type of feeding at five to six weeks. A mineral supplement such as Canovel or Stress should be added to one of their meals following the instructions on the tin. If on the other hand you feed one of the Complete Balanced Dry feeds, it should be soaked with warm water, additives are not necessary. Whichever brand you choose check that it contains at least 20% protein. The switchover to this type of feeding should be done gradually, it can be started when the puppy is six or seven weeks old.

A word about bones and toys, the only bone which is safe for either a puppy or adult dog is a marrow bone (in Scotland called a pipe bone).

Feeding Adults

There are four different types of diet which are suitable for an adult dog, it is up to the owner to choose which one they wish to use. Tinned foods are easy to handle with a long shelf life and a good choice of flavours. Some brands have a mixer meal to go with their tinned food or it can be mixed with a good quality biscuit. If a number of dogs are kept, this is an expensive way of feeding due to the high cost of packaging the product.

Fresh or frozen meat/tripe/offal should be cooked and mixed with a good quality biscuit or flaked meals. As this is not a complete diet it is suggested that one of the Vitamin/amino acid supplements should be added such as Canovel or Stress together with some sterilized bone meal.

Soft balanced moist diet is a convenience food with a limited shelf life. It can be mixed with biscuit meal.

Completely Balanced Expanded Dry Food, which can be obtained either as pellets or flakes, should be soaked with warm water to allow it to swell – no additives are required as it is a completely balanced food.

Fresh water in a clean bowl must always be available at all times to both dogs and puppies.

For a mild tummy upset fish and boiled rice is a good substitute for the normal diet. If the problem continues veterinary advice must be sought.

It need hardly be stressed too strongly that cleanliness must be paramount, not only in the preparation of food but also utensils and feeding dishes. Never feed food that is not 100% fresh; never be guilty of saying, 'Oh, it doesn't matter – it's only for the dog.'

A warning about toys. Pet shops and stands at shows sell a large variety of rubber and plastic balls, bones and other gimmicky toys as well as hide chews; these should only be given under supervision as they can easily be chewed up and swallowed with disastrous effects. A personal story – I received a panic phone call from a near neighbour saying her Cavalier had something stuck in her throat. She was rushed round in a very distressed state. I managed to get my finger down her throat and remove a soggy lump of hide chew. If this dog had been shut up on her own with a chew the story might have had a sad ending.

9

General Management and Training

Management and Training of a Puppy

Your puppy has come to a new home – your home. With patience, loving care and a regular routine he will settle in quickly. The puppy must have either a box or a collapsible wire cage to sleep in. A basket is not recommended as puppies love to chew them and in time the hair gets into the wicker work and it is difficult to clean. Whatever you choose, the puppy will soon realize he has a place of his own to sleep in.

If you decide on a box it should have three sides and a top, the front should have a 6-inch board nailed across it. This will not only keep the bedding in but allow the puppy access to his bed. Purchase four round door stops, either plastic or rubber; there is a hole in the middle to enable you to insert a screw. Fix one to each corner of the box which will raise it off the ground allowing a current of air to circulate underneath it, particularly important if the box is on a stone floor.

Alternatively, if the decision is to use one of the collapsible wire cages these are ideal if the puppy is to live in the house. The cages are expensive, but are versatile in their uses. If you buy a 22-inch or 24-inch cage it will be used not only when he is a puppy but right through his adult life. The advantage of a cage when travelling in a car is that not only is the dog secure but you can leave the windows open with safety while travelling. On holiday staying in a hotel or with non-doggie friends, the cage can easily be erected in your bedroom where the dog will happily settle in his own quarters.

If you decide on a cage when the puppy is very young, place a small cardboard box inside it and cut a six-inch section out of the front of the box so that the puppy has access to his bed. Place a newspaper in the tray so that when the puppy comes out to relieve himself it is easy to dispose of. As the puppy grows he will need the whole of the cage to sleep in.

For bedding the choice is either assimilated sheepskin pads which are made in a number of sizes, can be bought at a pet shop or from stalls at a dog show, and are non-allergic and machine-washable; or a woollen rug; or newspaper. Place a thick pad of newspaper in the box; it is warm, easily disposable and the puppy will enjoy tearing it and making a nest for itself.

It is, no doubt, distressing to hear a young pup expressing his feelings at the loss of the company of his brothers and sisters, particularly during the night, but if he is left alone he will settle down in a night or two just as he will equally quickly realize that a lot of howling will lead to a transfer to better quarters if the owner is weak enough to move him to the bedroom.

Now as to training; every effort should be made to do everything in connection with the dog at the same time and in the same manner every day. If this is done, the dog will train himself or herself on that point in a very short time. With regularity of conduct on the part of the owner the vast majority of dogs will soon learn to do all that is required of them. Many of the failures in the behaviour of dogs are due to carelessness, thoughtlessness, or irregularity on the part of the owner.

The first essential, particularly when the Cairn is to become the household pet, is to develop a sense of indoor cleanliness; a 'lavatorial location' can also reduce the work of cleaning up if more than one animal is involved. It is a good idea to start training a very young puppy to use newspaper. Place a newspaper on the floor, always on the same spot, and immediately after a meal place the puppy on the paper and keep him there until he has performed. Then give him a lot of praise and the puppy will soon learn to use the paper and will do so even in your absence.

When weather permits the puppy should be put out into the

garden to perform his 'lavatorial duties'. The golden rule is out first thing in the morning, last thing at night, after he has woken up from a sleep and after a meal. Always praise him when he has performed. At this stage, as in every other stage of training, the greatest patience may be called for because the slightest indication of temper may not only undo a deal of good work but may also make further training more difficult. Even in its earliest days the dog has a great desire to gain and keep the favour of those to whom it attaches itself.

Anyone setting out to train a dog has to realize that the four main requirements are patience, perseverance, firmness and kindness, and of these four the last, perhaps, is the most important.

The Cairn is one of the most intelligent of dogs and is usually quite anxious to respond to the orders, wishes and even the moods of the owner. There are at least two ways in which animals can be trained to obey human commands and the method that has been used can usually be identified by the manner in which the animal carries out its interpretation of the command. There is a great deal of difference between the happy tail-wagging movements of the dog that has been encouraged to do the right thing, and those of the dog that has been driven to do it. The idea behind the two approaches to dog training seems to be very clearly set out from the phrase 'breaking a dog to the gun' and contrasting it with 'training a dog to the gun'. This may seem to be merely juggling with words, but the two phrases do indicate two different approaches.

The first essential to be grasped by anyone who undertakes to train a dog is that all animals, including humans, are creatures of habit, and it is the purpose of all training to ensure that the good habits are developed and increased, and the bad ones are eliminated. The purpose of all elementary training or schooling is to ensure that certain things are done, and certain results achieved, by a repetitive process which calls for a minimum mental effort but achieves a uniform and unvarying final result. This may sound appalling to the adult human, but it must be remembered that we are dealing with a canine mind, and the foregoing description is exactly how we should set about our job. In other words, before we start on the dog let us try to place ourselves, as far as we can, on the level of the dog.

First decide on a simple vocabulary limited, as far as possible, to one word for each action required of the dog, and insist that everyone having anything to do with him uses the same word or words. Don't have one person saying 'no', another 'don't', and a third 'naughty, naughty', when the dog offends in some way. These words may all, more or less, be taken as indications of disapproval by a human, but to the dog they are entirely different sounds and can only confuse him. Despite the fact that we would all like to think that our dog 'understands every word we say to him', it is very doubtful if our words are any more than sounds to him, and his 'understanding' any more than an appreciation of our tone and the mental association with a pleasure which training or habit has developed.

Few of us have had lessons in elocution but we can all do something to express in the tone of voice what we are trying to convey in the word or sound we are making. Thus, we should try to say 'good' and 'bad' or 'no' in such a manner that the dog will differentiate between praise and blame. Shouting should never be resorted to; the hearing of a dog is so much more acute than our own that excessive noise may either frighten or confuse.

If the puppy was not inoculated when you purchased him, it is imperative that you make an appointment with the vet to have it done. The puppy must not be taken out into the street, meeting other dogs etc., until the inoculations are completed. When the puppy is between three and four months if you live in a busy neighbourhood take him out in your arms so that he gets used to the noise of the traffic and people, do this two or three times. The next move is to train him to a collar and lead. Put a light collar on him for a short time each day, gradually increasing the time the collar is on. He will probably object at first but he will soon get used to it. The next step is to attach a lead to the collar; let him trail it behind him round the house. When his objections to these additions to his person have subsided a little effort should be made to get him to walk while wearing them but, on no account, must he be dragged along. His first reaction may be to buck and struggle, and every effort should be made to prevent the lead from jerking him; on the other hand he may indulge in a 'sit-down' strike, when he should be joined by the trainer until he changes his mind and moves off, which may be in any direction, whereupon the good trainer becomes the follower in a game of 'follow my leader'.

Once the pup realizes that the lead is the precursor of a walk in the outside world there should be little difficulty, provided his training has been conducted with kindliness. In the early months a walk of about a quarter of a mile at a time is far enough; this distance can be gradually increased until he is able to take as much as time allows.

Once he has got thoroughy accustomed to the lead he must be trained to good behaviour while on it; he must not be allowed to strain ahead or lag behind. The proper place for a dog on the lead is on the left-hand side of and close to the handler, with the lead hanging loosely but not slackly so that instant control through the lead can be made if necessary. Should he attempt to pull ahead he should be admonished. Shorten the lead, at the same time pulling him back until he is walking by your side. It is seldom that a pup falls behind unless there is something ahead of which he is apprehensive, and should he be reluctant to proceed the handler should try to ascertain what that something is and then take steps to convince the pup that his fears are groundless. No dog should be on a road on which there is traffic without being on the lead; a loose dog is not only a danger to itself but can easily be the cause of an accident causing human deaths, as the person who lets a dog run free in such a place is unlikely to have much control over it.

When the puppy is completely happy on the lead, street manners should be taught. The handler, before setting out, should slip several small plastic bags into her pocket. Always walk on the outside of the pavement and train the puppy to relieve himself in the gutter. Should the puppy make a mess on the pavement, slip your hand into one of the plastic bags and pick up the offending mess. Draw your hand back through the bag, tie the bag into a knot and place it into the nearest waste bin; should one not be to hand, place the bag into a second plastic bag, knot it, take it home and dispose of it. The puppy should be taught not to jump up at passers by and also to pass other dogs without flying to greet them. It should always be remembered that each dog, as with each human being, has its own individuality and standard of mentality. The good trainer understands this and changes his approach to training to that most suitable to the dog. Fortunately the Cairn is a very adaptable dog, free of the dourness and stubbornness sometimes seen in his near relatives.

Occasionally one comes across a shy Cairn. He may have been bullied by his brothers and sisters or ill-treated by some uncaring human. With a lot of patience and loving care one should be able to restore his confidence though he may always remain a little apprehensive of sudden noises or strangers. Very occasionally, one comes across an aggressive Cairn. This can sometimes be expressed in possessiveness of their owner and resenting anyone coming too near them. Try making an extra fuss of the dog so he feels important. If this does not work discuss the situation with your vet.

GROOMING

One of the most pleasing features of the Cairn is that he is a breed that has been kept free of trimming and other forms of artificial 'improvement'. For this condition present-day devotees have to thank the early pioneers and their immediate successors who set their faces against any unnecessary interference with the coat. Of all the terriers, the Cairn needs less attention than most to keep him looking presentable. The fact that he is easy to keep in condition should not be made an excuse for periods of neglect. If he receives daily attention, not more than five or ten minutes' grooming is needed, and the individual who is not prepared to devote that much time to the comfort and condition of his dog should not have one.

The implements required are few and inexpensive, two combs and one brush being sufficient. Both combs should be made of metal, one having fairly widely spaced teeth, the other fine-toothed. The brush may be solely of bristle or of a double type, one side consisting of widely spaced metal prongs form-

ing a wire brush, the other of bristle. Most shops dealing with
pet requirements carry a wide selection.

The first step in grooming such a low-to-ground dog as a
Cairn is to place him on a table, as only there can the groom
see clearly what has to be done. Then he should be examined
to see if anything out of the ordinary has developed. This is
particularly necessary during summer and autumn when
there is the danger of grass seeds and parasites attaching themselves to the coat. Certain types of grass seed can work their
way through the coat and cause considerable irritation and if
they should get into the ears can cause not only irritation, but
more troublesome complications. If your dog shakes his head
or scratches one ear holding his head on one side take him to
your vet. It is a sure sign that a grass seed, some other foreign
body or an ear mite has entered the ear channel and needs
professional attention.

When the general inspection has revealed nothing calling
for special attention, the eyes should be inspected and any
foreign matter removed with cottonwool or a piece of soft
cloth; then attention should be given to the feet, to make certain that nothing which may lead to trouble has been picked
up. Any small piece of adhesive susbtance, not dangerous in
itself, can easily build up into something more serious.

Assuming all is well, the grooming can now proceed. First
the open comb should be used all over the body, legs, feet,
forehead, and muzzle. Then the brush should be used briskly,
particularly on the head furnishings, neck, body, and thighs.
Lastly the legs and feet should be tackled with the fine-toothed
comb.

When the general grooming is completed the dog should be
examined to see if any further treatment is necessary. There
may be some long hairs on the backs of the ears, under the tail,
at the rear of the legs, or round the feet, which require
removal. This can best be done with finger and thumb; if
grasped firmly and jerked the unwanted hair can be removed
with no trouble, if it is ready for removal.

Periodically the Cairn casts his coat. In this, as in many
other ways, each individual is a law unto himself or herself.
Some cast the coat approximately every six months, some
only once a year, and others have been known to go two years.

A few seem to cast and grow the coat continuously and are never really 'out of coat'. Every bitch casts her coat soon after whelping.

When coat-casting starts, the process should be assisted so that it will be completed as soon as possible and thus ensure uniformity in the succeeding coat. The process is referred to as 'stripping'. The first stage is to use the small comb to remove as much of the undercoat as is ready to be 'cast'. Combing with this implement should be continued as long as hair is being removed. Though a great deal of the coarse outer hair will come out on the brush and combs, much more can be removed with the finger and thumb. It will be found that the coarser hair on some part or parts of the body is more easily removed than that on others. These areas will vary from dog to dog, also from time to time. Obviously, no attempt should be made to jerk out hair not yet ready for removal. The process is sometimes completed in a day or two, at others it may take a week or so. Normally, the bitch after whelping completes the job very quickly. On one occasion, a litter bin and empty barrow being handy, a breeder stripped a bitch in the street while his wife did some shopping, much to the interest of some of the passers-by, and to the concern of others.

The hair on the edges of the ears sometimes becomes 'felted', but by rubbing in olive oil or some other emollient for a day or two the 'felted' hair can be detached with ease.

The use of trimming instruments is to be condemned but there are two places on the Cairn where the use of the knife and thumb is permissible. One is under the tail, where many Cairns develop a lengthy 'feather'; the other is behind the front legs, where a similar lengthy growth takes place. So far as his coat is concerned, no Cairn need ever be washed unless he has got himself into a particularly dirty or smelly condition.

Always keep your brush and combs clean. It is surprising how many people groom their dogs with dirty brushes. The mouth should be inspected from time to time. Should there be any sign of the formation of tartar this can be removed with a scaling instrument; despite statements that 'hard' feeding will prevent the formation of tartar it is doubtful if there is any method of prevention.

A Cairn which receives adequate exercise on hard roads

should require no special treatment for its feet and nails, but if the latter grow over-long they may be cut or filed. This, however, is an operation best left, in the first instance, to a skilled person.

If your Cairn has grown a very heavy coat and you feel you are unable to strip him out yourself, contact a breeder in your area. If they don't take on stripping themselves they will probably put you on to someone who does. A Cairn should never have its coat cut with electric clippers.

10

Accommodation

If you intend to keep two or three bitches and have not more than three litters a year, the dogs could be kept in the house. A downstairs room which has easy access to the garden should be turned into a dogroom. When equipping a dogroom the paramount objective should be that all surfaces should be able to be easily cleaned and durable. The floor should be covered with either vinyl or tiles. If a wood floor is preferred it should be varnished with several coats of a water-repellant varnish, for example a ship's varnish, so that urine cannot seep into the wood. The walls should be painted so that they can be washed down. Each dog should have its own box to sleep in; either a wooden box with a door which has a wire grid on the front so that there is plenty of ventilation, or alternatively one of the collapsible wire cages which make ideal sleeping quarters – plastic covers can be obtained for them for use in the winter. Each dog should be shut up in her box at night. This avoids any argument which can occur, particularly if someone has hidden a biscuit in the corner of the box under the bedding. I do want to emphasize most emphatically that dogs must not be shut in their boxes for hours on end during the day – they must have freedom and plenty of exercise.

If you intend keeping a number of dogs, the novice should visit some of the championship shows where several of the stands have kennels on display. Alternatively study the advertisement section in the dog papers and write to kennel manufacturers asking them to send you their illustrated brochures. Choose one that has big windows so that there is plenty of light in the kennels; these windows can also be opened for extra ventilation in very hot weather, ideally they should have a form of double glazing for the winter. If you decide to buy a big kennel which houses a number of dogs in individual stalls, it is also wise to buy two or three small kennels where a bitch in season or visiting can be housed away from the main kennel block. These could also be used as isolation kennels.

Thought must be given to positioning the kennel – it should not face due north or into the prevailing wind, but a south facing aspect can become unbearably hot in the summer. The ideal position is facing west. The kennel should be erected near the house so that a constant eye can be kept on the dogs; if it is pouring with rain or snowing the close proximity of the kennels to the house will be appreciated.

The run should be surrounded by a chain link fence, encircled by a strip of concrete a foot wide. The posts should be sunk into the concrete and the wire dropped four inches below the concrete strip on the outside of the run. This will prevent the enthusiastic digger with escaping in mind from burrowing underneath the wire. The surface of the run must be considered. Concrete has the advantage of being easily hosed down but against that it has the disadvantage of being extremely cold and slippery in wet and frosty weather, and again in summer it can become unbearably hot. Both conditions are bad for dogs' feet. Grass runs can become very muddy in wet weather, during the summer months there is a bit of extra work keeping the grass cut short. Grass can become very sour with continual urination and in time the run will have to be returfed. Gravel runs have taken the place of the old cinder runs of yesteryear, with central heating cinders are a thing of the past! Gravel makes an ideal surface, provides good drainage and is easily maintained. If the dogs dig holes, which they enjoy doing as the natural instinct of a terrier, they can easily be raked over. Excreta can be picked up with tongs and the run can be disinfected by watering it with a watering can containing disinfectant.

Accommodation must be available, preferably in the house, where a bitch can both whelp and nurse her puppies in peace and quiet away from the other dogs and at the same time under the supervision of the breeder. Small puppies

Above: The late Madge Hall and Dorothy Hall surrounded by Felshotts

Right: Peggy Wilson judging The Joint Cairn Show 1976

Ch. Felshott Bryany with her daughters Ch. Felshott Taste of Honey and Ch. Felshott Honey Dancer

Ch. Felshott Wine Taster

Left: Mrs Diana Hamilton with Ch. Oudenarde Fair Prospect in her arms (*The Field*)

Above: Ch. Oudenarde Queen of Light (*Thomas Fall*)

Group of Oudenarde Cairns (*Thomas Fall*)

Mrs Drummond

Ch. Blencathra Sandpiper

Ch. Blencathra Milord and Blencathra Rudolph, both b. 1956

Walter Bradshaw with Ch. Redletter McJoe, Ch. Redletter McMurran, Ch. Redletter Elford Morag and Ch. Redletter Marjose

Ch. Redletter Moonstruck (*Diane Pearce*)

Ch. Redletter McBryan, winner of 17 CCs and sire of 13 champions

need warmth, they can die very easily through hypothermia. One or two small kennels with their own runs must be provided for young stock. You can't put a five-month-old puppy in the same run as puppies of seven weeks, the older puppy would try and play with the baby puppies and be much too boisterous and frighten them. The puppy run should be of grass which is kept short. Gravel runs are not suitable as young puppies can play with small stones and swallow them. It is a good idea to nail a board between the gate posts at ground level, about ten inches high. This helps to keep the puppies in when you open the gate. Puppies can slip past you in a flash but with the board there it gives you time to shut the gate behind you before there is an escape.

11

Preparation for Shows

If an owner decides to enter the show ring, both he and his dog should undergo a period of preparation and training. The owner would be well advised to attend a number of shows of the various types from sanction to championship so that he can observe the routine and note what to do and what to avoid.

The main object when showing a dog, as in showing any animal, especially any 'fancier's' animal, is to present to the judge and to emphasize, by all legitimate means, the good points and to cover up, or at least to make less apparent, the weaker points.

When the owner has grasped show-ring procedure and, assuming the pup has become thoroughly accustomed to the lead, the time has come for the inculcation of ring manners. If the owner is fortunate enough to have a garden, part of which, by the proximity of walls, solid fences, or hedges, can be made to have some semblance of a show ring, this is where the preliminary training can be carried out. If he hasn't, he must improvise to the best of his ability.

The trainer should have, in his right-hand pocket, a good few titbits, and should put the dog through the routine usually carried out in the show ring. There is no need to duplicate the examination which takes place on the table as any well-groomed Cairn should be well accustomed to this part of the procedure. It is, however, quite a good idea to get any willing visitor to carry out the table routine so that the Cairn becomes familiar with the idea of strangers dealing with him in such circumstances.

As dogs are always moved in an anti-clockwise direction the lead should be held in the left hand, and the dog should be

walked round and up and down while his attention is held by
the movement of the disengaged hand containing one of the
titbits which he has been allowed to smell and which should
be given him as a reward at intervals, but only when he has carried out his movements correctly.

Not every Cairn will respond to ring training in the same
manner any more than he will respond uniformly on other
matters. No matter what is the response, the training must not
be prolonged at any one session, otherwise the dog may
become bored, a condition which can easily become habitual.
Five or ten minutes at a time is quite sufficient and, provided
the circumstances of the owner permit, it is not a bad idea to
train males in the forenoon and females in the afternoon,
which are the times when they are usually called upon 'to do
their stuff' in the show ring.

The greatest difficulty will, as a rule, be in getting the Cairn,
particularly bitches, to maintain a 'show' position while standing, and on this point every effort should be made and every
encouragement given to achieve the desired result.

Never train a Cairn for show by bouncing a ball. Its use in
the show ring, in addition to animating the handler's dog, will
also animate every other animal in the ring and lead to such
activity and jumping about as to render the judge's job more
difficult than it need be; it will almost certainly call forth a
sharp rebuke from him or her. To put it bluntly, the use of a
ball indicates a failure to apply proper training technique, and
a disregard for other handlers who are proceeding in a more
considerate manner.

In addition to training the Cairn to show behaviour at home
it is well to take him to places where there is much activity of
both humans and vehicles, and where he can be trained to
keep his attention on his handler despite all invitations to the
contrary. This is a job of patience, but, provided a start is made
in a moderately quiet spot, and the situation gradually inten-
sified by moving to busier environs, it can develop a very close
communion between handler and dog.

Once a Cairn has the 'show' idea well fixed in his mind, a
refresher course for a few days before a show is all that is
required.

It must always be remembered that, among canines, there

are good showmen, not so good showmen, and, unfortunately, some that may never be showmen. The first is the gift of the canine gods to any handler; the second, with an expert handler, can nearly equal the first, but he will require more work, attention and encouragement; and the third, in the hands of the gifted few, can be made to put up a good show, but is a disappointing handful for the majority.

The preparation of the physical condition of a Cairn is by no means difficult because the breed can truthfully be described as one of the most natural of all dogs. It is not too much to say that any Cairn that receives the daily attention he deserves should be in a fit condition to go into the show ring on very short notice, provided he is not out of coat. There is, fortunately, no need to be an efficient barber to put the finishing touches to a Cairn's appearance; he has, of course, to be tidied up, and this should be a gradual process, not left to be a rush job the day before the show. The long hair, if any, behind and round the ears has to be removed, as also has any excessive 'feathering' on the tail and behind the front legs; the nails should be filed down, though this should be unnecessary in well-exercised animals. Apart from these little attentions, and the removal of any long hairs beneath the stomach, all that is needed can be achieved by the effective use of the brush and comb.

The equipment needed at the show, in addition to brush, comb, and drinking dish, is a bench chain and a show lead. The bench chain should be as light as possible though strong enough to hold the dog and short enough to prevent his falling off the bench and hanging himself. The usual show lead is of cord, with a sliding grip on a loop which forms the collar; incidentally, the show training should be given with such a lead.

As straw is not used on the benches now (it never was a good thing anyway), a piece of old blanket, an old travelling rug, or, perhaps better than either, a few old newspapers which have been impregnated with some disinfectant and allowed to dry, can be taken to cover the bench. Though the benches are disinfected by the benching contractors nothing is lost by taking personal precautions.

Alternatively, some exhibitors take collapsible wire cages with them which they erect on their bench. This is a good idea as it gives the dog room to move around without getting tangled in the benching chain and while still remaining secure.

Once in the ring, the judge having started on his part of the day's work, it is up to the handler to divide his attention between his dog and the judge. If the dog is a good showman, more attention can be given to the judge after the table examination has been completed and the individual 'walkabout' carried out, but normally it is well to keep an eye on both. Every animal, including dog judges, can see round the corner of the eye so no slackness on the dog's part should be permitted.

Never crowd round the judge, never impede a fellow exhibitor, and *never* get into a prayerful position to hold up the head and tail of a Cairn; this is behaviour that has been strongly condemned from the earliest show days and if attempted may, at best, be dealt with by a caustic remark, or, at the worst, by an invitation to leave the ring.

After the judge has made his awards, take them with equanimity, win or lose. In winning do not crow too loudly – the next judge may have a different opinion; in losing, remember that every judge is entitled to his opinion, and the vast majority are doing their honest best; further, the appearance of your dog at the show is the result of a voluntary act on your part.

The responsibility for getting an exhibit into the ring rests on the handler who should always bear in mind that under a regulation of the Kennel Club an exhibit which misses a class is liable to be disqualified from all other classes in which it may be entered.

The mention of stewards prompts the suggestion that these hard-working amateurs deserve every assistance from exhibitors; no trade union would permit its members to work so long for so little.

This seems as good a place as any to give a brief description of the various types of shows held under Kennel Club control.

The most important is the championship show at which the Kennel Club grants challenge certificates, one for dogs and one for bitches; in a few shows these certificates are granted to all breeds catered for, but in the majority of shows to a limited and varying number of breeds. The number of pairs of challenge certificates issued in the course of a year to any breed is governed by the 'Breed Entry' figure which is determined by the total number of exhibits entered annually at General and Group Championship Shows where challenge certificates are on offer for the breed, averaged over the last three-year period. To this number is added the average number of exhibits at Breed Club Championship Shows over the same period.

This new system became effective in 1978 and the Kennel Club have allocated to the Cairns 26 sets of challenge certificates at General Championship shows, two sets at Group Championship shows, six sets at Breed Championship shows and one set at the Joint Cairn Breed Club show. The winning of three challenge certificates under three different judges approved by the Kennel Club confers on the winning dog the title of Champion. Certificates which are won at Championship Shows run by the six Cairn Clubs are the most highly regarded and prized by breeders and exhibitors.

General Championship shows held under the Kennel Club rules no longer give prize money for individual classes. Group winners and Best in Show receive prizes which are generally sponsored by commercial dog food firms. Breed Championship shows continue to give prize money for the first four in each class; this applies also to Open and Limited shows.

In the United States and in Eire, and in some other countries, the method of achieving the rank of champion is based upon a points system; the number of points secured in respect of the award of best in each sex varying according to the number of exhibits present at the show. The allocation of points varies from country to country, and in some instances calls for the winning of the maximum possible points on at least one occasion.

After the championship show the next in order of importance is the open show. This type differs from the other mainly in the absence of challenge certificates, and is therefore not considered of such a high standard. This does not mean that the exhibits may not be of equally high quality.

A limited show is similar to an open show but is limited to members of the promoting society or to exhibitors living within a specified area and dogs which have not won challenge certificates.

Sanction shows are confined to members of the promoting society and dogs which have not won challenge certificates. Also, no class higher than post-graduate may be scheduled at a sanction show.

Primary Show. The General Committee of the Kennel Club shall have the power to grant permission to hold a show in accordance with regulations laid down by the Kennel Club. Not more than eight classes may be scheduled, the highest of which is Maiden. Only bonafide members of the association, club or society may compete. All dogs competing must be Kennel Club registered. Entry fees may be taken on the day of the show. The exhibitor must complete and sign an entry form.

Matches. At a match, not more than 48 dogs owned by the members of the clubs engaged in the match may compete, and the class of animal is limited as in sanction shows. The match is carried forward on a knock-out principle until the two best meet in the final match, and to these two only may special prizes be awarded.

Exemption Shows. This type of show can best be described by quoting the Kennel Club:

The Committee of the Kennel Club or its Delegated Authority will, under special circumstances, grant to Agricultural and Horticultural Shows, Fêtes, and like, under the title of Exemption shows or Classes, permission to hold a Show of not more than four Classes for dogs at their Exhibitions, and the dogs exhibited at such Exemption Shows or in such Classes need not be registered, but any such Show or Classes and the Exhibitors in them will be subject to Kennel Club Rules 15, 17, 18 and 22.

In addition to the four authorized classes there are usually a number of novelty classes.

12

Points and Character

In writing on these two important subjects one cannot do
better than quote the opinion of that great authority the late
Mrs Alastair Campbell, expressed in a letter to Mr Beynon
some years ago. Her comments are as applicable to the breed
today as when they were first written. This is what she
wrote:

We do not wish the Fox Terrier front, but, can anything be nicer
than the broad shoulders and a straight front with toes slightly
turned out? Thick digging pads don't matter so much provided the
shoulder is in. The shelly Cairn is too common at present. We want
deep well-sprung ribs, with strong quarters, which are most important and so difficult to judge in a ring, but let a pack loose and then
you see the quarters; they should be light-footed and almost dance
along. I have always said they are like polo ponies, sturdy, but light
in their action and body.

They are difficult to describe, and why we say 'foxy outlook' is to
impress the wild look, or look of the wild. They have also the slyness
of the fox in many ways. I find my wildest are my best house dogs!
There is no need to think keeping them in the house will spoil them,
they love people and hate to be away from them. This I account for,
that for generations they have been about people and houses, living
in close daily contact with them. Good swimmers, they love water,
love boats and love hunting! It is little wonder they are considered
one of the most attractive of terriers.

As in all questions of working terriers, the size is the great difficulty, but when choosing or judging a Cairn Terrier one must always
remember that he is meant for bolting, not killing. One does not go
to work with one, but several terriers. In the West they prefer the
small ones. They may not be very light, so that weight is a very bad
guide; small sturdy terrier are what we want; lightly built ones with
narrow shoulders may be wonderful in the way of getting in and out

of a bad place, but they have not the strength for the work required. When a keeper chooses for work apart from gameness, he will always insist on the more compact terrier, not toys, which may be quite as game, but will be condemned as too small. I have seen large Cairns 13½ lb and small ones weighing 14 lb. The best are those with a fairly short jaw and broad in head, in fact, 'foxy'. Many are deceived by the baby face, but it very soon turns into a fierce, snarling face, and will hold on however badly wounded. They are a curious mixture of gentleness and fierceness.

Among kennels kept for work one certainly sees sometimes very soft coats, but the double coat, with the hard outer coat, is what is most desired. I think they simply were careless in selection in the old kennels. The very light eye is fast disappearing, also the bad mouths, and we hope soon the over-gay tail will disappear, but as two of these faults did not interfere with work, I fear fanciers did not trouble much about them in former days.

As this book is not particularly intended for kennel owners who keep their terriers purely for work and hunting, we will not say more about the working points of the Cairn Terrier, over which much ink has been spilled at various times, but as the Cairn is purely an Earth dog or working terrier the points should be entirely in agreement with those laid down for the Perfect Cairn Terrier. Some of our best Cairns have proved as good on the hillside as in the show ring; Ch. Gesto was a notable example.

A letter by the late Hon. Mary Hawke to the *Illustrated Kennel News* some years back, contained the following:

Two years ago I passed a very good little dog at the L.K.A. Show on account of his size, and the other day winning dogs in Scotland were not so large as he was. There were small Cairn Terriers in the olden days, but the Cairn Terrier Club decided that dogs and bitches should be about a certain size. It is more difficult to breed a medium-sized dog, and we Cairn breeders, both Scotch and English, must try to accomplish it; and do let us try and breed dogs with a good thick undercoat, which is hard to get.

The last sentence applies equally strongly today as it did when she wrote it all those years ago.

During the years there has been considerable controversy on the variation of type and size: any resemblance in conformation to either the West Highland or Scottie is not acceptable. The new standard for the Cairn Terrier agreed at the meeting of representatives of the six Cairn Terrier clubs on 23 and 24 January 1982 and approved by the Executive committee of the Kennel Club 20 November 1982 gives details of approximate height and weight acceptable to the breed.

Breed Standard
Revised 1982

Characteristics. Should impress as being active, game and hardy.

General Appearance. Agile, alert, of workmanlike natural appearance. Should stand well forward on forepaws. Strong quarters. Deep in rib, very free in movement. Weather-resistant coat.

Temperament. Fearless and gay disposition; assertive but not aggressive.

Head and Skull. Head small, but in proportion to body. Skull broad, a decided indentation between the eyes with a definite stop. Muzzle powerful, jaw strong but not long or heavy. Nose black. Head well furnished.

Eyes. Wide apart, medium in size, dark hazel. Slightly sunk with shaggy eyebrows.

Ears. Small, pointed, well carried and erect; not too closely set nor heavily coated.

Mouth. Large teeth. Jaw strong with a perfect, regular and complete scissor bite, i.e. the upper teeth closely overlapping lower teeth and set square to jaws.

Neck. Well set on, not short.

Forequarters. Sloping shoulders, medium length of leg, good but not too heavy bone. Forelegs never out at elbow. Legs covered with harsh hair.

Body. Back level, medium in length. Well-sprung deep ribs; strong supple loin.

Hindquarters. Very strong muscular thighs. Good, but not excessive, bend of stifle. Hocks well let down, inclining neither in nor out when viewed from the rear.

Feet. Forefeet, larger than hind, may be slightly turned out. Pads thick and strong. Thin, narrow or spreading feet and long nails, objectionable.

Tail. Short, balanced, well furnished with hair but not feathery. Neither high nor low set, carried gaily but not turned down towards back.

Gait. Very free-flowing stride. Forelegs reaching well forward. Hind legs giving strong propulsion. Hocks neither too close nor too wide.

Coat. Very important. Weather-resistant. Must be double-coated, with profuse, harsh but not coarse, outer coat; undercoat short, soft and close. Open coats objectionable. Slight wave permissible.

Colour. Cream, wheaten, red, grey or nearly black. Brindling in all these colours acceptable. Not solid black, or white, or black and tan. Dark points such as ears and muzzle very typical.

Weight and Size. Approximately 28 cms to 31 cms (11 to 12 inches) at the withers, but in proportion to weight – ideally 6 to 7½ kgs (14 to 16 pounds).

Faults. Any departure from the foregoing points should be considered a fault and the seriousness of the fault should be in exact proportion to its degree.

Note. Male animals should have two apparently normal testicles fully descended into the scrotum.

The following comments on the Standard are by Mr Fisher. Peggy Wilson, the previous reviser, wrote in her introduction to the 6th Edition 'provided Mr Fisher's classic interpretation to the Standard is understood and accepted by breeders, exhibitors and judges in every part of the world then the essential true type and character of the Cairn will be safe.' I can only echo the sentiment.

Characteristics. The phrase means that the Cairn while moving through life, and particularly when in the show ring, should appear to be enjoying its life; should carry its tail, if not perpendicularly, at least well up from the horizontal, but never hooked over the back.

General Appearance. The first few words are Characteristics expressed in another way. It is when we come to the words 'natural appearance' that we are called upon to exercise discretion. These words do not mean ungroomed, untidy, or neglected; they do mean there should be none of that excessive preparation which has turned other terrier breeds into what are little more than animated examples of the china dogs formerly so popular as shelf decorations.

Standing well forward on forepaws implies the possession of a well-developed brisket and the absence of any indication of a straight-line appearance of the forelegs and chest, as seen in long-legged terriers when viewed from the side.

Very free in movement means that the forelegs should reach well forward and the hind legs give every indication of a strong push when the Cairn is moving at the trot. Standing to the rear and slightly to one side it should be possible to get a good view of the pads of both front and rear feet at the completion of each step.

The reference to the head is obviously intended to condemn any exaggeration of this very important item in the make-up and general appearance of the Cairn; there should be no coarseness, and no undue length of the whole head or of the foreface.

There are those who describe the Cairn as having a general foxy appearance, the writer cannot accept this as a good description of the Cairn whose proportions and outline are, in his opinion, very different from those of 'Brock', of whom it would not be unkind to say that he lacks the attributes of a 'fearless and gay disposition', there being in his appearance more evidence of the furtive and the sly.

Head and Skull. Here the statement covering the development of the skull in the vicinity of the eyes is, perhaps, not too clear. While there is an indentation running up the skull between the eyes, the real essential is the possession of a decided 'stop'. 'Stop' means a sudden and short rise in the bone structure, carrying the level of the foreface up to that of the skull, but this rise should not continue in such a manner as to produce the condition known as 'apple-headed' but should be delicately rounded to the occiput. The phrase 'very strong jaw, which should be neither undershot nor overshot' could mislead one to imagine that the incisors (front teeth) should meet point to point, but the correct 'bite' can best be described as a 'scissors grip', i.e. the incisors of the lower jaw fitting evenly and tightly but slightly behind those of the upper jaw.

Eyes. Little need be added to the Standard except to stress the colour; some judges have a preference for black eyes, but the possession of these deprives the Cairn of its correct expression.

Ears. The correct placement of these external organs is of considerable importance in the make-up of the head; when they are carried too close, too wide, too far forward or too far back they mar the appearance of the whole head. It is difficult to give a description of the correct placement, but a glance at a head with well-placed ears and at others not so happily situated will soon demonstrate.

Mouth. In a hunting dog this is very important. There has been in recent years a tendency for some Cairns to have small teeth, but fortunately this is diminishing, though care must be taken as such things have a tendency to move in cycles. This is a good point at which to state that the adult dog of any breed should have 42 teeth distributed as follows: six incisors in each jaw, two large canine teeth (commonly called tusks), four pre-molars in each side of the upper and lower jaws, two molars in each side of the upper jaw, and three molars in each side of the lower. The position of these teeth, starting from the back of the jaw, is: molars, pre-molars, canines, and incisors. These details of dentition are given because a few Cairns have been shown with fewer than the natural number of incisors and, while the Standard makes no mention of the number of teeth, nature apparently intended the number to be as stated, and some judges look on a lower number as a fault though not necessarily a serious one.

Neck, Forequarters, and Body. These three can be treated as a whole, as they deal with bodily construction. While it is difficult to define the word in all its connotations the main factor in the Cairn's construction can be summed up in the word 'medium'. This means that the Cairn must be built up to a well-proportioned and well-balanced animal free of exaggerations in any shape or form. The shoulders must be sloping and the upright form of shoulder must be avoided for two reasons: first, and most important, is that a sloping shoulder gives freedom of movement to the forelegs; secondly, the Cairn's chest does not rest on the forelegs but is placed between them so that with the well-sprung ribs, which are essential, the arch of the sound straight forelegs and sloping shoulders should be complete.

The writer (A.F.) confesses that what is meant by 'strong sinews' is not quite clear to him. His dictionary gives 'sinew: that which unites a muscle to a bone; a tendon'. Not being gifted with X-ray eyes he fails to understand how this can be ascertained by ordinary judging technique. It is possible that the two words are meant to imply that the animal is well knit and well held together with an absence of flabbiness or softness.

The need for strength in the hindquarters is obvious when one considers the terrain of the original home of the breed. This strength can be obtained only by muscular development associated with a well-bent stifle. Straight stifles are a sign of weakness and should be heavily condemned, apart from the fact that no Cairn with straight stifles can move as a Cairn should.

The forelegs should be wider apart than the hind legs but both sets should, in movement, be carried forward in a straight line and should not be swung inwards or outwards. At the present time quite a number of Cairns, particularly youngsters, advance their forefeet with a skating motion.

Coat. As stated in the Standard, this is very important and there is very little to add to the description except that the Cairn is, or should be, blessed with a coat that is one of the easiest to keep in condition.

Colour. It could be said with safety that the only colours to which anyone could take exception are white or pure black, provided the colour, whatever it may be, is evenly distributed over the body and there are no *patches* of any other colour.

Under *Faults* the statement condemning any resemblance to the Scottish Terrier is interesting, as in the original Standard this item read: 'In order to keep this breed to the best old working type, any cross with a *modern* Scottish Terrier will be considered objectionable.'

While the pet or show Cairn Terrier of today is seldom, if ever, called on to emulate the hunting activities of his remote ancestors, it is of interest to compare the results of years of more or less selective breeding with what a practical gamekeeper thought the ideal for his purpose 40-odd years ago.

During the early part of 1914 there was some correspondence in *Dogs Weekly* as to the correct size and conformation of the breed. One writer, who described himself as a humble gamekeeper, and who claimed to have had 15 years fox and otter hunting in the Highlands of Scotland, wrote:

Give me the medium-lengthed backed dog, strong hindquarters, good feet, and not too short-legged, a powerful jaw, good teeth, lots of spirit – none of your liver-coaxed dead heads' – a weather-resisting top coat (cannot be hard enough), a woolly undercoat, and weight about 14 lbs, a scale such as bitches 11 to 12 lb, dogs 12 to 14 lb.

In the 1982 Breed Standard reference is made to weight and size – approximately 28 cm to 31 cm (11 to 12 inches) at the withers but in proportion to weight – ideally 6 to 7½ kgs (14–16 pounds). From the physical conformation point of view it would seem that what the practical man wanted in 1914 was very much what the lover of the breed wants today.

Writing in the previous edition, John Beynon asked, 'What is type?' and the remainder of this chapter comes from his answer to this question.

TYPE AND COMMON FAULTS

Probably more ink has been spilled in trying to find the answer to the three words 'what is type?' than to any other question relating to dogs.

Most judges and breeders find their own answer, and judge

the breed according to their own conception and interpretation of the standard of points. It is a case of many men, many
minds, and certainly it lends that sporting element to showing
dogs which always appeals to the average individual. Diversity
of opinion, if not carried to extremes, is beneficial, for it helps
to bring out the best in each side, but, if carried too far, causes
endless confusion and does much harm.

In 1914 there was a tremendous controversy as to what
really constituted a correct Cairn Terrier; there were so many
different 'types' and varying sizes that no one quite knew
where they were. The arguments did a lot of good, cleared the
air, and led to a better understanding. The 'Scottish Terrier'
cross was banned for good, those who favoured a cross with
the West Highland White Terrier carried out their pro-
gramme, and the remainder stuck to the original stock.

The true Cairn Terrier is a much smaller dog than the Scottish Terrier, also smaller than the West Highland White
Terrier, which has many points in common with the Cairn but
is broader in skull, wider in ear carriage, and built on stronger
and sturdier lines. The chief distinction, however, lies in the
expression for no other terrier that I know of has that furtive,
foxy look, and the deep red-brown eye, which simply fas-
cinates one. The eye of the Cairn Terrier is where many go
astray, for they look for the boot-button black eye of the Scottish Terrier, which is all wrong because no Cairn can have the
correct expression with such an eye. The Cairn eye is of
medium size, dark hazel or rich red-brown in colour, and well
fringed with eyelashes, the want of which gives a decided
Scottie expression.

The skull should be broad between small pointed ears,
which at attention should incline outwards. Ears set too close
together and upright generally give a Scottie character to the
expression, and particularly so if accompanied by a too long
foreface or jaw, which, to be correct in a Cairn, should be short
and very strong – distinctly a fox jaw. The front and legs
should be straight, with the elbows placed well in, feet small,
sound and cat-like, with good pads (*see* Figure 18). In body he
should be of moderate length to enable him to turn and work
in the cairns, or underground. A good thick undercoat and a

moderately long harsh outercoat are essential to protect him from the elements.

At one time there was a craze for 'short' backs, but luckily for the good of the breed it eventually died out to a very great extent. We want a compactly built, but at the same time a lithe, lissom terrier, with just sufficient length of leg to give great agility. A good deal of stress is laid on tails. A long, gaily carried tail is most unsightly; the tail should be short, thickly covered with hair, and carried nearly erect.

The drawings illustrate the various points mentioned in the foregoing. Figure 2 is an admirable illustration of the correct type of Cairn Terrier: moderate in length of body, forelegs straight and true, with correctly placed elbows. The carriage of ears and tail should be particularly noted.

Now compare this with figure 3. Study it and note the thick-set, blocky body as compared with the agile-looking dog in figure 2. Note, too, the longer and stronger muzzle, the close-set ears, and the different expression the eye gives, all of which tend to give a Scottie appearance to a terrier built on these lines. It is, unfortunately, a type of terrier which at one time too often found a place in the prize lists. In this sketch the artist has cleverly and distinctly shown two other common and prevalent faults not confined to any 'type' but to be observed in specimens of varying types, and that is the straight stifles and hocks. Any dog with these faults is bound to be an indifferent mover, lacking in agility and propelling power through this malformation.

Figure 4 is another 'type' to be met with. Its faults are most apparent: weak in face, too high in the leg, which the want of coat, or furnishings, accentuate; it is light in bone, lacks substance in body, and is, in doggy parlance, a 'weed'.

It does not follow that a dog with such a body as depicted in this sketch will have a similar head. Unfortunately, it is not uncommon to see a most beautiful true Cairn head attached to such a framework, and such dogs do the breed considerable harm. Many people are fascinated by the beauty of the head and expression and are tempted to breed from it – losing sight of the fact that the many deformities may be reproduced in the progeny – with the remote hope of breeding a puppy with a

Figure 2   *Correct type*

Figure 3   *Wrong type*

Figure 4   *Bad type – a 'weed'*

body to equal the head of the parent. It has happened now and then, but at what a cost to the progress of the breed. One 'chance-bred' champion may set the clock back several generations because of the hereditary taints behind him.

Having given the *tout ensemble* of three different types to be met with, we will now go into a few details which I hope will prove helpful. In figure 5 we have the correct front, shoulder placement, and feet. Figure 6 gives the reverse of this: elbows wrong, feet turned too far out, and weak in pasterns, all of which are structural failings.

We have several times remarked upon the importance of the ears, their shape, placement, and carriage. Figure 7 is the ideal ear, set nicely at the angle of the skull and pointing outwards and forwards. The Scottie type of ear is plainly indicated in figure 8.

Figure 9, known as the 'Bat' ear, was at one time very common, but fortunately is now seldom seen. The rounded tips, and broad base which usually accompanied it, destroyed the alert, sharp expression which one looks for in the breed, giving instead a dull, almost clownish, appearance.

Tails have generally been more or less a source of trouble to the average breeder, and a bad tail is not only an abomination,

Figure 5   *Correct front*

Figure 6   *Bad and weak front*

Figure 7   *Correct ears*

Figure 8   *Scottie ears*   Figure 9   *Bat ears*

but very difficult to breed out. Figure 10 depicts the ideal tail, and figures 11 and 12 faulty tails; both are bad, but the 'Hound' tail, if not too long, is less objectionable. The 'Gay' tail is generally condemned and all thoughtful breeders now do their best to avoid it.

In figure 13 we have an example of the perfect hind-quarters, while figure 14 shows the other side, which I have previously referred to in my remarks on figure 3.

Coat, texture, and eyes I have referred to elsewhere.

Figure 10   *Correct tail*

Figure 11   *Gay tail*

Figure 12   *Hound tail*

Figure 13
Good hindquarters

Figure 14
Incorrect hindquarters

Figure 15
Thin pad

Figure 16
Weak pastern

Figure 17
Correct foot

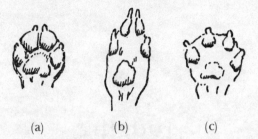

(a)   (b)   (c)

Figure 18   *Feet and pads*
(*a*) is correct, while the open pads depicted in (*b*) and (*c*) are incorrect

13

Judging

With the passing of time and the achievement of a little success the novice may pass from novitiate stage and find himself elected to the list of judges of one or more of the breed clubs. Then, sooner or later, will come the invitation to judge the breed for the first time.

Throughout the years there has been built up a more-or-less stereotyped procedure which judges have accustomed themselves to follow, and there seems little reason for departing from it.

After the stewards have reported all available dogs in the ring, and given the numbers of any absentees, the first step is to check in the judge's book the numbers worn by the handlers of the dogs actually present. Satisfied that his book is correctly entered the judge usually orders the handlers to move round in a circle, taking full advantage of the size of the ring. Having thus obtained a general impression of the dogs, the parade is stopped and the detailed individual examination of each exhibit begun; in low-to-ground dogs such as Cairns this should always be done on the table.

First, the handler should be asked to show the mouth (the Kennel Club has 'suggested' that judges should not personally handle each animal's mouth in case his hands carry infection); the teeth should be examined as to size, placement, and condition, bearing in mind the words of the Standard which calls for 'large teeth'. Then the head should receive attention, the colour, size, and placement of the eyes being noted, the existence of 'stop' being verified, the position and carriage of the ears noted, and the presence or absence of adequate 'furnishings' on the forehead observed.

Proceeding backwards, the following points should be observed and noted:

Adequate length of neck, or its absence.

Brisket, shoulders and forelegs; the brisket should be well in evidence without giving the Cairn the appearance of being 'pouter-chested'*, the shoulders should be sloping and laid well back and never upright, the forelegs should be straight, fairly wide apart, and covered with short hard hair.

The pads of the forefeet should be round and thick and the feet may turn slightly outwards but, if so, both must turn outwards; not one foot straight and the other outwards, as sometimes happens.

The ribs should be handled to make certain that they are well sprung, and the coat examined as to the texture of the rough outer coat and the presence of the essential woolly undercoat. The back and loins are examined to verify strength without excessive shortness or weakness through too great length. The thigh should be strong and well rounded and the stifle well bent. The hind feet should be smaller than the front, and there should be no sign of 'cow hock' in the rear legs.

At this point a check should be made as to whether the dog is 'entire' (both testicles fully descended into the scrotum). The Kennel Club permit either a monorchid or a cryptorchid to be shown. It is left to the discretion of the judge as to whether they place the dog. However, judges' attention must be drawn to the footnote in the Breed Standard which states 'Male animals should have two apparently normal testicles fully descended into the scrotum'.

After the judge has completed the examination on the table they will ask the exhibitor to walk the dog in a triangle, i.e. making a straight line into the top right-hand corner, then across the ring to the left-hand corner, then straight back to the judge. Using this method the judge can assess the back movement, the top line and stride, and front movement.

Bad movement should be penalized as it is generally due to incorrect skeletal construction or lack of muscle tone. A little leniency can be shown to a very young puppy (in the minor

*'Pouter-chested' a Scottish word for pigeon chested.

puppy class) who is full of *joie de vivre* and takes time to settle and move correctly.

After all the dogs have been examined they should again be scrutinized with the details discovered on the table and in movement born in mind.

Then comes the task of picking out, and placing in order of merit, the four which have come nearest to satisfying the ideas of the judge. If this is done fearlessly and decisively there is little danger of repercussions. Hesitant and dithery judging always causes comment.

The bases of all sound judging are a thorough knowledge of the Standard, and a clear mental picture of the dog that has never been and never will be – the perfect Cairn.

It is wise for a judge before each judging appointment to read the Breed Standard and the article on 'Anatomy and its Influence' by W. L. McCandlish which is published in the 'Cairn Club Rules – Breed Standard' booklet.

The general appearance of the dog is most important. It is not impossible for a dog whose body is examined piecemeal to seem to have many excellent features, if each part is considered without reference to the rest, yet the whole, when considered as such, can present a most undesirable appearance.

The condition of the coat is one about which there can be many differences of opinion. There can be only one decision on a soft coat, which must be penalized, but a difficulty may arise over the relative merits of two coats, one of which is the correct length though not so hard as it might be, and the other which is harder but shorter, either through having been stripped recently, or from a natural shortness. In such a case, previous knowledge of the dog may be permitted to influence a judge's decision. If the dog has been known to carry a correct coat in the past, the condition could be viewed more leniently than that of a dog which consistently bears a short coat. This is the only point on which any judge should give any thought to past or future conditions.

Apart from the question of coat in such rare cases as I have just mentioned, the judge should place the animals as he sees them, not only on the day but also at the time when he is making his final decision. There should be no thought of how they looked last week or how they may look tomorrow.

Some judges have been known to use the words 'not my type', a phrase which, on the kindliest interpretation, may be taken to mean 'does not comply with my idea of the Standard' but which can mislead novices into thinking there are a number of correct types. While there are variations in the individual appearance of each of any collection of animals of the same breed there are always some which conform more nearly to the judge's idea of what is correct but this does not justify his referring to 'my type'.

In carrying out his duties it is essential that the judge should put from his mind any impression any of the exhibits may have made on previous appearances in the ring, and to ignore the reputation (good or bad) that may have been built up round any dog. Further, the reputation and record of any handler must not be allowed to influence any judge in making his or her decisions. The biggest and best-known kennels have been known to exhibit not-so-good ones on occasions, and novices have bred 'fliers'. The judge is there to make awards on the appearance and behaviour of the dogs as they are on the day and at the time at which his decision is made, and these awards should not be influenced by any other factor.

The question of who shall judge at primary, sanction or open shows is one for the committee of the club or society running such shows, but the judge at championship shows must be approved by the Kennel Club which has compiled a list of the names of people who are considered of such experience and standing as to justify their appointment to award challenge certificates. At present, the qualifications so far as 'specialist' (i.e. judges confining their judging activities to one breed) judges are concerned are: at least five years knowledge of the breed, and five years intermittent judging of the breed at open shows. Also of importance is the number of dogs or bitches they have bred which have qualified for entry in the Kennel Club Stud Book.

TABLE OF COMPARATIVE MEASUREMENTS OF EARLY 'SHORT-HAIRED SKYE', EARLY SCOTTISH TERRIERS AND RECENT CAIRN TERRIERS

	Flora (Bitch) working type of Skye*	Ch. Dunolly (Dog) Scottish Terrier†	Ch. Dundee (Dog) Scottish Terrier†	Glengogo (Bitch) Scottish Terrier†	Ch. Brindie of Twobees	Ch. Blencathra Redstart	Ch. Broc o' the Braes	Ch. Merrymeet Jason	Ch. Redletter McMurran	Ch. Fimor Katrine	Ch. Oudenarde Souvenir	Ch. Redletter Elford Mhorag
	in.	in.	in.	in.	in.	in.	in.	in.	in.	in.	in.	in.
Occipital bone to eye	3¼	4⅞	5	4½	4	3¾	4	4	3⅝	3½	3¼	3½
Inner corner of eye to nose	2¼	3	3	3	2½	2¾	2½	2	2½	2	2¼	2¼
Shoulder to root of tail	17	15	15	16	13	14	12	12¼	15	12	12½	14½
Length of tail	–	–	7	7½	5	5½	5½	6¼	5¾	5½	6	5½
Round muzzle	8½	6⅞	7¼	6½	7	8	7½	6½	7	6	6½	7
Round skull	12	11½	11¾	11½	12½	12½	12½	12¼	11¾	11½	11½	11
Round chest	16	17¾	17½	17½	19½	19	17½	18	18½	17½	17¼	17
Round loin	15	14¾	15	15	18½	18½	14½	16½	17	15½	16	16
Round arm	4	4⅞	5	4½	4½	5¼	5	5	4	4½	4½	4⅝
Height	10½	10	10	10	11½	11	11	11¼	12	10½	11½	11

* From *The Illustrated Book of the Dog*, by Vero Shaw, published *circa* 1880.

† From *Dogs of Scotland*, by D. J. Thomson Gray, published 1981.

The measurements of recent Champion Cairns were supplied by the owners: those of Ch. Merrymeet Jason were taken by a veterinary surgeon.

14
Breed Clubs and the Kennel Club

Breed Clubs and their Honorary Secretaries

THE CAIRN TERRIER CLUB: Mr J. A. Berrecloth,
6 Duff Street, Dundee. DD4 7AN

SOUTHERN CAIRN TERRIER CLUB: Mrs M. Towers,
Turn again Lodge, Hook Green, Wilmington, Kent.
DA2 7AT

THE CAIRN TERRIER ASSOCIATION: Mrs B. Dewhurst,
68 Rosehill Road, Burnley, Lancs. BB11 2QX

MIDLAND CAIRN TERRIER CLUB: Mrs Linda Firth,
The Bungalow, Columbia Avenue, Sutton-in-Ashfield,
Notts. NG17 2GL

SOUTH WALES AND WEST OF ENGLAND CAIRN TERRIER CLUB:
Mr John Radford, Skimmerton, Chapel Rise, Atworth,
Melksham, Wilts.

NORTH OF IRELAND CAIRN TERRIER CLUB: Mr Joe Dean,
19 Terryhoogan Road, Scarva, Craigavon, Northern Ireland.

THE CAIRN TERRIER ASSOCIATION OF IRELAND: Mr McCoy,
59 Oliver Plunket Road, Dun Laoghaire, Co. Dublin.

SWEDISH CAIRN TERRIER CLUB: Inger Hansson,
Wictoryf Cairns, Viktoria-Vgen, MO 30, Alysjö, Sweden.

DUTCH CAIRN TERRIER CLUB: Mevr. L. E. von Winning-
Reepmaker, Buurtweg 44, 6971 K M Oeken-Brummen,
Nederland.

CAIRN TERRIER CLUB OF VICTORIA: Mrs Hutchison,
c/o Box 38, Lancefield, Victoria 3435, Australia.

CAIRN TERRIER CLUB OF NEW SOUTH WALES: Mrs Hill,
47 Abbotsford Road, Homebush, N.S.W., 2140, Australia.

THE CAIRN TERRIER CLUB OF AMERICA: Mrs Lawrence
Griffith, PO Box 58, Port Allegahany, PA 16743, USA.

THE CAIRN TERRIER CLUB OF CANADA: Mrs A. P. G. Joy,
39 Rivercove Drive, Islington, Ontario, M9B 4Y8, Canada.

THE CAIRN TERRIER CLUB. It would seem that the earliest
movements towards the formation of a club to look after the
interests of the breed, then usually described as Short-haired
Skye Terriers, followed a show held at Inverness in 1909, but
the final steps were taken after the judging at the Scottish
Kennel Club's show of October 1910. Mrs Alastair Campbell
was appointed Hon. Secretary and she carried on in that
capacity until after the end of the First World War, when she
was succeeded by Major I. Ewing who, in turn, was succeeded
by Lieutenant-Colonel Whitehead who devoted some 20 years
to guiding the club with integrity and wise counsel. The
welfare of both the breed and the club were paramount to
him.

The club had the great honour of having as their Patron
from 1923–34 HRH The Prince of Wales later to become
Duke of Windsor, a devotee of the breed.

In common with all other breed clubs the main functions of
the Cairn Terrier Club were and are to outline and lay down a
standard of points by which judging should be done and to
which judges were expected to adhere; to elect a panel of
judges who were accepted as being qualified to apply the Standard; to guarantee general clubs against a certain proportion
of any loss that might be incurred on classes scheduled for the
breed; and to offer cups and silver spoons for their members,
as special or extra prizes, at shows where approved judges
made the awards. Cups are awarded at the club shows, the

silver spoon has been replaced by money prizes. This principle has also been adopted by the other clubs.

In 1986 the membership stood at approximately 400 British member sand 200 overseas members.

THE SOUTHERN CAIRN TERRIER CLUB. This club seems to have been formed either in 1914 or earlier, as the first record that can be traced is of a minute of a general meeting held at the Ladies' Kennel Association show of June 1915.

The first secretary was Miss Viccars, who held the post until the end of the First World War when she and Mrs Dixon acted jointly for a year or two, after which Mrs Dixon held the post until 1932, when Mrs Prichard started her long and devoted service which only ended at the beginning of 1958 after 25 years.

The Southern Club had the honour of running the first breed championship show. This was on 14 September, 1916, when Lady Sophie Scott judged, and Inverness Doran and Cloughton Lorna won the challenge certificates. The show was held in aid of war charities.

The first breed show held by this club was in November 1929, but the first championship show (apart from that in 1916) was not until November 1936. Today the club holds one championship show and two open shows.

Mr Alex Fisher OBE became patron of the club from 1965 until his death in 1971. When Mr Beynon's health deteriorated he asked Mr Fisher to collaborate with him to revise the second edition of this book, then called *The Popular Cairn Terrier*. Mr Fisher revised the third and fourth editions on his own.

In 1986 the membership of this club was approximately 450.

THE CAIRN TERRIER ASSOCIATION. The association, formed in 1925 and becoming effective in 1926, was, in a way, a break away from the Southern Club. However, though it was then the youngest of the breed clubs it was the first to venture into one-breed shows.

The first secretary was Mr Caspersz who held the post for

some years and was succeeded by Major Townley, who, in turn, handed to Mr Wilding Jones on whose sudden death Major Townley had again to resume control until 1947 when he handed over the secretaryship to Mrs Diana Hamilton (Oudenarde) who gave 25 years of devoted service to running a happy and successful club. In 1972 she handed the administration to Mrs Bessie Dewhurst who, 16 years later, is still carrying on the tradition.

The club holds a championship show and an open show each year. In 1986 the membership stands at approximately 400.

The Cairn Terrier Club, The Southern Cairn Terrier Club and The Cairn Terrier Association run a Joint Cairn Clubs Show annually, each club taking it in turn to organize and run the show.

THE MIDLAND CAIRN TERRIER CLUB. Founded in 1981 this is a new enthusiastic club holding its first championship show in December 1985. It also runs two open shows each year.

SOUTH WALES AND WEST OF ENGLAND CAIRN TERRIER CLUB. South Wales and West of England is an area which tends to be isolated from Cairn activities; it was therefore decided to form the South Wales and West of England Cairn Terrier Club in 1982. They were awarded challenge certificates, holding their first championship show in October 1985. Each year they also hold an open and a primary show.

THE NORTH OF IRELAND CAIRN TERRIER CLUB. Founded in 1930 to further the interest of the breed, it played an active part in Cairn affairs. From 1960 onwards membership dwindled owing to political unrest; in the late 70s a fresh interest was rekindled and in 1982 they held their first championship show. They are now a flourishing club with a close liaison with the mainland. Both Mrs Warmsley and Ben Simpson have been members for over 50 years, giving loyal service and support to the club.

Hazel Small with 2 of the Avenelhouse Cairns

Avenelhouse Golden Phesant

Ch. Avenelhouse Golden Oriole

Sally Ogle holding Pinetop Rough Diamond

Ch. Pinetop Priscilla

Ch. Pinetop Montana – who said a
champion couldn't catch rats?

Miss Clark and Miss Howes

Above: Ch. Courtrai John Julius

Left: Ch. Robinson Crusoe of Courtrai, sire of 16 champions

Above: Mrs Proudlock

Right: Affectionate greeting from a young
Proudlock to a young Seltirk

Above: Seltirk Burnt Sugar

Left: Seltirk head studies over a
period of 20 years

THE CAIRN TERRIER ASSOCIATION OF IRELAND. Founded in 1928, it was granted championship status by the Irish Kennel Club in 1971. They hold a championship show each year.

Each of the British Clubs arrange educational programmes, i.e. grooming demonstrations, matches against other clubs, talks from veterinary surgeons and other authoritative people in dogdom, videos on movement and judging. These are primarily for the novice breeder and exhibitor but no one is too old to learn though there are those who think they know it all!

The Kennel Club

The Kennel Club are the governing body on all facets of pedigree dogs and all other activities connected with dogdom. Their administration includes issuing registrations, transfers and export certificates. All categories of shows have to comply with Kennel Club Rules and Regulations. Championship show judges, i.e. those who award challenge certificates, have to be passed by the Kennel Club, who keep a strict eye on their ability to judge. Those who err by breaking the rules set down by the Kennel Club or those whose behaviour is unacceptable or detrimental to dogdom come before a disciplinary court held by the Kennel Club who may issue a fine, a disqualification of an award, or a suspension or ban from exhibiting or owning dogs. The Kennel Club has working agreements with similar bodies throughout the world.

No dog or bitch can be exhibited unless registered with the Kennel Club. If you buy a puppy or an adult dog, be adamant at the time of purchase that you are given the registration papers. The Kennel Club alter the registration system from time to time; it is wise for the novice breeder to write to the Kennel Club, 1–5 Clarges Street, London W1Y 8AB, requesting an application form for Litter Recording, on the back of which is information on how to complete the form and the current registration fees.

Formerly the Kennel Club ran its annual show under the

title The Kennel Club Show, but after the last war it acquired from the representatives of the late Mr Charles Cruft, the name and title of Crufts, so that Crufts Dog Show, held in February each year, is now the official event.

Details from the Catalogues of Crufts Show 1909–1913
In 1909 four Cairns – Roy-Mohr, Doran Bhan, Sporgan McLeod, and Cuilean Bhan – all owned by Mrs Campbell, were shown in a special class headed 'Short-haired Skyes'. There was considerable objection to the use of the word 'Skye'.

In 1910, at the same show, two classes for 'Cairns or Short-haired Terriers' were scheduled: Limit D or B and Open D or B. These two classes attracted two and three entries respectively. In the limit class these were:

Mr F. Linton. Ossian (br. Mr J. Campbell) – Uan of Sligachan – Gateshead Fanny
Mr J. B. Hamilton. Rose of Kepstom (br. D. Kemp) – Sgithanach Bhan – Culag
(Rose of Kepstom was obviously a half-sister to Ch. Gesto.)

In the Open class these two were joined by:

Mrs Fjellstedt. Cabhag (br. Owner) – Bodach – Theorag

For some reason, which was not given, all five entries were noted as disqualified.

The dam of Ossian – Gateshead Fanny – was observed as having been shown in a Scottish Terrier class in an earlier Crufts show. In the same year, 1910, but in the Skye Terrier, Limit Dog, and Bitch class, Mrs Campbell had entered Doran Bhan and Roy Mohr and Miss Hawke had entered Bride, while in the Novice Dog and Bitch class Mrs Campbell had entered MacLeod of MacLeod; Mrs Campbell had also entered in Brace and Team classes.

In 1911, when Mr Ferrier of Dundee judged, four classes, brace and team, were scheduled; the classes, entries, and winners were:

Open dog, 8 entries; winner – Gesto
Open bitch, 8 entries; winner – Mrs McDonald's Vixen by

Talisker × Daisy
Limit dog or bitch, 8 entries; winner – Gesto
Novice dog or bitch, 9 entries; winner – Vixen
Brace, 4 entries, and team, 3 entries, both won by Mrs Campbell

In 1912, when Mr G. J. Ross judged, there were six classes with brace and team in addition. These were:

Open dog, 5 entries; winner – Gesto
Limit dog, 6 entries; winner – Sandy
Open bitch, 7 entries; winner – Tibbie of Harris
Limit bitch, 10 entries; winner – Tibbie of Harris
Graduate dog or bitch, 8 entries; winner – Strathpeffer Tassy
Junior dog or bitch, 8 entries; winner – Strathpeffer Tassy
Brace and team classes held only Mrs Campbell's dogs

In 1913 certificates were on offer at Crufts for the first time. The judge was Mr R. Leighton. There were three classes for each sex, one mixed class and brace and team. Details:

Open dog, 4 entries; winner – Gesto
Limit dog, 7 entries; winner – David
Novice dog, 8 entries; winner – Brocaire Saitress
Open bitch, 12 entries; winner – Tighru Fiona
Limit bitch, 12 entries winner – Tighru Fiona
Novice bitch, 9 entries; winner – Frag of Harris
Special limit dog or bitch, 12 entries; winner – David
The certificates were won by Gesto and Tighru Fiona

Details from the Catalogues of the Kennel Club Shows of 1912 and 1913
The Kennel Club were much slower than Crufts in providing classes for Cairns, and it was not until after the breed had been granted championship status that they appeared in the schedule of the governing body's show. This was in 1912 when, in the index to the catalogue, they were placed in the non-sporting list. Six breed classes were provided with brace and team.

Puppy dog or bitch, 8 entries; winner – Keystone Laddie
Novice dog or bitch, 12 entries; winner – Loch Handa
Limit dog, 4 entries; winner – Loch Handa
Open dog, 6 entries; winner – Gesto

Limit bitch, 9 entries; winner – Brocaire Speireag
Open bitch, 9 entries; winner – Tibbie of Harris
Gesto and Tibbie of Harris won the certificates

In 1913 nine classes, brace and team, were scheduled. Mr C. McNeill was the judge.

Puppy dog or bitch, 8 entries; winner – Inverness Badger
Novice dog, 9 entries; winner – Bard of Harris
Special limit dog, 9 entries; winner – Firring Fox
Limit dog, 7 entries; winner – Firring Frolic
Open dog, 8 entries; winner – Firring Frolic
Novice bitch, 8 entries; winner – Inverness Vixen
Special limit bitch, 6 entries; winner – Inverness Vixen
Limit bitch, 6 entries; winner – Sheila of Harris
Open bitch, 5 entries; winner – Sheila of Harris
The certificates were won by Firring Frolic and Sheila of Harris

Popularity of the Cairn at Home and Abroad

While every pure-bred dog is not registered at the Kennel Club, it is fairly reliable to take the figures of registrations as an indication of the popularity of any breed.

Details of Cairn registrations for the years 1947–86 are as follows:

1947 – 3645	1957 – 2628	1967 – 3670	1977 – 945
1948 – 3131	1958 – 2759	1968 – 3862	1978 – 2442
1949 – 3296	1959 – 2969	1969 – 4001	1979 – 3162
1950 – 2896	1960 – 3078	1970 – 3860	1980 – 3141
1951 – 2756	1961 – 3426	1971 – 3163	1981 – 2571
1952 – 2269	1962 – 3375	1972 – 3493	1982 – 2384
1953 – 2391	1963 – 3264	1973 – 3336	1983 – 2411
1954 – 2341	1964 – 3206	1974 – 3358	1984 – 2427
1955 – 2513	1965 – 3642	1975 – 2864	1985 – 2509
1956 – 2643	1966 – 3354	1976 – 1345	1986 – 2322

An even more realistic assessment of the popularity of the Cairn is that they consistently remain in the second half of the top twenty of the breeds registration list.

Steady consistency is the principal feature of these figures;

this is good, since a breed which becomes too popular can deteriorate when – as often happens – commercial breeders who have little thought for the welfare of the breed 'cash in' on the situation. This occurred in the late 1960s when dealers were selling puppies of all breeds wholesale, particularly to Japan; the phase has now passed and breeders are more aware of their responsibilities when placing puppies. None the less, it is still vitally important to ensure that every puppy which is sold finds a proper home in a good environment, especially when exporting overseas. Similarly, anyone purchasing a Cairn for the first time should make sure that he buys from a reputable breeder. Should advice be needed, potential purchasers should approach the nearest Cairn Club – Secretaries are always happy to put them in contact with genuine and reliable Cairn breeders in the locality.

The American Kennel Club Gazette also lists details of annual registrations. The first Cairn was registered in 1913, and numbers steadily climbed to reach a total of 1899 in 1964. Since then, however, they have rocketed to reach 7100 registrations in the year 1972. Approximately 100 American Champions have been made annually in recent years, compared with an annual average of 10 in the United Kingdom.

Details of registrations in European countries are not readily available, but export pedigrees indicate that a steady number are exported each year.

15

Minor Illnesses
by Ruth Wadman Taylor, MRCVS

In previous editions of *The Cairn Terrier* a chapter has been included on 'minor illnesses and mishaps'. In this new edition Bunty Proudlock has asked me to review the advice previously proferred. During the last fifteen to twenty years there have been great changes not only in the knowledge available to doctors and veterinary surgeons but also, through the media – especially TV programmes – to the general public. Everyone knows much more about the working (i.e. physiology) of the body, human and animal, and much more also of the diseases that are likely to be encountered.

All dog owners regard inoculation against the major canine diseases as a routine protection policy nowadays. Thus canine distemper, with its mutant, hard pad disease; leptospirosis and liver virus infection (hepatitis) are no longer a serious threat to the kennel owner. Canine parvovirus infection, our newest member of the epidemic diseases, is proving to be much more intractable. At the time of writing there is still great controversy about times of inoculation and one can only suggest taking local veterinary advice on this matter.

Kennel Cough covers a range of adenovirus infections plus a bacterial one, *Bordetella bronchisepticus*. Some distemper vaccines include adenoviruses and Intrac – the intra-nasal inoculation – protects against Bordetella. Unfortunately kennel cough vaccines, rather like the common cold vaccines for humans, only give protection for a short time. Some of the manufacturers advise six-monthly boosting. With the cost of other vaccinations, particularly parvovirus vaccine, being so high it is not likely that the average kennel owner would feel that routine vaccination for kennel cough was practicable.

However it is not usually a serious complaint unless the very young or very old are the victims. It is very infectious and can last a long time. A quiet life, good food and the use of cough syrups such as Benylin eventually produce a cure. On the whole antibiotics do not greatly shorten the course of the illness unless chest complications have arisen. This disease is endemic at dog shows in some years.

There has been a great change in dog showing over the last twenty years or so. Instead of the majority of exhibitors being owners of large kennels with kennel staff employed, the average fancier has a small number of dogs, often few enough to keep in the house and has no outside help with the management of the dogs. In many ways this means that any illness or divergence from the norm is picked up much more quickly and dealt with immediately.

Apart from the main epidemic diseases, parasites – external and internal – are the next important thing to consider. It is well worth being ruthless about worms and fleas. Livestock will never look in full bloom when infested with fleas, and worms cause damage to the bowel wall allowing parvovirus for example to gain easy access. In fact where parasites flourish there is a lowered resistance to disease.

Nowadays there are excellent preparations available for skin diseases including mange, ringworm, flea allergy, lice and tick infestations. Similarly there are preparations for internal parasites such as round and tapeworms, whip and hook worms and coccidiosis (caused by a protozoan parasite) which causes diarrhoea with bloody streaks and is not so uncommon as it was. Ear parasites too must not be forgotten, especially (as Peggy Wilson pointed out in her editions) if there is a cat in the household. Cats often carry the ear mite, *otodectes felis*, which is easily transferable to dogs.

Each individual has his own idea of a first-aid or medicine kit. The first item should be a clinical thermometer. Be sure you know how to use it and can read it correctly before an emergency occurs. Normal temperature for a dog is 101.5°F or 38.4°C. A little vaseline put on the end of the thermometer before inserting it into the rectum is helpful. An antiseptic such as Savlon or Dettol should be kept; some bandages, cotton wool and elastoplast (in a roll, not the individual dressings), scissors, and nail clippers; a buffered Aspirin such as Disprin or Codis – ordinary aspirin tends to cause gastric irritation followed by vomiting. The new drug Nurofen is very helpful as a painkiller in dogs as well as humans.

A dog which looks unwell and has a rise in temperature should have veterinary attention soon. If the temperature is not up the owner has 24 hours to 'home-doctor' then re-assess the condition.

There has been quite a revolution in the feeding of dogs during the last decade or so. One can still get fresh foods but the commercial diets especially those termed 'Complete Diets' contain all the nutriments including vitamins and minerals that the dog requires. It is realized nowadays that adding a bit of cod liver oil here and some calcium there as we used to do is not without danger. I think on the whole a mixture of foods is best. I tend to feed a complete biscuit plus raw tripe – which is excellent – during the week and perhaps tinned food and ordinary biscuit or wholemeal rusks at the weekend. With this type of dryish food, teeth collect less tartar and, as good firm motions are passed, anal glands tend to empty themselves. To keep up with the modern vogue for vegetarian food there is even a vegetarian Complete Diet for dogs, still high in protein – soya bean being the source. An interesting sidelight on this diet called 'Happidog' is that it is turning out to be very helpful to dogs suffering from pancreatic deficiency, mostly German Shepherd dogs, where animal protein cannot be digested without the addition to the diet of *very expensive* pancreatic extract.

Constipation was mentioned in the last edition of this work; not now a major problem unless your dogs have been eating bones. It is important that only raw bones are offered. Cooked bones, being brittle, splinter easily when chewed and can cause obstruction at worst and at least great discomfort. Diarrhoea is a much commoner complaint in kennels and if it persists in several inmates at once, infection must be thought of and veterinary advice sought.

Allied to vomiting, diarrhoea can quickly cause dehydration. Ordinary water will not do for fluid replacement, a special formula such as Lectade mixed with water must be used for rehydration, obtainable in sachets from veterinary surgeons. This is a most useful addition to the medicine chest. It can be used in the first days of nursing after surgical procedures or for feeding weakly pups.

These days one can scarcely keep up with the number of books published on all aspects of the dog world, but here is a short list of those I have found most readable:

The Doglopaedia: Complete Guide to Dog Care, J. M. Evans and Kay White, (Henston, 1985).

Dog Breeding: A Guide to Mating & Whelping, Kay White, (Bartholomew Pet Care Services, 1985).

– for those interested in alternative medicine – *Homoeopathic Medicine for Dogs*, H. G. Wolff, (Thorson Publishers Ltd., 1984).

First Aid for Pets, Dr Barry Bush – paperback (Adam & Charles Black, 1984).

APPENDIX A

PEDIGREE OF
CH. SPLINTERS OF TWOBEES

Ch. Trashurst Chip

- **Trashurst Sandyman**
  - **Donnington Gillie**
    - **Ch. Gillie of Hyver**
      - Ch. Carngowan Murran
        - Raeburn Conas
        - Lugate Lively
      - Gillassie of Ninfield
        - Strathpeffer Gillie Ruadh
        - Raits Ranhaich
    - **Chip of Hardings**
      - Firefly of Hardings
        - Inverness Mac
        - Lassie
      - Moccasin Kirsty Vic
        - Moccasin Mac
        - Moccasin Lassie
  - **Eaton Wendy**
    - **Sweep of Frimley**
      - Ch. Breakwater Jock
        - Firring Forge
        - Eiley of Ninfield
      - Lassie of Frimley
        - Ch. Firring Frolic
        - Frimley Pixie
    - **Dochfour Flora Ruadh**
      - Doran
        - Ornsay Dhoran
        - Spleach
      - Caillack
        - Ballach
        - Caffag

- **Cherry McBryan**
  - **Ch. Dud of Hyver**
    - **Ch. Gillie of Hyver**
      - Ch. Carngowan Murran
        - Raeburn Conas
        - Lugate Lively
      - Girlie
        - Little Bruce
        - Yorna
    - **Knipton Dian**
      - Ross-shire Glenara
        - Rags
        - Rockfield Shieling
      - Inverness Culaig
        - Cairn Reich
        - Moccasin Ruby
  - **Haggis of Sandiacre**
    - **Strathblane Chaillean**
      - Little Bruce
        - Bruce
        - Pickles
      - Strathpeffer Vixen
        - Strathpeffer Sionnach
        - Strathpeffer Mhor Ruadh
    - **Stew of Sandiacre**

Pedigree of **Sorag of Twobees**

```
Sorag of Twobees
├─ Ch. Quicksand Out of the West
│  ├─ Offley Brimon
│  │  ├─ Ch. Harviestoun Brigand
│  │  │  ├─ Harviestoun Jet
│  │  │  │  ├─ Harviestoun Wisp
│  │  │  │  └─ Harviestoun Jean
│  │  │  └─ Ardgay Frenchie
│  │  │     ├─ Brocaire Simon
│  │  │     ├─ Judy
│  │  │     ├─ Shiela
│  │  │     ├─ Bealty
│  │  │     └─ Fairy
│  │  └─ Canna of Frimley
│  └─ She
│     ├─ Ch. Quicksilver Out Of the West
│     │  ├─ Doughall out of the West
│     │  │  ├─ McDonald of Crastock
│     │  │  └─ Morag
│     │  └─ Shinnel Silver
│     │     ├─ Cairn Reich
│     │     └─ Dochfour Bidrach
│     └─ Dderfel Caraid
│        ├─ Dochfour Gesto
│        │  ├─ Gesto Footprint
│        │  └─ Scotish Meg
│        └─ Smut
│           ├─ Ch. Macsporran
│           └─ Patsy
└─ Mulaidh of Twobees
   ├─ Glenmhor Rascal
   │  ├─ Harviestoun Raider
   │  │  ├─ Harviestoun Kim
   │  │  │  ├─ Harviestoun Yorrick (W.H.W.T.)
   │  │  │  └─ Glenmhor Crougach
   │  │  └─ Harviestoun Tibbie
   │  │     ├─ Cairn Reich
   │  │     └─ Moccasin Topsy
   │  └─ Sorag
   │     ├─ Bodach Ruadh
   │     │  ├─ Inverness Doran
   │     │  └─ Soraig
   │     └─ Rona
   │        ├─ Sockan
   │        └─ Fanny
   └─ Glenmhor Coullie
      ├─ Harviestoun Raider
      │  └─ Ch. Castlehill Dan
      │     ├─ Dochfour Davie
      │     └─ Brocaire Dorette
      └─ Mulaidh
         └─ Cloughton Spider
            ├─ Brocaire Lorne
            └─ Erna Girl
```

APPENDIX B

CHAMPIONS

Championship shows resumed in 1946. Between then and 1960, 132 Cairn Terriers achieved the title of Champion. The numbers in each year are:

Year	No. of champions	Year	No. of champions
1946	1	1956	9
1947	5	1957	11
1948	8	1958	11
1949	10	1959	5
1950	5	1960	11
1951	15		
1952	14		
1953	6		
1954	11		
1955	10		

The following list gives the names of these 132 champions in alphabetical order, and sets out the particulars of parentage and ownership as well as the date of birth and the year in which each won its title. The total number of certificates won is also given, as are the line and family of which each is a member.

Name of champion	Sex	Sire	Dam	Breeder	Owner	Born	Title won in	Total number of certs. won	Line and family
Ailsa of Crondall	B	Ch. Simon of Twobees	Rollick of Crondall	Mrs Sparrow-Wilkinson	Mrs Sparrow-Wilkinson	28. 6.54	1957	3	SD—89
Ainsty Zillah	B	Blencathra Chatabov	Ainsty Matilda	Mrs M. E. Carr	Mrs M. E. Carr	26.12.58	1960	3	DGS—90

Name	Sex	Sire	Dam	Breeder	Owner	Born	Year		Ref
Altbeck Clever Girl	B	Altbeck Athlete	Fluffy Joan	Mrs P. H. Brierley	Mr H. E. Robinson	8. 5.47	1952	3	DGS—3
Balshagray Bomber	D	Beechacre Bellman	Achilti Effie	Mr R. McEwan	Mr N. B. Rintoul	15. 9.48	1952	3	DG—82
Balshagray Bombshell	B	Ch. Balshagray Bomber	Sinclairtown Sheila	Mr and Mrs N. B. Rintoul	Mr N. B. Rintoul Jun.	1.11.49	1952	3	DG—15
Battling Bloom	B	Ch. McJoe of Twobees	Battling Beana	Rev. and Mrs A. Hybart	Rev. and Mrs A. Hybart	7. 8.50	1952	4	SD—48
Blencathra Clivegreen Timothy	D	Classic of Cornerstone	Jill of Barksholme	Mrs W. A. Shelley	Mrs E. H. Drummond	7. 8.49	1951	4	I—59
Blencathra Elford Chiefton	D	Ch. Bonfire of Twobees	Foundation Sylvia	Mrs G. Vickers	Mrs E. H. Drummond	19. 7.52	1955	3	DGS—59
Blencathra Galgate Lady Piper	B	Ch. Blencathra Sandpiper	Brown Owl of Barassie	Mrs A. Bramley	Mrs E. H. Drummond	23. 7.48	1950	4	GB—80
Blencathra Milord	D	Ch. Blencathra Elford Chiefton	Blencathra Milady	Mrs E. H. Drummond	Mrs E. H. Drummond	26. 9.56	1958	4	DGS—80
Blencathra Pipit	B	Ch. Blencathra Sandpiper	Brown Owl of Barassie	Mrs A. Bramley	Mrs E. H. Drummond	19. 2.49	1951	4	GB—80
Blencathra Redberry	B	Ch. Blencathra Redstart	Blencathra Rowanberry	Mrs E. H. Drummond	Mrs E. H. Drummond	9. 6.56	1958	4	I—91
Blencathra Redstart	D	Ch. Blencathra Clivegreen Timothy	Ch. Blencathra Galgate Lady Piper	Mrs E. H. Drummond	Mrs E. H. Drummond	12. 1.51	1952	4	I—80
Blencathra Rosanne	B	Ch. Blencathra Redstart	Blencathra Rowanberry	Mrs E. H. Drummond	Mrs E. H. Drummond	9. 6.56	1960	3	I—91
Blencathra Rosemary	B	Blencathra Ruffan	Lytheside Candy Floss	Mrs Hutchinson	Mrs E. H. Drummond	28. 4.59	1960	4	DGS—45
Blencathra Rowanna	B	Ch. Blencathra Redstart	Blencathra Rowanberry	Mrs E. H. Drummond	Mrs E. H. Drummond	5.11.53	1955	6	I—91

Name of champion	Sex	Sire	Dam	Breeder	Owner	Born	Title won in	Total number of certs. won	Line and family
Blencathra Sandboy	D	Donnington Sandboy	Blencathra Radiance	Mrs E. H. Drummond	Mrs E. H. Drummond	1. 2.42	1948	4	GB–71
Blencathra Sandpiper	D	Donnington Sandboy	Blencathra Radiance	Mrs E. H. Drummond	Mrs E. H. Drummond	26.10.44	1947	4	GB–71
Blencathra Sprig	B	Ch. Blencathra Sandboy	Allenglen Sprig	Mrs E. H. Drummond	Mrs E. H. Drummond	12. 1.44	1948	3	GB–34
Blencathra Stonechat	B	Ch. Blencathra Redstart	Lady Isle	Mr J. G. MacFarlane	Mrs E. H. Drummond	8. 8.53	1955	6	I–91
Bonfire of Twobees	D	Ch. Splinters of Twobees	Mitsie of Zellah	Mrs E. L. Hazell	Miss Bengough Mrs Butterworth	10. 4.43	1948	5	DGS–3
Brackendene Brig of Cona Lynn	D	Ch. Valiant Rob Roy of Rhosbridge	Bunty of Brackendene	Mrs E. G. Walker	Dr J. M. Young	12.11.46	1949	3	DG–4
Brilliant o' the Braes	D	Buster o' the Braes	Dorrit o' the Braes	Mrs H. M. M. Rhodes	Mrs H. M. M. Rhodes	1. 3.55	1957	4	GR–2
Brindie of Twobees	D	Ch. Bonfire of Twobees	Foundation Sylvia	Mrs G. Vickers	Miss Bengough	5. 7.49	1952	8	DGS–59
Broc o' the Braes	D	Capture o' the Braes	The Braes Bunty of the Shieling	Mrs H. M. M. Rhodes	Mrs H. M. M. Rhodes	19. 6.52	1954	7	DGS–5
Cairntop Nicholas	D	Ch. Elford Shanty	Cairntop Piper Lass of the Shieling	Mrs M. Sangar	Mrs M. Sangar	7. 2.58	1960	4	GB–6
Cinders o' the Braes	B	Ch. Hillston Ian Dhu	My Shadow	Rev S. A. Clark	Mrs H. M. M. Rhodes	26. 3.50	1952	3	DR–85

Name	Sex	Sire	Dam	Breeder	Owner	Date	Year	No.	Reg.
Cloverpark Cornflower	B	Broadwater	Cloverpark Silver Chime	Mrs E. A. Callaghan	Mrs E. A. Callaghan	6.12.52	1956	3	GB—94
Crowtrees Coraline	B	Hillston Bruiser of Barassie	Crowtrees Coral	Mrs N. Swires	Mrs N. Swires	5. 3.52	1955	3	DG—90
Daleace Jerogi	D	Ch. Blencathra Sandpiper	Daleacre's Maurie's Gift	Mr and Mrs A. W. Sibbons	Mr and Mrs A. W. Sibbons	27. 3.52	1953	4	GB—5
Dirk of Twytchett	D	Ch. Blencathra Sandpiper	Janice of Aviemore	Mrs K. N. Corbould-Ellis	Mrs K. N. Corbould-Ellis	1. 1.48	1950	3	GB—74
Dochfour Bean-Mormhair	B	Dochfour Jake	Oubeck Countess	Baroness Burton	Baroness Burton	10. 7.55	1958	3	DG—80
Dochfour Eacob	D	Dochfour Jake	Cleesandra Dinkie Daisy	Baroness Burton	Baroness Burton	25.10.49	1951	4	DG—12
Dochfour Langach	B	Dochfour Jake	Dochfour Cudaig	Baroness Burton	Baroness Burton	28. 7.48	1951	3	DG—69
Dochfour Suisaidh	B	Ch. McEan of Ellandee	Dochfour Suenach	Baroness Burton	Baroness Burton	5.11.48	1951	3	GB—81
Doughall of Pledwick	D	Rhu Rory O'More of Pledwick	Salome of Pledwick	Mrs I. M. Summers	Mrs I. M. Summers	31. 1.47	1949	5	DGS—77
Elford Shanty	D	Broadwater	Foundation Sylvia	Mrs G. M. Vickers	Miss I. V. Bengough	22. 3.53	1957	4	GB—59
Fimor Katrine	B	Rufus of Garratts	Fimor Jewel	Mr A. Fisher	Mr A. Fisher	15. 3.50	1954	3	GB—1
Fincairn Gillian	B	Ch. Brackendene Brig of Cona Lynn	Fincairn Jennifer	Mrs J. Finlay	Mrs J. Finlay	10. 2.49	1951	7	DG—6
Gerolf of Mistyfell	D	Ch. Blencathra Redstart	Sadie of Mistyfell	Miss M. D. W. Gibson	Miss M. D. W. Gibson	4.11.55	1957	10	I—63
Glenmacdhui Marilyn	B	Ch. Blencathra Redstart	Glenmacdhui Marigold	Mrs M. Mawson	Mrs M. Mawson	5.10.54	1957	4	I—59
Glenmacdhui Mohra	B	Ch. Blencathra Redstart	Glenmacdhui Marigold	Mrs M. Mawson	Mrs M. Mawson	4.11.57	1959	5	I—59

Name of champion	Sex	Sire	Dam	Breeder	Owner	Born	Title won in	Total number of certs. won	Line and family
Glenmacrobin Five Finches	B	Ardenvohr Corngleam	Glenmacrobin Forked Elm	Mr M. Hammill	Dr J. M. Young	1. 9.45	1949	6	SD–4
Greetavale Mickey Boy	D	Greetavale Blondey	Sandie of Blarnyestone	Mrs E. Cooper	Mrs E. Cooper	16. 8.58	1960	4	DGS–90
Heidi of the Mountains	B	Yeendsdale Merry Minstrel	Pixie of the Poplars	Mrs J. Hole	Mrs G. F. Stickley	28. 1.57	1960	3	GB–73
Hillston Bonny Briar	B	Hillston Monarch	Hillston Sweet Briar	Mrs M. Garbutt	Mrs M. Garbutt	15. 8.44	1947	3	GR–63
Hillston Ian Dhu	D	Hillston Seawrack	Quarrydene Flinders	Mrs M. Garbutt	Mrs M. Garbutt	22.10.45	1948	6	DR–10
Hillston Madcap Madame	B	Ch. Hillston Ian Dhu	Kellach of Newbold	Mr F. Harris	Mrs M. Garbutt	12. 4.48	1951	3	DR–3
Hillston Sally Anne	B	Hillston Shantyman	Tulloch Gorum	Miss E. P. McCulloch	Mrs G. M. Hodgkinson	31. 1.45	1947	5	DR–76
Ilidach of Inchture	B	Thistleclose Zip	Iscyllach of Inchture	Miss E. F. D. Fulton	Miss E. F. D. Fulton	28. 1.54	1955	7	DGS–60
Joyous o Yeendsdale	B	Masterman of Yeendsdale	Jean of Yeendsdale	Mrs E. M. Yeend	Mrs E. M Yeend	28.10.49	1951	4	GB–17
Kilallan Bunty	B	Sionnach o' the Braes	Maytime Serenade	Mr J. Cameron	Mr A. Arthur	26. 7.44	1949	3	DGS–34
Lady Jane of Cyrisorene	B	Jon of Blarneystone	Auchtergaven Midge of Blarneystone	Mrs M. MacNeill	Mrs M. Maceill	28. 3.53	1957	4	GR–80
Lanimer Zeanah	B	Lanimer Trumpeter	Lanimer Crannog Rose	Mrs N. S. Nicoll	Mrs N. S. Nicoll	27. 2.51	1953	3	GR–86

Name	Sex	Sire	Dam	Breeder	Owner	Date	Year		
Lofthouse Geryon of Mistyfell	D	Ch. Blencathra Redstart	Sadie of Mistyfell	Miss M. D. W. Gibson	Mrs Manley	4.11.55	1959	3	I—63
Lofthouse Golden	B	Ch. Uniquecottage Sir Frolic	Greetavale Golden Girl	Mrs E. Cooper	Mrs Manley	7. 1.57	1958	3	DGS—80
Lofthouse Sundew	D	Ch. Lofthouse Geryon of Mistyfell	Lofthouse Primrose	Mrs H. L. Manley	Mrs H. L. Manley	4. 9.57	1960	3	I—59
Lynwil Lady Maclan	B	Ch. Lynwil Maclan Dhu	Ch. Fincairn Gillian	Mrs J. Finlay	Miss E. P. McCulloch	6. 1.52	1955	3	DR—6
Lynwil Maclan Dhu	D	Ch. Hillston Ian Dhu	Lynwil Elizabeth	Miss E. P. McCulloch	Miss E. P. McCulloch	23. 9.48	1951	10	DR—76
McEan of Ellandee	D	Woodthorpe Ronnie	Lassie of Ellandee	Mr J. L. Baines	Mr J. L. Baines	21. 3.46	1949	3	GB—17
McJoe of Twobees	D	Joe of Twobees	Gem of Twobees	Miss I. V. Bengough and Mrs Butterworth	Miss I. V. Bengough and Mrs Butterworth	18. 6.45	1947	6	SD—10
Macushla of Blarneystone	B	Rex of Maylea	Jura of Maylea	Mr W. Ross	Mrs M. A. MacNeil	12. 6.46	1949	3	GR—47
Marauder of Pledwick	D	Hamish of Pledwick	Woodthorpe Volante	Mrs I. M. Summers	Mrs I. M. Summers	17. 1.54	1956	3	GB—9
Merryman of Yeendsdale	D	Masterman of Yeendsdale	Jean of Yeendsdale	Mrs E. M. Yeend	Mrs E. M. Yeend	26. 9.47	1950	5	GB—17
Merrymeet Cornelian	B	Ch. McJoe of Twobees	Merrymeet Merle	Mrs E. F. Leverton	Mrs E. F. Leverton	11. 6.51	1953	3	SD—74
Merrymeet Jason	D	Merrymeet Jennar Silver	Ch. Merrymeet Medea	Mrs E. F. Leverton	Mrs E. F. Leverton	12. 8.53	1955	5	GB—78
Merrymeet Medea	B	Broadwater	Ch. Merrymeet Novera Diana	Mrs E. F. Leverton	Mrs E. F. Leverton	17. 8.50	1951	4	GB—78
Merrymeet Novera Diana	B	Ch. Blencathra Sandpiper	Novera Sylvia	Mr J. Spencer	Mrs E. F. Leverton	26. 9.48	1950	4	GB—78

Name of champion	Sex	Sire	Dam	Breeder	Owner	Born	Title won in	Total number of certs. won	Line and family
Merrymeet Perseus	D	Ch. Merrymeet Jason	Jennar Flicka	Mrs J. K. Riley	Mrs E. F. Leverton	13. 3.55	1956	3	GB—74
Merrymeet Tathwell Therese	B	Ch. Merrymeet Jason	Toptwig Sorag	Mrs Hawdon	Mrs E. F. Leverton	26.12.56	1958	11	GB—17
Michelcombe Fay	B	Hillston Shantyman	Michelcombe Fury	Miss O. I. Nicholls	Miss O. I. Nicholls	6. 9.45	1948	3	DR—59
Michelcombe Mr Chips	D	Michelcombe Fearless	Fabercairn Netta	Mr S. C. Smith	Miss O. I. Nicholls	1. 5.52	1954	3	SD—6
Michelcombe Starry	D	Michelcombe Fearless	Michelcombe Sunshine	Miss O. I. Nicholls	Miss O. I. Nicholls	25. 7.49	1953	3	SD—45
Normanhurst Penelope	B	McLarry	Cherimie	Mrs M. Summerford	Miss J. F. Maxfield (later Mrs Greatrex)	5. 1.44	1947	5	DG—15
Oudenarde Duskie Belle	B	Wellaway Bobolink	Wendy of Harwell	Mr C. Coombes	Mmes Hamilton and Temple	19.10.45	1949	3	DGS—3
Oudenarde Joyful Light	B	Peripor of Oudenarde	Oudenarde Blue Moon	Mmes Hamilton and Temple	Mmes Hamilton and Temple	13. 4.49	1951	3	DG—84
Oudenarde Light Melody	B	Ch. Broc o' the Braes	Oudenarde Starlight	Miss F. A. Hamilton	Mmes Hamilton and Temple	11. 9.55	1960	6	DGS—84
Oudenarde Live Spirit	B	Pansa of Oudenarde	Ch. Oudenarde Souvenir	Mmes Hamilton and Temple	Mmes Hamilton and Temple	15. 6.54	1956	3	DG—3
Oudenarde Queen of Light	B	Ch. Redletter McJoe	Oudenarde Blue Moon	Mmmes Hamilton and Temple	Mmes Hamilton and Temple	26. 6.52	1954	3	DGS—84

Name	Sex	Sire	Dam	Breeder	Owner	Date	Year	No.	Reg.
Oudenarde Sandboy	D	Oudenarde Fire Light	Anna of Moran	Mrs Holness	Mmes Hamilton and Temple	3. 3.58	1960	5	DGS—96
Oudenarde Souvenir	B	Oudenarde Conservative	Oudenarde Trinket	Mmes Hamilton and Temple	Mmes Hamilton and Temple	23. 1.52	1954	4	DGS—3
Philomena of Blarneystone	B	Scot of Blarneystone	Flora of Blarneystone	Mr C. Dunlop	Mrs MacNeill	16. 5.58	1960	3	DG—45
Redletter Elford Mhorag	B	Ch. Redletter McJoe	Foundation Sylvia	Mrs G. M. E. Vickers	Mr W. N. Bradshaw	6. 5.51	1952	18	DGS—59
Redletter Fincairn Frolic	D	Ch. Redletter McJoe	Ch. Fincairn Gillian	Mrs J. Finlay	Mr W. N. Bradshaw	30. 7.50	1954	3	DGS—6
Redletter McBrach	D	Ch. Redletter McJoe	Maybe of Mercrogia	Mr W. L. Donovan	Mr W. N. Bradshaw	6. 9.52	1955	3	DGS—92
Redletter McBrigand	D	Ch. Redletter McMurran	Ch. Redletter Miss Splinters	Mr W. N. Bradshaw	Mr W. N. Bradshaw	31. 1.57	1958	3	DGS—4
Redletter McBryan	D	Ch. Redletter McMurran	Ch. Redletter Miss Splinters	Mr W. N. Bradshaw	Mr W. N. Bradshaw	31. 1.57	1958	17	DGS—4
Redletter Mac E Boy	D	Ch. Redletter McMurran	Greetavale Golden Girl	Mrs E. Cooper	Mr W. N. Bradshaw	21. 5.56	1958	3	DGS—80
Redletter McJoe	D	Ch. Bonfire of Twobees	Redletter My Choice	Mr W. N. Bradshaw	Mr W. N. Bradshaw	22. 8.48	1950	10	DGS—79
Redletter McMurran	D	Ch. Redletter McJoe	Cairncragg Binky	Mr H. Craig	Mr W. N. Bradshaw	6. 6.50	1951	26	DGS—59
Redletter McRuffie	D	Ch. Redletter McJoe	Rosefield Rebecca	Mr W. E. Parry	Mr W. N. Bradshaw	18. 6.52	1953	3	DGS—89
Redletter McRufus	D	Ch. Redletter Mac E Boy	Ch. Redletter Miss Muffit	Mr W. N. Bradshaw	Mr W. N. Bradshaw	15.11.57	1959	4	DGS—3
Redletter Magnet	B	Stanholmes Dusty Prince	Carnochan Lass	Mr W. N. Bradshaw	Mr W. N. Bradshaw	11. 8.43	1948	6	SD—72

Name of champion	Sex	Sire	Dam	Breeder	Owner	Born	Title won in	Total number of certs. won	Line and family
Redletter Marjose	B	Ch. Redletter McJoe	Ch. Fincairn Gillian	Mrs J. Finlay	Mr W. N. Bradshaw	30. 7.50	1952	4	DGS—6
Redletter Matelot	D	Ch. Redletter McJoe	Redletter Bonny Kilmeny	Mr W. N. Bradshaw	Mr W. N. Bradshaw	12. 9.53	1955	3	DGS—59
Redletter Midas	B	Ch. Redletter McMurran	Ch. Redletter Elford Mhorag	Mr W. N. Bradshaw	Mr W. N. Bradshaw	16. 6.54	1957	3	DGS—59
Redletter Miss Muffit	B	Ch. Redletter Fincairn Frolic	Uniquecottage Goldigger	Misses Longmore and Marshall	Mr W. N. Bradshaw	15. 4.54	1957	7	DGS—3
Redletter Miss Splinters	B	Crowtrees Splinters	Foxearle Goldfinch	Mrs M. Swires	Mr W. N. Bradshaw	29. 7.55	1956	3	DGS—4
Redletter Mona of Cambwll	B	Redletter Memory	Daffy of Cambwll	Miss M. G. Jones	Mr W. N. Bradshaw	13. 1.55	1957	4	I—95
Redletter Monalize	B	Ch. Redletter McMurran	Ch. Redletter Mona of Cambwll	Mr W. N. Bradshaw	Mr W. N. Bradshaw	8. 6.56	1958	3	DGS—95
Redletter Penny of Blarneystone	B	Killearn Mr Chips	Hopeful of Strath	Mr S. F. Gray	Mr W. N. Bradshaw	11. 5.50	1954	3	DGS—5
Redstacks Demoiselle	B	Curveside Cascade	Redstacks Naomi	Mrs B. Shea	Mrs B. Shea	30.12.57	1959	8	DGS—5
Redstacks Kerry Dancer	D	Yeendsdale Ringmaster	Dhumossie Lucinda	Mrs B. Shea	Mrs B. Shea	21.10.54	1956	4	DGS—5
Rob of Yeendsdale	D	Masterman of Yeendsdale	Jean of Yeendsdale	Mrs E. M. Yeend	Mr F. Hancox	12.10.48	1952	4	GB—17

Name	Sex	Sire	Dam	Owner	Breeder	Date	Year	No.	Code
Rogie of Rossarden	D	Ch. Rufus of Rhu	Red Devil of Rossarden	Miss B. M. Dixon	Miss B. M. Dixon	11.11.48	1952	3	DGS—63
Rosie of Rabling	B	Andrew of Twobees	Mandy of Crondall	Mrs C. Ross	Mrs C. Ross	15.10.47	1949	3	DGS—73
Rufus of Rhu	D	Killearn Mr Chip	Morag of Rhu	Mr J. Keay	Mr J. Keay	6. 5.44	1948	3	DGS—68
Shadow of Attic	B	Broadwater	Fairway of Carysfort	Mrs L. Bentley-Carr	Mrs L. Bentley-Carr	27. 2.53	1954	5	GB—48
Shelagh of Glen	B	Ch. Bonfire of Twobees	Sorag of Glen	Mrs E. D. Stonhouse Williams	Mrs G. Marsh	2. 3.52	1953	3	DGS—88
Shonru of Blarneystone	B	Ch. Rufus of Rhu	Crowtrees Snippet	Mr M. Currie	Mrs E. Gardner	22. 9.51	1954	3	DGS—90
Simon of Twobees	D	Ch. McJoe of Twobees	Oldcastleview Sandra of Twobees	Miss I. V. Bengough	Miss I. V. Bengough and Mrs Butterworth	31.10.48	1951	5	SD—11
Tags of Twobees	D	Ch. Elford Shanty	Bonnethill Juno	Miss I. V. Bengough	Miss I. V. Bengough	8. 8.57	1960	4	GB—59
Thistleclose Fling	B	Thistleclose Dauntless of Twobees	Thistleclose Rosette	Mrs D. G. Leigh	Mrs D. G. Leigh	17. 8.43	1948	4	DGS—59
Thistleclose MacGregor	D	Thistleclose Twig	Ch. Thistleclose Marigold	Mrs D. G. Leigh	Mrs D. G. Leigh	24.10.54	1956	4	DGS—59
Thistleclose Marigold	B	Thistleclose Hamon	Thistleclose Juliet	Mrs D. G. Leigh	Mrs D. G. Leigh	18. 1.50	1952	3	DGS—59
Thistleclose Pennyroyal	B	Thistleclose Royalist of Rhu	Thistleclose Harmony	Mrs D. G. Leigh	Mrs D. G. Leigh	4. 2.50	1952	3	DGS—59
Thistleclose Posy	B	Thistle of Thistleclose	Thistleclose Rosette	Mrs D. G. Leigh	Mrs D. G. Leigh	26. 3.44	1951	3	DGS—59

Name of champion	Sex	Sire	Dam	Breeder	Owner	Born	Title won in	Total number of certs. won	Line and family
Thistleclose Rosada	B	Thistleclose Royalist of Rhu	Thistleclose Rosalys	Mrs D. G. Leigh	Mrs D. G. Leigh	31. 8.49	1951	3	DGS—59
Uiseag o'the Braes	B	Ch. Rufus of Rhu	Thistleclose Rhona	Mrs J. Ogilvie	Mrs Hamilton (later Mrs Rhodes)	6.10.46	1949	3	DGS—59
Uniquecottage Blackgold	B	Ch. Redletter Fincairn Frolic	Uniquecottage Goldigger	Misses J. Marshall and H. Longmore	Misses J. Marshall and H. Longmore	15. 4.54	1957	5	DGS—3
Uniquecottage McAilenmor	D	Thistleclose Royalist of Rhu	Jollee Gay Memory	Misses J. Marshall and H. Longmore	Misses J. Marshall and H. Longmore	18.10.51	1954	3	DGS—3
Uniquecottage Maningray	D	Thistleclose Royalist of Rhu	Jollee Gay Memory	Misses J. Marshall and H. Longmore	Misses J. Marshall and H. Longmore	18.10.51	1957	3	DGS—3
Uniquecottage Sir Frolic	D	Ch. Redletter Fincairn Frolic	Uniquecottage Goldigger	Misses J. Marshall and H. Longmore	Misses J. Marshall and H. Longmore	15. 4.54	1955	17	DGS—3
Valiant Rab	D	Valiant James	Rhosbridge Rosemary	Miss A. D. Moody	Miss E. M. R. Reoch	9. 4.46	1949	3	DG—2
Valiant Rob Roy of Rhosbridge	D	Valiant Drummer	Rhosbridge Rosalind	Miss A. D. Moody	Miss E. M. R. Reoch	1. 4.45	1946	8	DG—2
Warberry Frederick of Dalry	D	Novera Kim	Fanhams Dilys	Mrs K. M. Carins	Mrs M. F. Hoyle	28. 7.53	1956	3	GB—93

Wencoly Maid Marion	B	Ch. Elford Shanty	Wencoly Twinkle of Talbotheath	Mr E. Pearce	15. 2.56	1958	3	GB—68
Whinyeon of Rossarden	B	Ch. Uniquecottage Sir Frolic	Ailsa of Rossarden	Miss B. M. Dixon	5.11.56	1959	5	DGS—63
Woodthorpe Clansman	D	Woodthorpe Merryman	Woodthorpe Dairymaid	Miss M. N. Morgan	29. 3.48	1952	3	DG—9
Yeendsdale Inspiration	D	Ch. Yeendsdale Merry Fiddler	Yeendsdale Never Say Die	Mrs M. Brookes	2.11.56	1958	14	DGS—17
Yeendsdale Masterpiece	D	Ch. Redletter McJoe	Ch. Joyous of Yeendsdale	Mrs E. M. Yeend	11. 1.52	1954	3	DGS—17
Yeendsdale Merry Fiddler	D	Ch. Yeendsdale Masterpiece	Gay Girl of Yeendsdale	Mrs E. M. Yeend	4. 5.53	1956	3	DGS—2

During the years 1961–1968 the number of Cairns gaining the title of champion increased by 84:

Year	No. of champions	Year	No. of champions	Year	No. of champions
1961	10	1964	12	1967	7
1962	10	1965	15	1968	8
1963	10	1066	13		

Name of champion	Sex	Sire	Dam	Breeder	Owner	Born	Title won in	number of certs. won	Line and family
Ainsty Therese	B	Ch. Lofthouse Geryon of Mistyfell	Ch. Ainsty Zillah	Mrs M. E. Carr	Mrs M. E. Carr	15.10.62	1965	3	1—90

Name of champion	Sex	Sire	Dam	Breeder	Owner	Born	Title won in	Total number of certs. won	Line and family
Ainsty Wilspoon Donna	B	Bracken of Ainsty	Treanfield Katrina	Messrs Wilson and Spooner	Mrs Carr	4. 7.63	1966	3	DGS—45
Beaver of Klinchy	B	Ch. Blencathra Reynard	Doonrae Elfin Gay	Mrs Goronowitch	Mr & Mrs R. W. Woods	30. 1.63	1966	5	I—9
Blencathra Barbara	B	Blencathra Rudolph	Blencathra Bonnie Girl	Mrs Drummond	Mrs Drummond	20. 9.59	1961	3	I—97
Blencathra Bravo	D	Ch. Blencathra Elford Badger	Blencathra Renata	Mrs Drummond	Mrs Drummond	10. 4.65	1968	3	DGS—9
Blencathra Brochter	D	Ch. Cairncrag Caesar	Blencathra Bittern	Mrs Drummond	Mrs Drummond	21. 4.61	1963	3	DGS—3
Blencathra Elford Badger	D	Ch. Blencathra Brochter	Elford Sprat	Mrs Vickers	Mrs Drummond	27. 2.64	1965	6	DGS—59
Blencathra Elford Lisa	B	Ch. Blencathra Brochter	Elford Sprat	Mrs Vickers	Mrs Drummond	17. 3.65	1966	5	DGS—59
Blencathra Renata	B	Ch. Blencathra Reynard	Keithview Mitzie	Mrs Bloor	Mrs Drummond	18.10.62	1964	4	I—9
Blencathra Reynard	D	Blencathra Smiler	Blencathra Rhoda	Mrs Drummond	Mrs Drummond	17. 3.61	1962	3	I—97
Cairncrag Caesar	D	Ch. Redletter McBryan	Dochfour Jeanie	Mrs D. D. Lewis	Mrs D. D. Lewis	2. 5.59	1963	3	DGS—69
Cairndow Goldilocks	B	Ch. Blencathra Brochter	Cairndow Saucy Sue	N. Roskell	N. Roskell	4. 9.64	1967	3	DGS—106
Campanologia Pricket	D	Ch. Oudenarde Fellamelad	Campanologia Merrymeet Diana	Miss Churchill	Miss Churchill	21. 3.64	1965	11	DGS—74

Name	Sex	Sire	Dam	Breeder	Owner	Date	Year	No.	Reg.
Catriona of Crondall	B	Ch. Dorseydale Tammy	Catriona of the Shieling	Mrs Sparrow-Wilkinson	Mrs Sparrow-Wilkinson	12. 9.65	1968	3	I—5
Craiglyn Cavalier	D	Ch. Redletter McBryan	Ewandale Cherry	Mrs Scruby	Miss E. Campbell	21. 2.62	1965	5	DGS—80
Craiglyn Easter Parade	B	Bobsacre Stoneyjacket	Craiglyn La Salle	Miss E. Campbell	Mr R. Gardner	7. 7.60	1962	3	DGS—90
Crispin of Mistyfell	D	Ch. Redletter McBryan	Moonshine of Mistyfell	Miss M. D. W. Gibson	Miss M. D. W. Gibson	14. 3.62	1964	3	DGS—63
Dorseydale Tammy	D	Ch. Lofthouse Geryon of Mistyfell	Justeena	Mrs D. Seymour	Mrs D. Seymour	6.12.61	1964	3	I—34
Felshott Annalisa	B	Ch. Redletter Master Mac	Felshott Arabella	Misses Hall and Wilson	Misses Hall and Wilson	22.10.62	1965	4	DGS—11
Felshott Bryany	B	Ch. Redletter McBryan	Felshott Shenandoah	Misses Hall and Wilson	Misses Hall and Wilson	2. 5.61	1963	3	DGS—11
Felshott Honey Dancer	B	Ch. Redletter Master Mac	Ch. Felshott Bryany	Misses Hall and Wilson	Misses Hall and Wilson	8. 9.64	1966	3	DGS—11
Felshott Red Shadow	B	Felshott Lordling	Silhouette of Mistyfell	Mrs M. Leitch	Misses Hall and Wilson	4. 4.62	1964	3	DGS-102
Felshott Taste of Honey	B	Ch. Redletter Master Mac	Ch. Felshott Bryany	Misses Hall and Wilson	Misses Hall and Wilson	4. 1.64	1965	5	DGS—11
Glenmacdhui Doonrae Memsie	B	Ch. Lofthouse Davey	Doonrae Beattie of Walaimor	Mrs Jennings	Mrs Mawson	11.12.65	1968	6	I—9
Glenmacdhui Gillie Gold	D	Hillston Bracken of Lapdown	Ch. Glenmacdhui Mohra	Mrs Mawson	Mrs Mawson	10. 4.62	1964	6	I—59
Glenmacdhui Ginger Lady	B	Ch. Redletter McBryan	Ch. Glenmacdhui Mohra	Mrs Mawson	Mrs Mawson	8.12.60	1963	3	DGS—59
Glenmacdhui Tearlach	D	Glenmacdhui Doran	Glenmacdhui Una	Mrs Mawson	Miss J. M. Hudson	28. 7.62	1965	3	GB—59

Name of champion	Sex	Sire	Dam	Breeder	Owner	Born	Title won in	Total number of certs. won	Line and family
Hallion of Rossarden	B	Ch. Ronaldshay of Rossarden	Skene of Rossarden	Miss Dixon	Miss Dixon	11.12.61	1966	3	DGS—63
Heshe Idaberry of Nunsfield	B	Ch. Redletter Marshall	Nunsfield Jenny Wren	Mrs Brooke	F. A. Edwards	23. 6.63	1965	4	DGS—89
Hillston Bonny Sweet Briar	B	Ch. Lofthouse Geryon of Mistyfell	Moonbeam of Mistyfell	Mrs Garbutt	Mrs Garbutt	5.12.59	1962	3	I—63
Impstown Jenny Geddes	B	Warberry Beau Brocade	Bonfire of Impstown	Miss J. Hall	Miss Hall	6. 9.62	1964	3	DGS—5
Lofthouse Copperplate	B	Ch. Lofthouse Geryon of Mistyfell	Copper of Twomegs	Mrs Coates	Mrs Manley	26. 4.60	1962	3	I—99
Lofthouse Davey	D	Ch. Lofthouse Geryon of Mistyfell	Dorseydale Justeena	Mrs Seymour	Mrs Manley	16. 5.63	1965	3	I—34
Lofthouse Larkspur	D	Ch. Lofthouse Geryon of Mistyfell	Ch. Lofthouse Golden	Mrs Manley	Mrs Manley	28. 6.63	1966	3	I—80
Lofthouse Rough Tweed	D	Ch. Lofthouse Larkspur	Dorseydale Cindy	Mrs Manley	Mrs Manley	12. 6.66	1968	3	I—34
Lofthouse Victoria	B	Ch. Lofthouse Geryon of Mistyfell	Ch. Lofthouse Golden	Mrs Manley	Mrs Manley	10. 3.61	1964	4	I—80

Name	Sex	Sire	Dam	Breeder	Owner	Date	Year		Ref
Merrymeet Marcella	B	Ch. Blencathra Milord	Ch. Merrymeet Tathwell Therese	Mrs Leverton	Mrs Leverton	12.10.59	1963	0	DGS—17
Merrymeet Marksman	D	Ch. Cairntop Nicholas	Ch. Merrymeet Tathwell Therese	Mrs Leverton	Mrs Leverton	20.12.60	1962	3	GB—17
Merrymeet Marlin	D	Ch. Blencathra Milord	Ch. Merrymeet Tathwell Therese	Mrs Leverton	Mrs Leverton	12.10.59	1961	3	DGS—17
Oudenarde Capital Case	D	Ch. Redletter McBryan	Oudenarde Light Case	Mmes Hamilton and Temple	Mmes Hamilton and Temple	26. 5.65	1968	4	DGS—84
Oudenarde Carefree Pete	D	Ch. Oudenarde Special Edition	Bellhammer Audacity	Mrs S. Manning	Mmes Hamilton and Temple	24. 8.66	1968	3	DGS—104
Oudenarde Fair Prospect	B	Oudenarde Radiant Light	Oudenarde Light Fantastic	Mmes Hamilton and Temple	Mmes Hamilton and Temple	2. 7.61	1963	4	DGS—3
Oudenarde Fancy Light	B	Ch. Oudenarde Special Edition	Ch. Oudenarde Light Melody	Mmes Hamilton and Temple	Mmes Hamilton and Temple	12. 9.62	1965	5	DGS—84
Oudenarde Fellamelad	D	Ch. Blencathra Milord	Oudenarde Silver Spray	Mmes Hamilton and Temple	Mmes Hamilton and Temple	27.12.61	1964	3	DGS—84
Oudenarde Madame Caroline	B	Ch. Merrymeet Marlin	Oudenarde Catchlight	Mmes Hamilton and Temple	Mmes Hamilton and Temple	19. 9.61	1964	3	DGS—11
Oudenarde Midnight Chimes	D	Ch. Oudenarde Sandboy	Mickleham Lady Susan	Miss Innes Hutchinson	Mmes Hamilton and Temple	6.12.64	1966	4	DGS—9
Oudenarde Rambling Rose	B	Ch. Redletter McBryan	Oudenarde Veronica	Mmes Hamilton and Temple	Mmes Hamilton and Temple	29.11.59	1963	3	DGS—59
Oudenarde Special Edition	D	Oudenarde Game Bird	Oudenarde Dahlia	Mmes Hamilton and Temple	Mmes Hamilton and Temple	12. 2.60	1962	5	DGS—3

Name of champion	Sex	Sire	Dam	Breeder	Owner	Born	Title won in	Total number of certs. won	Line and family
Pledwick Drusilla	B	Ch. Blencathra Elford Badger	Doonrae Elfin Gay	Mrs Goronovitch	Mrs Summers	16.10.65	1967	3	DGS—9
Pledwick Trojan	D	Ch. Redletter McBryan	Redletter Miss Frolic	Mrs Summers	Mrs Summers	3. 5.59	1961	3	DGS—59
Redletter Charming	B	Ch. Redletter McBryan	Redletter Margaret	W. N. Bradshaw	W. N. Bradshaw	9. 9.64	1967	3	DGS—3
Redletter Maestro	D	Ch. Redletter McBryan	Redletter Maura	W. N. Bradshaw	W. N. Bradshaw	23.11.63	1965	5	DGS—59
Redletter Marshall	D	Redletter Mr Frolic	Redletter Maura	W. N. Bradshaw	W. N. Bradshaw	30. 1.61	1962	5	DGS—59
Redletter Master Mac	D	Ch. Redletter McBryan	Ch. Redletter Miss Muffit	W. N. Bradshaw	W. N. Bradshaw	3. 8.59	1961	11	DGS—3
Redletter Maymorn	B	Redletter My Bobbie	Redletter Mistrip	W. N. Bradshaw	W. N. Bradshaw	20. 8.64	1966	8	DGS—103
Redletter Michael	D	Ch. Redletter Marshall	Ch. Redletter Miss Melody	W. N. Bradshaw	W. N. Bradshaw	27. 6.63	1966	4	DGS—52
Redletter Miss Fenella	B	Ch. Redletter Master Mac	Glenlanna Gold Gauntlet	Miss Abraham	W. N. Bradshaw	9. 5.66	1967	5	DGS—3
Redletter Miss Madam	B	Ch. Redletter McMurran	Ch. Redletter Miss Muffit	W. N. Bradshaw	W. N. Bradshaw	22. 2.60	1961	9	DGS—3
Redletter Miss Melody	B	Ch. Redletter Mac E Boy	Redletter Foggyfurze Snow Belle	W. N. Bradshaw	W. N. Bradshaw	3.12.59	1963	3	DGS—52
Redletter Twinlaw Seaspirit	D	Ch. Redletter Maestro	Felshott Araminta	Mrs Henderson	W. N. Bradshaw	1. 2.66	1967	17	DGS—11

Name	Sex	Sire	Dam	Owner	Breeder	D.O.B.	Year	No.	Ref.
Redstacks Kelly	D	Flora Cottage Colonel	Redstacks Shooting Star	Mrs Shea	Mrs Shea	31. 8.62	1964	5	GB—3
Ronaldshay of Rossarden	D	Riskin of Rossarden	Scutra of Rossarden	Miss B. M. Dixon	Miss B. M. Dixon	23.11.57	1961	5	DGS—63
Rossarden McDougall of Wimpas	D	Ch. Merrymeet Marlin	Moragtwo of Wimpas	Mrs Heery	Miss B. M. Dixon	4. 6.62	1964	6	DGS—101
Seiyun Neon	D	Blencathra Rudolph	Redstacks Lobelia	J. H. Dean	J. H. Dean and Mrs Dewhurst	30.10.59	1963	4	I—3
Seiyun Sheba	B	Blencathra Chataboy	Redstacks Lobelia	J. H. Dean and Mrs Dewhurst	J. H. Dean and Mrs Dewhurst	21. 9.62	1964	3	DGS—3
Toptwig Miss Defoe	B	Ch. Tolptwig Mr Defoe	Toptwig Speireag	Mrs G. Marsh	Mrs G. Marsh and J. H. Danks	18. 8.66	1968	3	DGS—100
Toptwig Mr Defoe	D	Toptwig Oudenarde Glendawn	Terriwin Silvia	Mrs German	Mrs G. Marsh	4.10.64	1966	3	DGS—9
Toptwig Tilden	D	Toptwig Cathmhor	Toptwig Gorgeous Gussie	Mrs G. Marsh	Mrs G. Marsh and J. H. Danks	1. 1.67	1968	14	DGS—100
Toptwig Token	B	Ch. Redletter McBryan	Toptwig Mulaidh	Mrs G. Marsh	Mrs G. Marsh	28. 3.59	1962	3	DGS—100
Truelove of Yeendsdale	B	Ch. Yeendsdale Masterpiece	Yeendsdale Perfection	Mrs Yeend	Mrs Yeend	18. 7.60	1963	3	DGS—104
Twinlaw Blithe Spirit	B	Ch. Redletter Maestro	Felshott Araminta	Mrs Henderson	Mrs Henderson	1. 2.66	1967	6	DGS—11
Uniquecottage Gold Goblet	D	Ch. Ronaldshay of Rossarden	Uniquecottage Miss Gold	Misses Marshall and Longmore	Misses Marshall and Longmore	25. 9.63	1965	3	DGS—3
Uniquecottage Gold Melody	B	Ch. Uniquecottage Sir Frolic	Uniquecottage Sorcha	Misses Marshall and Longmore	Misses Marshall and Longmore	22.12.59	1963	3	DGS—3

Name of champion	Sex	Sire	Dam	Breeder	Owner	Born	Title won in	Total number of certs. won	Line and family
Uniquecottage Gold Moi Dor	B	Ch. Uniquecottage Maningrey	Ch. Uniquecottage Blackgold	Misses Marshall and Longmore	Misses Marshall and Longmore	30. 9.59	1962	3	DGS—3
Uniquecottage Gold Rouble	D	Ch. Ronaldshay of Rossarden	Ch. Uniquecottage Gold Moi Dor	Misses Marshall and Longmore	Misses Marshall and Longmore	25. 2.64	1966	3	DGS—3
Uniquecottage Mr Bradshaw	D	Warberry Regency of Rossarden	Uniquecottage Gold Memory	Misses Marshall and Longmore	Misses Marshall and Longmore	18. 8.59	1961	3	DGS—3
Uniquecottage Powder Monkey	D	Ch. Dorseydale Tammy	Adrigole Alves	Mrs Seymour	Misses Marshall and Longmore	7.12.59	1966	3	I—105
Uniquecottage Terrible Twin	D	Ch. Redletter McBryan	Uniquecottage Silver Flame	Misses Marshall and Longmore	Misses Marshall and Longmore	1. 4.60	1961	6	DGS—3
Vinovium Graham	D	Vinovium Dominic	Glonmor Vinovium Gem	Mrs Graham	Mrs M. Jagger	3. 4.65	1966	3	DR—90
Vinovium Pledwick Tiger	D	Ch. Lofthouse Sundew	Pledwick Roamer	Mrs Summers	Mrs M. Jagger	21. 2.59	1962	3	I—98
Warberry Watagirl	B	Warberry Rob Roy	Warberry Quicksilver	Mrs Hoyle	Misses Marshall and Longmore	29. 1.62	1965	4	GDS—93
Warberry Wild Honey	B	Warberry Beau Brocade	Gay Girl of Warberry	Mrs Hoyle	Misses Marshall and Longmore	20.11.61	1965	4	DGS—93
Wendanny Coquette	B	Ch. Lofthouse Davey	Ch. Wendanny Pirouette	Miss T. P. Browne	Miss T. P. Browne	9.11.65	1967	7	I—48
Wendanny Pirouette	B	Wendanny Mr Wanderer	Attic Moonide	Miss T. P. Browne	Miss T. P. Browne	1.11.59	1961	3	GB—48
Witch of Mistyfell	B	Ch. Gerolf of Mistyfell	Delightful Shandy	Mrs H. Hall	Miss Gibson	6. 5.59	1961	3	I—9

During the years 1969–1973 the number of Cairns gaining the title of Champion increased by 48:

Year	No. of champions
1969	10
1970	8
1971	13
1972	8
1973	9

Name of champion	Sex	Sire	Dam	Breeder	Owner	Born	Title won in	Total number of certs. won	Line and family
Ainsty Tabatha	B	Felshott Tom Brown	Ch. Ainsty Therese	Mrs Carr	Mrs Carr	2. 6.68	1970	3	DGS—90
Attic Wallisheath Mid Day Chimes	D	Ch. Oudenarde Midnight Chimes	Wallisheath Sweet Memory	Mrs Brasnett	Miss Bentley-Carr	22. 6.69	1971	4	DGS
Avenal House Cloth of Gold	D	Ch. Lofthouse Rough Tweed	Uniquecottage My Fair Lady	Major and Mrs Small	Major and Mrs Small	5. 7.69	1972	5	1—2
Blencathra Barrett	D	Ch. Blencathra Barrie	Blencathra Brora	Mrs Drummond	Mrs Drummond	21. 6.69	1971	6	1—2
Blencathra Barrie	D	Blencathra Derryvale Tara	Blencathra Rosabel	Mrs Drummond	Mrs Drummond	7. 5.67	1969	4	DGS—45
Blencathra Brat	D	Blencathra Derryvale Tara	Blencathra Britt	Mrs Drummond	Mrs Drummond	6. 3.68	1969	9	DGS—80

Name of champion	Sex	Sire	Dam	Breeder	Owner	Born	Title won in	Total number of certs. won	Line and family
Blencathra Buccaneer	D	Blencathra Derryvale Tara	Blencathra Rosabel	Mrs Drummond	Mrs Drummond	7. 5.67	1971	3	DGS—45
Brucairns Crackerjack	D	Dorseydale Red Admiral	Brucairns Pearly Queen	Mrs Harding	Mrs Harding	15. 4.69	1971	3	I—108
Brucairns Juliet	B	Ch. Oudenarde Capital Case	Brucairns Silver Belle	Mrs Harding	Mrs Harding	7. 4.69	1971	3	DGS—108
Brucairns Merrybelle	B	Ch. Oudenarde Midnight Chimes	Brucairns Liberty Belle	Mrs Harding	Mrs Harding	4.11.69	1972	3	DGS—108
Brucairns Red Robin	D	Dorseydale Red Admiral	Brucairns Pearly Queen	Mrs Harding	Mrs Harding	21. 2.67	1970	3	I—108
Charlotte of Camcairn	B	Brav o' the Braes	Wendy o' the Braes	Mrs H. Rhodes	Messrs Cammish and Williams	3. 9.71	1973	3	GR—90
Courrai Mary Lou	B	Oudenarde Raebrook Cavalier	Attic Christmas Carol	Miss Bentley-Carr	Mmes Howes and Clark	18. 7.71	1973	3	DGS—48
Craiglyn Commodore	D	Ch. Blencathra Elford Badger	Craiglyn Woodland Belle	Miss E. Campbell	Miss E. Campbell	24. 4.69	1972	3	DGS—90
Craiglyn Easter Bonnet	B	Ch. Blencathra Elford Badger	Craiglyn Woodland Belle	Miss E. Campbell	Miss E. Campbell	11.10.67	1970	3	DGS—90
Craiglyn Morag	B	Ch. Craiglyn Cavalier	Craiglyn Carla	Miss E. Campbell	Miss E. Campbell	9. 7.67	1969	3	DGS—90
Craiglyn Stornoway	D	Ch. Blencathra Elford Badger	Craiglyn Woodland Belle	Miss E. Campbell	Miss E. Campbell	11.10.67	1969	7	DGS—90

Name	Sex	Sire	Dam	Breeder	Owner	Date	Year	No.	Reg.
Dalemoss Jillywood	B	Kilticlan Doonrae Kilrenny	Kilticlan Dearest Kate	Mr and Mrs Woods	Mrs Moss	17. 9.66	1970	3	1—80
Delia of Bankfoot	B	Redletter Son of Marshall	Alexa of Bankfoot	Miss J. Pascoe	Mrs Holne	30.11.68	1973	4	DGS—2
Early Bird of Unique Cottage	B	Ch. Heshe Donovan	Avenal House Cinderella	Major and Mrs Small	Mrs Parker-Tucker	21. 4.72	1973	4	DGS—3
Felshott Anita	B	Felshott Tom Brown	Felshott Alexandra	Misses M. and D. Hall and M. D. Wilson	Misses M. and D. Hall and M. D. Wilson	16. 9.66	1969	3	DGS—11
Felshott Coolin	D	Felshott Honey Badger	Ch. Felshott Anita	Misses M. and D. Hall and M. D. Wilson	Misses M. and D. Hall and M. D. Wilson	21. 3.71	1973	4	DGS—11
Felshott Honey Bird	B	Ch. Redletter Master Mac	Ch. Felshott Bryany	Misses M. and D. Hall and M. D. Wilson	Misses M. and D. Hall and M. D. Wilson	4. 2.67	1969	3	DGS—11
Felshott Honey Dew of Rossarden	B	Ch. Redletter Master Mac	Ch. Felshott Bryany	Misses M. and D. Hall and M. D. Wilson	Miss C. H. Dixon	4. 2.67	1971	3	DGS—11
Felshott Sari Sara	B	Blencathra Derryvale Tara	Felshott Lonicera	Misses M. and D. Hall and M. D. Wilson	Misses M. and D. Hall and M. D. Wilson	19.12.69	1971	3	DGS—11
Felshott Tarantara	B	Blencathra Derryvale Tara	Felshott Lonicera	Misses M. and D. Hall and M. D. Wilson	Misses M. and D. Hall and M. D. Wilson	30.10.68	1970	6	DGS—11
Felshott Tulloch	D	Ch. Craiglyn Cavalier	Ch. Felshott Anita	Misses M. and D. Hall and M. D. Wilson	Messrs Cammish and Williams	16. 6.70	1973	3	DGS—11
Felshott Wine Taster	D	Ch. Unique Cottage Gold Goblet	Felshott Lonicera	Misses M. and D Hall and M. D. Wilson	Misses M. and D. Hall and M. D. Wilson	18. 4.67	1969	3	DGS—11

Name of champion	Sex	Sire	Dam	Breeder	Owner	Born	Title won in	Total number of certs. won	Line and family
Ghilepatric Girtle	B	Kilticlan Doran	Ghilepatric Sally St Clair	Dr D. and Miss F. MacLenan	Mrs Mawson	28. 8.69	1971	6	DGS—90
Gregor of Crondall	D	Seasand of Crondall	Ch. Catriona of Crondall	Mrs Sparrow-Wilkinson	Mrs Sparrow-Wilkinson	1. 8.69	1972	4	DGS—5
Heshe Donovan	D	Ch. Blencathra Brat	Drusilla of Rossarden	F. A. Edwards	F. A. Edwards	6. 1.71	1972	5	DGS
Lofthouse Geryon	D	Ch. Lofthouse Larkspur	Dorseydale Cindy	Mr Pauling	Mrs Manley	24. 1.67	1971	4	I—34
Myaldour My Jo Janet	B	Ch. Glenmacdhui Gillie Gold	Redstacks Linnhe	Mrs N. G. Hogg	Mrs N. G. Hogg	26. 6.68	1971	4	I—3
Oudenarde Be Joyful	B	Ch. Campanologia Pricket	Ch. Oudenarde Madame Caroline	Mesdames Hamilton and Temple	Mesdames Hamilton and Temple	31. 3.67	1969	4	DGS—11
Oudenarde Midnight Magic	D	Ch. Oudenarde Midnight Chimes	Ch. Oudenarde Be Joyful	Mrs D. and Miss Helen Hamilton	Mrs D. and Miss Helen Hamilton	4.12.69	1972	5	DGS—11
Oudenarde Midnight Marauder	D	Ch. Oudenarde Midnight Chimes	Ch. Oudenarde Fair Prospect	Mesdames Hamilton and Temple	Mesdames Hamilton and Temple	4.10.66	1969	5	DGS—3
Oudenarde Raiding Light	D	Ch. Oudenarde Midnight Marauder	Oudenarde Bright Eyes	Mrs D. and Miss Helen Hamilton	Mrs D. and Miss Helen Hamilton	25. 2.69	1970	4	DGS—59
Pledwick Glenda of Wildmoor	B	Vinovium Irwin	Ch. Pledwick Drusilla	Mrs Summers	Mr A. Price	11. 9.68	1970	5	DR—9

Name	Sex	Sire	Dam	Breeder	Owner	Date	Year	No.	Ref.
Pledwick Hazel of Wildmoor	B	Vinovium Irwin	Ch. Pledwick Drusilla	Mrs Summers	Mr A. Price	23. 3.70	1971	4	DR—9
Redletter Magic Orb	D	Ch. Redletter Twinlaw Sea Spirit	Ch. Redletter Miss Fennella	W. N. Bradshaw	W. N. Bradshaw	23. 3.68	1971	3	DGS—3
Redletter Marcel	B	Ch. Redletter Michael	Redletter Miss Marshall	W. N. Bradshaw	W. N. Bradshaw	2. 8.68	1970	17	DGS—59
Redletter Moonracker	B	Ch. Redletter Moon Tripper	Ch. Redletter Marcel	W. N. Bradshaw	W. N. Bradshaw	23.11.70	1972	21	DGS—59
Redletter Moon Tripper	D	Ch. Redletter Michael	Redletter Mistrip	W. N. Bradshaw	W. N. Bradshaw	29. 9.69	1973	3	DGS—103
Redletter Twinlaw Melissa	B	Ch. Redletter Maestro	Felshott Araminta	Mrs A. Henderson	W. N. Bradshaw	1. 3.67	1969	4	DGS—11
Star Turn of Rossarden	D	Reactor of Rossarden	Ch. Felshott Honey Dew of Rossarden	Miss C. H. Dixon	Miss C. H. Dixon	11. 9.69	1971	3	DGS—11
Toptwig Adam	D	Toptwig Brigadier	Nicola of Baraburn	Mrs Evans	Mrs Marsh and Mr J. Danks	18. 8.67	1972	3	DGS—91
Twinlaw Phillippa	B	Ch. Redletter Michael	Ch. Twinlaw Blithe Spirit	Mrs A. Henderson	Mrs A. Henderson	11. 9.69	1973	12	DGS—11
Wandering Willie of Toptwig	D	Ch. Toptwig Tilden	Uniquecottage My Fair Lady	Major and Mrs Small	Mrs Marsh and J. Danks	26.11.71	1973	7	DGS—2
Wendanny Cockaigne	D	Ch. Gregor of Crondall	Ch. Wendanny Coquette	Miss T. P. Browne	Miss T. P. Browne	16. 3.72	1973	5	DGS—48

During the years 1974–1976 the number of Cairns gaining the title of Champion increased by 32:

Year	No. of champions
1974	12
1975	10
1976	10

Name of champion	Sex	Sire	Dam	Breeder	Owner	Born	Title won in	Total number of certs. won	Line and family
Avenel House Golden Oriole	D	Ch. Blencathra Brat	Avenel House Tumbler	Owners	Major and Mrs Small	2. 4.73	1975	9	DGS—3
Bankfoot Devoran	D	Ch. Redletter Moonstruck	Ch. Delia of Bankfoot	Mrs Holme	Major and Mrs Small	17. 2.75	1976	4	DGS—2
Brucairn Jason	D	Brucairn Romeo	Brucairn Ballerina	Owner	Mrs Harding	24. 9.71	1974	3	DGS—108
Brucairn Quality Street	D	Ch. Oudenarde Midnight Chimes	Brucairn Honeysuckle	Owner	Mrs Harding	22. 2.72	1975	4	DGS—108
Cairncrag Huntsman	D	Cairncrag John Peel	Cairnstone Lady Wilder	Mr J. M. Shenton	Mrs Dickens-Lewis	1.10.71	1974	3	DGS—3
Detchmont Catriona	B	Ch. Craiglyn Stornoway	Isla of Detchmont	Owner	Mrs McKinlay	16. 7.71	1976	3	DGS—3
Felshot Hilarity	B	Felshot Honey Badger	Ch. Felshot Anita	Owners	Misses M. and D. Hall and M. D. Wilson	15. 7.72	1975	4	DGS—11

Name	Sex	Sire	Dam		Breeder	Date	Year		DGS
Felshott Russell	B	Felshott Honey Badger	Ch. Felshott Anita	Owners	Misses M. and D. Hall and M. D. Wilson	16. 5.73	1975	3	DGS—11
Greetavale Super Honey	B	Ch. Felshott Wine Taster	Greetavale Suzette	Mrs Newton	Mrs Cooper	5. 5.71	1974	3	DGS—80
Heshe Miss Emm Dee	B	Felshott Honey Badger	Heshe Jan-Ela of Nunsfield	Owner	F. A. Edwards	24. 9.72	1975	3	DGS—
Heshe Izawyche	B	Ch. Blencathra Brat	Drusilla of Rossarden	Owner	F. A. Edwards	19. 1.72	1974	4	DGS—109
Myaldour Mally Lee	B	Doonrae Quixote	Ch. Myaldour My Jo Janet	Owner	Mrs Hogg	27. 1.71	1974	4	1—3
Oudenarde Bold and Free	D	Ch. Oudenarde Raiding Light	Oudenarde Streamlight	Owners	Mrs D. and Miss H. Hamilton	28. 5.71	1974	3	DGS—84
Oudenarde Fair Nicola	B	Ch. Oudenarde Raiding Light	Oudenarde Sea Belle	Owners	Mrs D. and Miss H. Hamilton	25. 2.72	1974	3	DGS—9
Oudenarde Sea Hawk	D	Ch. Oudenarde Midnight Marauder	Oudenarde Sea Romance	Owners	Mrs D. and Miss H. Hamilton	9. 4.72	1974	5	DGS—9
Redletter Marcella	B	Ch. Redletter Moon Tripper	Ch. Redletter Marcel	Owner	W. N. Bradshaw	10. 7.74	1976	3	DGS—59
Redletter Miss Millie	B	Ch. Redletter Magic Orb	Ch. Redletter Twinlaw Melissa	Owner	W. N. Bradshaw	20. 9.71	1975	3	DGS—11
Redletter Midsummer	B	Ch. Redletter Moonstruck	Ch. Redletter Miss Millie	Owner	W. N. Bradshaw	8. 6.74	1976	6	DGS—11
Redletter Miss World	B	Ch. Redletter Michael	Ch. Redletter Twinlaw Melissa	Owner	W. N. Bradshaw	7. 4.73	1975	3	DGS—11

Name of champion	Sex	Sire	Dam	Breeder	Owner	Born	Title won in	Total number of certs. won	Line and family
Redletter Moonstruck	D	Ch. Redletter Moon Tripper	Ch. Redletter Marcel	Owner	W. N. Bradshaw	23.11.70	1974	7	DGS—59
Rossarden Minerva	B	Ch. Blencathra Brat	Drumy of Rossarden	Owner	Miss C H. Dixon	20. 1.72	1976	3	DGS—109
Schottische of Selirk	B	Selirk Barry	Killearn Meg	Misses H. and J. Todd	Mrs D. Proudlock	20. 1.74	1976	4	DGS—34
Sine of Clanranald	B	Ch. Glenmacdhui Tearlach	Queen Maxine	M. and J. Spence	Miss Hudson	14. 9.72	1975	4	GB—112
Tablin Rolle	D	Ch. Oudenarde Raiding Light	Tablin Thisbe	Owner	Mrs J. Meyrick	27.11.72	1975	6	DGS—
Toptwig Dawnlight of Oudenarde	B	Ch. Oudenarde Raiding Light	Duntiblae Top Score of Toptwig	Mrs G. Marsh	Mrs D. and Miss H. Hamilton	17.10.74	1976	3	DGS—4
Toptwig Fly By Night of Oudenarde	D	Ch. Oudenarde Raiding Light	Duntiblae Top Score of Toptwig	Mrs G. Marsh	Mrs D. and Miss H. Hamilton	17.10.74	1976	6	DGS—4
Twinlaw Barnstormer	D	Ch. Redletter Magic Orb	Ch. Twinlaw Blithe Spirit	Owner	Mrs A. Henderson	11.10.73	1976	3	DGS—11
Twinlaw Spring Song	B	Ch. Redletter Magic Orb	Ch. Twinlaw Phillippa	Owner	Mrs A. Henderson	11. 3.73	1974	7	DGS—11
Uniquecottage Gold Pippit	B	Ch. Avenelhouse Golden Oriole	Ch. Uniquecottage Gold Wings	Owner	Mrs Parker-Tucker	4. 1.75	1976	4	DGS—11

	Sex	Sire	Dam	Breeder	Owner	Born	Title won in	Total number of certs. won	Line and family
Uniquecottage Gold Wings	B	Ch. Avenelhouse Cloth of Gold	Uniquecottage Wingletang	Owner	Mrs Parker-Tucker	7.10.72	1974	3	I—11
Uniquecottage Grey Wagtail	D	Craiglyn Caledonian	Ch. Early Bird of Uniquecottage	Owner	Mrs Parker-Tucker	10. 7.74	1976	6	DGS—3
Wimpas Mark	D	Doublet of Wimpas	Gypsy Girl of Wimpas	Owner	Mrs E. Heery	27.12.73	1975	7	DGS—

During the years 1977–1986 the number of Cairns gaining the title of Champion increased by 121:

Year	No. of champions	Dogs	Bitches
1977	12	5	7
1978	14	7	7
1979	10	5	5
1980	12	5	7
1981	9	3	6
1982	10	5	5
1983	12	7	5
1984	13	6	7
1985	18	9	9
1986	11	5	6

Name of champion	Sex	Sire	Dam	Breeder	Owner	Born	Title won in	Total number of certs. won	Line and family
Avenelhouse Acrobat Bird	B	Uniquecottage Golden Eagle	Avenelhouse Gold Lanie	Mrs H. Small	Mrs H. Small	14.8.78	1981	3	DGS—2

Name of champion	Sex	Sire	Dam	Breeder	Owner	Born	Title won in	Total number of certs. won	Line and family
Avenelhouse Dark Gentleman	D	Ch. Uniquecottage Flycatcher	Ch. Avenelhouse Acrobat Bird	Mrs H. Small	Mrs H. Small	15.4.82	1984	3	DGS—2
Avenelhouse King's Frolic	D	Ch. Craiglyn Caledonian	Ch. Early Bird of Uniquecottage	Mrs Parker-Tucker	Mr A. Price	20.1.76	1978	4	DGS—3
Avenelhouse King's Guard	D	Avenelhouse King's Councillor	Avenelhouse Devil Me Care	Mrs H. Small	Mrs H. Small	30.6.81	1983	5	DGS—3
Avenelhouse Noble Hindrance	D	Uniquecottage Bushchat	Ch. Avenelhouse Acrobat Bird	Mrs H. Small	Mrs H. Small	29.10.83	1985	3	DGS—2
Brindle Oak Bianca	B	Ch. Robinson Crusoe of Courtrai	Tamroy Lassio	Mr K. Holmes	Mr K. Holmes	23.4.79	1982	4	DGS—
Brucairn Chimes Beau Belle	B	Ch. Oudenarde Midnight Chimes	Brucairn Ballerina	Mrs J. E. Harding	Mrs J. E. Harding	14.11.74	1977	3	DGS—108
Brucairn Jonnie	D	Ch. Oudenarde Raiding Light	Ch. Brucairn Juliet	Mrs J. E. Harding	Mrs J. E. Harding	20.8.73	1977	3	DGS—108
Cairntop Master Simon	D	Ch. Robinson Crusoe of Courtrai	Cairntop Cyrene	Mrs Sanger	Mrs M. Shuttleworth	8.8.77	1979	5	DGS—17
Camcairn Beaulah	B	Camcairn Calvin	Ch. Camcairn Cordelia	Messrs W. H. Cammish & W. J. Williams	Messrs W. H. Cammish & W. J. Williams	3.2.78	1981	3	DGS—90
Camcairn Claudette	B	Camcairn Cabor	Ch. Charlotte of Camcairn	Messrs W. H. Cammish & W. J. Williams	Messrs W. H. Cammish & W. J. Williams	23.4.77	1979	3	DGS—90

Name	Sex	Sire	Dam	Breeder	Owner	Date	Year	No.	Ref.
Camcairn Cordelia	B	Ch. Felshott Tulloch	Camcairn Country Girl	Messrs W. H. Cammish & W. J. Williams	Messrs W. H. Cammish & W. J. Williams	24.1.76	1977	3	DGS—90
Captivating Lady of Orior	B	Ir. Ch. Celtic Ayr of Uniquecottage	Uniquecottage Chilfchaff	Mrs W. Dean	Mr J. Dean	3.10.82	1985	4	DGS—3
Clanranald Foxy Lady	B	Ch. Clanranald Tam O'Shanter	Ch. Clanranald Laetare	Miss J. Hudson	Miss J. Hudson	18.11.82	1986	3	DGS—112
Clanranald Laetare	B	Foxgrove Jeff of Ljekarna	Ch. Sine of Clanranald	Miss J. Hudson	Miss J. Hudson	12.6.78	1980	3	DGS—112
Clanranald Tam O'Shanter	D	Ljekarna Valentine	Clanranald Stella Maris	Miss J. Hudson	Miss J. Hudson	13.10.80	1982	5	DGS—112
Correnie Warrior in Silver	D	Ch. Robinson Crusoe of Courtrai	Velora Quick Silver of Correnie	Mrs Weinberger	Mrs Weinberger	9.12.81	1984	6	DGS—113
Courtrai Culty Boy of Skimmerton	D	Ch. Robinson Crusoe of Courtrai	Ch. Courtrai Triella Trudy	Misses D. Howes & C. Clark	Mr & Mrs J. Radford	27.9.80	1985	3	DGS—90
Courtrai John Julius	D	Ch. Robinson Crusoe of Courtrai	Ch. Courtrai Triella Trudy	Misses D. Howes & C. Clark	Misses D. Howes & C. Clark	28.11.81	1984	5	DGS—90
Courtrai Sally Ann	B	Petersden Prince	Courtrai Pollyanna	Misses D. Howes & C. Clark	Misses D. Howes & C. Clark	27.8.75	1978	3	GR—48
Courtrai Triella Trudy	B	Felshott Honey Badger	Camcairn Cavalcade	Misses D. Howes & C. Clark	Misses D. Howes & C. Clark	25.12.76	1978	5	DGS—90
Craiglyn Caledonian	D	Ch. Craiglyn Commodore	Craiglyn Christmas Carol	Miss E. Campbell	Mrs Parker-Tucker	24.12.72	1977	5	DGS—90
Cruzo Carousel	B	Ch. Robinson Crusoe of Courtrai	Courtrai Penelope Prue	Mrs G. Robinson	Mrs G. Robinson	6.2.78	1980	4	DGS—48

Name of champion	Sex	Sire	Dam	Breeder	Owner	Born	Title won in	Total number of certs. won	Line and family
Cruzo Cornelian	D	Ch. Stanedykes Pete	Ch. Cruzo Carousel	Mrs G. Robinson	Mr C. A. Guest	15.9.83	1986	4	DGS—48
Cruzo Drummer Boy of Chezaku	D	Ch. Robinson Crusoe of Courtrai	Cruzoe Brocade	Mrs G. Robinson	Mr D. J. Kippen & Mrs A. C. Kippen	28.12.78	1983	3	DGS—48
Cruzo Henna Holly	B	Courtrai Buffalo Bill	Cruzo Delilah	Mrs G. Robinson	Mrs G. Robinson	21.6.80	1982	4	DGS—48
Curveside Crofter	D	Wildmoor Cameron	Curveside Clementine	Miss A. Turton	Miss A. Turton	20.4.78	1983	3	DGS—
Daleletty Adam	D	Velora Proper Charlie	Velora Evergreen	Miss B. Whittaker	Miss B. Whittaker	1.11.80	1984	3	DGS—113
Dear Gabriella at Phildickers	B	Ch. Mistyridge Magic Solo	Monary Conni	Mrs J. Smith	Mesdames Shuttleworth & Dickers	24.12.83	1986	9	DGS—4
Dechmont Christopher	D	Ch. Uniquecottage Treecreeper	Dechmont Maud	Mrs M. McKinlay	Mrs M. McKinlay	3.12.81	1983	3	DGS—110
Felshott Silly Season of Oudenarde	B	Ch. Oudenarde Raiding Light	Ch. Felshott Hilarity	Misses M. & D. Hall & M. D. Wilson	Mrs D. Hamilton	6.9.76	1978	4	DGS—11
Glenbrae Avena	B	Dormerhall Apple Catcher	Glenbrae Wheatear	Mr I. M. Kettle	Mr I. M. Kettle	23.3.84	1985	5	I—103
Glencara Bright Spark	D	Ch. Ugadale Leadall	Twinlaw Lucky Fortune	Mr & Mrs Carruthers	Mr & Mrs Carruthers	11.8.77	1980	4	DGS—11

Name	Sex	Sire	Dam	Owner 1	Owner 2	Date	Year	No.	Code
Greetavale Honey Dew of Harlight	B	Ch. Robinson Crusoe of Courtrai	Greetavale Moon Girl	Mr A. Cooper	Mrs L. Spence	9.7.81	1984	3	DGS—80
Hamish of Seltirk	D	Killearn King's Ransom	Killearn Blaeberry	Mr R. Gardner	Mrs A. D. Proudlock	29.9.76	1980	3	GB—90
Harlight Heidi	B	Ch. Uniquecottage Treecreeper	Harlight Honeybunch	Mrs L. Spence	Mrs L. Spence	4.5.82	1984	3	DGS—80
Harlight Hilary	B	Ch. Robinson Crusoe of Courtrai	Harlight Honeybunch	Mrs L. Spence	Mrs L. Spence	18.10.81	1985	3	DGS—80
Harlight Honeysuckle	B	Ch. Robinson Crusoe of Courtrai	Greetavale Honey Star	Mrs L. Spence	Mrs L. Spence	31.10.77	1980	3	DGS—80
Heshe Charmer	B	Ch. Oudenarde Sea Hawk	Ch. Heshe Miss Emmdee	Mr F. A. Edwards	Mr F. A. Edwards	19.7.75	1979	3	DGS—110
Heshe Happy Talk	B	Heshe The Ghillie	Heshe Hot Spice	Mr F. A. Edwards	Mr F. A. Edwards	17.9.77	1980	3	DGS—109
Heshe Rough Cut of Kinkim	D	Ch. Lofthouse Rough Tweed	Ch. Heshe Izawyche	Mr F. A. Edwards	Mr & Mrs Birch	7.3.75	1979	3	I—109
Honeyhall Houdini	D	Ch. Pinetop Montana	Ugadale Warbonnet	Mrs E. B. Shaw & Mr I. L. B. Shaw	Mrs E. B. Shaw & Mr I. L. B. Shaw	12.10.84	1986	3	DGS—90
Kinkim Lohna Ladycan	B	Heshe Flashman	Kinkim Wyche Maid	Mrs B. D. Birch	Mrs B. D. Birch	4.1.78	1979	4	I—90
Kinkim Zarina Chafay	B	Kinkim Yoman Chad	Kinkim Fay Girl	Mr & Mrs R. Birch	Mr & Mrs R. Birch	2.2.85	1986	3	DGS—90
Larchlea Here's Harvey	D	Ch. Stanedykes Pete	Dougrie Terrie of Larchlea	Mrs C. Templeton	Mrs C. Templeton	30.3.83	1985	5	DGS—90
Larchlea Look at Me	D	Ch. Larchlea Here's Harvey	Larchlea Blue Jaye	Mrs C. Templeton	Mr & Mrs D. A. Burns	23.6.84	1986	3	DGS

Name of champion	Sex	Sire	Dam	Breeder	Owner	Born	Title won in	Total number of certs. won	Line and family
Larchlea Winner Takes All	B	Ch. Dechmont Christopher	Larchlea Blue Jaye	Mrs C. Templeton	Mrs C. Templeton	23.11.83	1986	3	DGS—
Lindcoly Miss Simply Super	B	Courtrai Duncan of Lindcoly	Lindcoly Miss Dizzy Lizzy	Mr C. J. & Mrs L. M. Saich	Mr C. J. & Mrs L. M. Saich	17.3.83	1984	3	GR—90
Ljekarna Gay Lord	D	Seltirk Barry	Ch. Ljekarna Jolly	Mr D. Wright	Mr D. Wright	3.9.80	1983	4	DGS—114
Ljekarna Jolly	B	Foxgrove Jeff of Ljekarna	Merry of Ljekarna	Mr D. Wright	Mr D. Wright	14.2.77	1979	3	DGS—114
Lynwil Sarah Jane	B	Felshott Honey Badger	Stanedykes Iona	Mr W. McCulloch	Mr W. McCulloch	24.4.74	1977	3	DGS—111
Macbean Procyon	D	Ch. Wandering Willie of Top Twig	Macbean Josephine Solitaire	Mrs Flint	Mrs Flint	19.11.73	1977	3	DGS—
Mistyridge Magic Solo of Monary	D	Monary Cruda	Mistyridge Magic Sprite	Miss J. Oakley	Mrs M. Shuttleworth	20.4.82	1985	3	DGS—
Monary Roda	B	Ch. Robinson Crusoe of Courtrai	Mitcham Dana	Mrs M. Shuttleworth	Mrs M. Shuttleworth	21.11.78	1980	5	DGS—89
Monary Saucy Kristina	B	Ch. Monary Something Special	Ch. Saucy Miss of Monary	Mrs M. Shuttleworth	Mrs M. Shuttleworth	30.10.83	1985	5	DGS—2
Monary Something Special	D	Dutch Ch. Heshe Haggis	Ch. Monary Roda	Mrs M. Shuttleworth	Mrs M. Shuttleworth	14.4.82	1985	7	DGS—89
Monary Susanella	B	Dutch Ch. Heshe Haggis	Ch. Monary Roda	Mrs M. Shuttleworth	Mrs M. Shuttleworth	14.4.82	1984	10	DGS—89

Name		Sire	Dam	Breeder	Owner	Date	Year		DGS
Orior Jaunty Jane	B	Ir. Ch. Celtic Ayr of Uniquecottage	Uniquecottage Chiffchaff	Mrs W. Dean	Mrs W. Dean	5.11.80	1985	3	DGS—3
Oudenarde Fair Thrill	B	Ch. Oudenarde Midnight Marauder	Oudenarde Sea Romance	Mrs D. & Miss H. Hamilton	Mrs D. & Miss H. Hamilton	4.6.75	1977	4	DGS—9
Oudenarde Night Watch	D	Oudenarde Night March	Oudenarde What Joy	Mrs D. & Miss H. Hamilton	Mr S. W. Somerfield	28.5.77	1980	3	DGS—11
Oudenarde Sea Venture	B	Ch. Oudenarde Sea Hawk	Campanologia Bright Beam	Mrs D. & Miss H. Hamilton	Mrs D. & Miss H. Hamilton	10.6.75	1977	6	DGS—11
Oudenarde What Next	D	Ch. Oudenarde Raiding Light	Oudenarde Midnight Dream	Mrs D. & Miss H. Hamilton	Mrs D. & Miss H. Hamilton	5.7.76	1978	7	DGS—84
Oudenarde Wot a Lad	D	Ch. Oudenarde What Next	Oudenarde Fair Wind	Mrs F. Somerfield	Mrs F. Somerfield	27.3.83	1985	3	DGS—9
Penticharm Catherine	B	Ch. Robinson Crusoe of Courtrai	Penticharm Calamity Jane	Mr & Mrs P. D. Hooton	Mr & Mrs P. D. Hooton	5.11.79	1981	3	DGS—2
Penticharm Charlie Girl	B	Ch. Redletter Moonstruck	Penticharm Calamity Jane	Mr & Mrs P. D. Hooton	Mr & Mrs P. D. Hooton	29.3.79	1981	4	DGS—2
Penticharm Gold Digger	B	Ainsty Marcus of Ophone	Avenelhouse Young Charm	Mr & Mrs P. O. Hooton	Mr & Mrs P. O. Hooton	19.1.75	1979	3	DGS—2
Penticharm Guy Fawkes	D	Ch. Robinson Crusoe of Courtrai	Penticharm Calamity Jane	Mr & Mrs P. D. Hooton	Mr & Mrs P. D. Hooton	5.11.79	1983	3	DGS—2
Penticharm Sparkler	B	Ch. Penticharm Guy Fawkes	Penticharm Primrose	Mr & Mrs P. D. Hooton	Mr & Mrs P. D. Hooton	28.10.83	1985	3	DGS—2
Petersden Sweet Morag	B	Selurk Barry	Petersden Gailsa	Mrs B. A. Clark	Mrs B. A. Clark	8.5.82	1984	3	DGS—90

Name of champion	Sex	Sire	Dam	Breeder	Owner	Born	Title won in	Total number of certs. won	Line and family
Petersden The Monarch of Carthian	D	Camcairn Claudius	Petersden Gailsa	Mrs Barbara Clark	Mrs M. A. Stuart	1.10.81	1983	3	DGS—90
Pinetop Hopscotch	B	Ch. Pinetop Montana	Pinetop Sorrel	Mrs S. Ogle	Mrs S. Ogle	2.4.82	1984	3	DGS—90
Pinetop Montana	D	Ch. Avenelhouse King's Frolic	Ch. Pinetop Simply Super	Mrs S. Ogle	Mrs S. Ogle	11.5.78	1981	6	DGS—90
Pinetop Playboy	D	Ch. Pinetop Montana	Pinetop Sorrel	Mrs S. Ogle	Mrs S. Ogle	9.11.80	1982	7	DGS—90
Pinetop Priscilla	B	Ch. Pinetop Playboy	Ch. Pinetop Victoria	Mrs S. Ogle	Mrs S. Ogle	22.5.83	1985	10	DGS—90
Pinetop Raffles of Croyanda	D	Ch. Robinson Crusoe of Courtrai	Pinetop Sorrel	Mrs S. Ogle	Mr & Mrs R. A. Croyman	28.4.81	1984	3	DGS—90
Pinetop Savannah of Birselaw	•B	Ch. Pinetop Montana	Ch. Pinetop Victoria	Mrs S. Ogle	Miss Y. Catto	5.5.81	1983	3	DGS—90
Pinetop Simply Super	B	Craiglyn Minstrel Boy of Pinetop	Craiglyn Curiosity	Mrs S. Ogle	Mrs S. Ogle	27.11.74	1977	4	DGS—90
Pinetop Skye of Duncraig	D	Craiglyn Minstrel Boy of Pinetop	Pinetop Silver Dollar	Mrs S. Ogle	Miss K. Wiggen	12.12.78	1982	3	DGS—90
Pinetop Victoria	B	Craiglyn Minstrel Boy	Pinetop Silver Dollar	Mrs S. Ogle	Mrs S. Ogle	15.6.77	1978	3	DGS—90
Redhackle of Ferniegair	D	Ferniegair Rustler	Littlegala Sherry	Mrs M. Frame	Mr W. Craig	5.2.84	1985	4	DGS—90
Redletter Martini	B	Ch. Redletter Moonstruck	Ch. Redletter Midsummer	Mr W. N. Bradshaw	Mr W. N. Bradshaw	31.12.78	1981	5	DGS—11

Name	Sex	Sire		Dam					Ref
Redletter Matthew	D	Ch. Bankfoot Devoran	Mr W. N. Bradshaw	Ch. Redletter Midsummer	Mr W. N. Bradshaw	2.5.77	1978	3	DGS—11
Redletter Moon Marcel	B	Ch. Redletter Moon Tripper	Mr W. N. Bradshaw	Ch. Redletter Marcel	Mr W. N. Bradshaw	17.6.75	1977	3	DGS—59
Robinson Crusoe of Courtrai	D	Ch. Heshe Donavon	Mrs G. Robinson	Courtrai Nimble Nell	Misses D. Howes & C. Clark	7.6.75	1977	5	DGS—80
Roseview Lancelot	D	Ch. Robinson Crusoe of Courtrai	Mr F. D. Sutton	Roseview Femin	Mr F. D. Sutton	25.2.78	1980	3	DGS—59
Rossarden Drambui	B	Ch. Robinson Crusoe of Courtrai	Miss C. H. Dixon	Rossarden Cognac	Miss C. H. Dixon	11.11.79	1982	3	DGS—109
Rossarden Eye Catcher	B	Uniquecottage Flycatcher	Miss C. H. Dixon	Rossarden Candleshine	Miss C. H. Dixon	28.8.82	1985	3	DGS—109
Rossarden Royal Star	D	Ch. Star Turn of Rossarden	Miss C. H. Dixon	Rossarden Amazing Grace	Miss C. H. Dixon	26.6.77	1979	4	DGS—109
Rustlebury Tarragon of Ramslow	D	Heshe Kid Currie	Mrs Susan Poole	Heshe Izadonna of Rustlebury	Mr V. Anton	17.8.76	1978	3	I—110
Sandaig Salade Days	B	Velora Proper Charlie	Mrs P. Jeffrey	Sandaig Sheigra	Mrs P. Jeffrey	20.5.83	1985	3	DGS—11
Sandaig Sula Rhu	B	Ch. Felshott Coolin	Mrs P. Jeffrey	Sandaig Stroma	Mrs P. Jeffrey	3.5.77	1980	3	DGS—11
Saucy Miss of Monary	B	Ch. Cairntop Master Simon	Mr J. McCartney	Penticharm Slightly Saucy	Mrs M. Shuttleworth	13.3.80	1981	8	DGS—2
Seneley Captain Poldark of Uniquecottage	D	Ch. Felshott Coolin	Mrs Sumner	Uniquecottage Lorikeet	Mrs Parker-Tucker	21.8.80	1982	3	DGS—11

Name of champion	Sex	Sire	Dam	Breeder	Owner	Born	Title won in	Total number of certs. won	Line and family
Spirecairn Andy Lad	D	Dutch Ch. Heshe Haggis	Thinswarra Solitaire	Mrs J. E. Bunting	Mrs J. E. Bunting	17.10.81	1984	3	DGS—4
Spirecairn Charmer of Cairngold	B	Ch. Courtrai John Julius	Monary Miss Becky	Mr J. M. P. Bunting	Mr J. & Mrs L. Firth	25.7.84	1986	6	DGS—2
Stanedykes Pete	D	Ch. Redletter Moonstruck	Stanedykes Candy	Mr J. Pollock	Mr J. Pollock	1.12.75	1978	8	DGS—111
Strathinver Red Regent	D	Ch. Avenelhouse King's Frolic	Strathinver Sweet Sherry	Mrs N. Newton	Mrs N. Newton	22.5.78	1980	4	DGS—80
Strathinver Red Rufus	D	Am-Can Ch. Foxgrove Jeronimo	Strathinver Sweet Sherry	Mrs N. Newton	Mrs N. Newton	29.8.79	1981	3	DGS—80
Sugar Plum of Courtrai	B	Courtrai Buffalo Bill	Courtrai Trixie	Mrs Martin	Misses D. Howes & C. Clark	16.8.80	1983	3	DGS—5
Thinswarra Estelle	B	Ch. Thinswarra Roulette	Thinswarra Babette	Mr A. Arrowsmith	Mr & Mrs Firth Mr & Mrs Jones	20.5.78	1980	5	DGS—4
Thinswarra Roulette	D	Ch. Tablin Rolle	Ugadale Honeydew of Thinswarra	Mr A. Arrowsmith	Mr A. Arrowsmith	6.3.76	1978	5	DGS—90
Thurso of Stanedykes	D	Felshott Honey Badger	Stanedykes Iona	Mr W. McCulloch	Mr J. Pollock	24.7.74	1980	3	DGS—111
Tristess of Tribannon	B	Velora Proper Charlie	Velora Evergreen	Miss B. Whittaker	Mrs Waugh	4.11.80	1984	6	DGS—113
Tweenus Georgina of Uniquecottage	B	Ch. Uniquecottage Grey Wagtail	Mostly Mary of Tweenus	Mrs J. Keech	Mrs Parker-Tucker	22.2.77	1978	9	DGS—109

Name	Sex	Sire	Dam	Breeder	Owner	Date	Year	No.	Ref.
Ugadale Leadall	D	Redletter Moondust of Ugadale	Ugadale Baroness	Mr J. Alexander	Mr J. Alexander	12.2.75	1977	4	DGS—90
Uniquecottage Brier Fox	D	Uniquecottage Gold Brick	Uniquecottage Gold Harrier	Mrs Parker-Tucker	Mrs Parker-Tucker	26.11.81	1984	4	DGS—3
Uniquecottage Bristle Bird	D	Ch. Uniquecottage Brier Fox	Uniquecottage Tergoirmoo	Mrs Parker-Tucker	Mrs Parker-Tucker	20.7.84	1986	10	DGS—11
Uniquecottage Flycatcher	D	Uniquecottage Bushchat	Uniquecottage Gold Solo	Mrs Parker-Tucker	Mrs Parker-Tucker	30.4.78	1979	15	DGS—11
Uniquecottage Gold Diver	D	Ch. Uniquecottage Flycatcher	Uniquecottage Gold Harrier	Mrs Parker-Tucker	Mrs Parker-Tucker	27.6.82	1985	4	DGS—3
Uniquecottage Gold Feather	B	Uniquecottage Bushchat	Uniquecottage Gold Solo	Mrs Parker-Tucker	Mrs Parker-Tucker	21.7.81	1983	6	DGS—11
Uniquecottage Gold Kinloch	B	Wendanny Rhum	Uniquecottage Kiskerdee	Mrs Parker-Tucker	Mrs Parker-Tucker	29.1.81	1982	8	DGS—109
Uniquecottage Gold Spark	B	Ch. Uniquecottage Treecreeper	Uniquecottage Gold Mimosa	Mrs Parker-Tucker	Mr W. McCulloch	12.12.80	1982	5	DGS—11
Uniquecottage Grey Swift	D	Ch. Craiglyn Caledonian	Ch. Early Bird of Uniquecottage	Mrs Parker-Tucker	Mr & Mrs Hooton	10.7.74	1978	4	DGS—13
Uniquecottage Soleil D'Or.	B	Ch. Uniquecottage Gold Diver	Uniquecottage Mimosa	Mrs Parker-Tucker	Mrs Parker-Tucker	23.1.85	1986	3	DGS—11
Uniquecottage Treecreeper	D	Ch. Uniquecottage Flycatcher	Ch. Tweenus Georgina of Uniquecottage	Mrs Parker-Tucker	Mrs Parker-Tucker	17.7.79	1981	14	DGS—109
Uniquecottage Whinchat	B	Ch. Heshe Donavon	Ch. Early Bird of Uniquecottage	Mrs Parker-Tucker	Mrs Parker-Tucker	10.1.75	1978	3	DGS—3
Velora Dancing Light	B	Felshott Hot Toddy	Velora Prim and Proper	Mrs E. M. Morrison	Mrs E. M. Morrison	30.6.75	1978	3	DGS—113

Name of champion	Sex	Sire	Dam	Breeder	Owner	Born	Title won in	Total number of certs. won	Line and family
Velora Proper Madam of Tribannon	B	Velora Proper Charlie	Velora Scarlet	Mrs E. M. Morrison	Mrs A. Waugh	3.12.79	1983	3	DGS—113
Wendanny Carigroyale	D	Ch. Clanranald Tam O'Shanter	Ch. Wendanny Spinette	Miss T. P. Browne & Miss H. Mathew	Miss T. P. Browne & Miss H. Mathew	4.2.84	1986	3	DGS—
Wendanny Spinette	B	Ch. Uniquecottage Flycatcher	Wendanny Coll	Miss T. P. Browne & Miss H. Mathew	Miss T. P. Browne & Miss H. Mathew	23.6.80	1983	3	DGS—
Wimpas Skebo	D	Ch. Wimpas Mark	An Airidh Anneg	Mrs E. Heery	Mrs E. Heery	2.4.78	1982	4	DGS—90

APPENDIX C

INFLUENTIAL STUD DOGS AND BROOD BITCHES 1946–1986

Stud dogs who have sired two or more Champions

Name	Line/Family	No. of Champions sired
Ch. Robinson Crusoe of Courtrai	DGS/80	16
Ch. Redletter McBryan	DGS/4	13
Ch. Redletter McJoe	DGS/79	9
Ch. Oudenarde Raiding Light	DGS/59	8
Ch. Lofthouse Geryon of Mistyfell	I/63	8
Ch. Blencathra Redstart	I/80	7
Felshott Honey Badger	DGS/11	7
Ch. Redletter Master Mac	DGS/3	6
Ch. Redletter McMurran	DGS/59	6
Blencathra Derryvale Tara	DGS/59	5
Ch. Blencathra Sandpiper	GB/71	5
Ch. Oudenarde Midnight Chimes	DGS/9	5
Ch. Redletter Moonstruck	DGS/11	5
Ch. Blencathra Elford Badger	DGS/59	5
Ch. Uniquecottage Flycatcher	DGS/11	5
Ch. Thistleclose Royalist of Rhu	DGS/59	4
Ch. Bonfire of Twobees	DGS/3	4
Broadwater	GB/-	4
Ch. Redletter Moon Tripper	DGS/103	4
Ch. Redletter Michael	DGS/52	4

Ch. Blencathra Brat	DGS/45	4
Velora Proper Charlie	DGS/113	4
Ch. Pinetop Montana	DGS/90	4

Ch. McJoe of Twobees	SD/10	3
Ch. Blencathra Milord	DGS/80	3
Dochfour Jake	DG/–	3
Ch. Hillston Ian Dhu	DR/10	3
Ch. Oudenarde Midnight Marauder	DGS/3	3
Ch. Uniquecottage Sir Frolic	DGS/3	3
Ch. Redletter Magic Orb	DGS/3	3
Ch. Heshe Donavon	DGS/109	3
Ch. Rufus of Rhu	DGS/68	3
Ch. Redletter Fincairn Frolic	DGS/6	3
(all in one litter)		
Ch. Redletter Maestro	DGS/59	3
Craiglyn Minstrel Boy of Pinetop	DGS/96	3
Dutch Ch. Heshe Haggis	DGS/109	3
Uniquecottage Bushchat	DGS/3	3
Seltirk Barry	DGS/84	3
Ch. Blencathra Brochter	DGS/63	3
Ch. Ronaldshay of Rossarden	DGS/59	3
Masterman of Yeendsdale	GB/-	3
Ch. Craiglyn Cavalier	DGS/80	3

Ch. Felshott Coolin	DGS/11	2
Ch. Avenelhouse King's Frolic	DGS/3	2
Foxgrove Jeff of Ljekarna	DGS/114	2
Ch. Lofthouse Larkspur	I/80	2
Ch. Lofthouse Davy	I/34	2
Ch. Oudenarde Special Edition	DGS/3	2
Ch. Redletter Marshall	DGS/59	2
Ch. Redletter Mac E Boy	DGS/80	2
Blencathra Rudolph	I/80	2
Irish Ch. Celtic Ayr of Uniquecottage	DGS/90	2
(both in the same litter)		
Blencathra Chataboy	DGS/91	2
Ch. Blencathra Reynard	I/97	2
Felshott Tom Brown	DGS/11	2
Duntiblae Top Score of Toptwig	DGS/4	2
Ch. Merrymeet Marlin	DGS/17	2
Courtrai John Julius	DGS/–	2
Vinovium Irwin	DR/9	2

Killearn Mr Chips	DGS/-	2
Ch. Craiglyn Caledonian	DGS/90	2
Ch. Stanedykes Pete	DGS/111	2
Courtrai Buffalo Bill	DGS/90	2
Ch. Merrymeet Jason	GB/78	2
Michelcombe Fearless	SD/59	2
Donnington Sandboy	GB/-	2
Hillston Shantyman	DR/-	2
Ch. Dorseydale Tammy	I/34	2
Ch. Yeendsdale Masterpiece	DGS/17	2
Dorseydale Red Admiral	I/90	2
Ch. Dutch Heshe Haggis		2
(both in the same litter)		
Warberry Beau Brocade	DGS/45	2
Ch. Clanranald Tam O'Shanter	DGS/112	2

Brood Bitches who have become the dam of two or more Champions

Name	Line/Family	No. of Champions produced
Ch. Felshott Bryany	DGS/11	4
Foundation Sylvia	DGS/59	4
Ch. Felshott Anita	DGS/11	4
Ch. Early Bird of Uniquecottage	DGS/3	4
Ch. Redletter Marcel	DGS/59	4
Ch. Courtrai Triella Trudy	DGS/90	4
Ch. Merrymeet Tathwell Therese	GB/17	3
Craiglyn Woodland Belle	DGS/90	3
Ch. Felshott Araminta	DGS/11	3
(all in one litter)		
Felshott Lonicera	DGS/11	3
Jean of Yeendsdale	DGS/17	3
Ch. Fincairn Gillian	DGS/6	3
Ch. Redletter Miss Muffit	DGS/3	3
Ch. Pinetop Victoria	DGS/90	3

Pinetop Sorrel	GB/90	3
Penticharm Calamity Jane	DGS/2	3
(two in one litter)		
Uniquecottage Gold Digger	DG/3	3

Blencathra Radiance	GB/71	2
Blencathra Rosabel	DGS/45	2
Brown Owl of Barassie	DGS/80	2
Doonrae Elfin Gay	I/90	2
Dorseydale Cindy	I/34	2
Elford Sprat	DGS/59	2
Glenmacdhui Marigold	DGS/59	2
Ch. Glenmacdhui Mohra	I/59	2
Harlight Honeybunch	DGS/80	2
Velora Evergreen	DGS/113	2
Oudenarde Sea Romance	DGS/9	2
Strathinver Sweet Sherry	DGS/80	2
Ch. Avenelhouse Acrobat Bird	DGS/2	2
Uniquecottage Gold Harrier	DGS/3	2
Uniquecottage Gold Solo	DGS/11	2
Ch. Monary Roda	DGS/89	2
(both in the same litter)		
Petersden Gailsa	DGS/90	2
Larchlea Blue Jay	DGS/-	2
Uniquecottage Gold Mimosa	DGS/11	2
Uniquecottage Chiffchaff	DGS/3	2
(both in the same litter)		
Greetavale Golden Girl	GB/80	2
Jollee Gay Memory	DG/3	2
Dorseydale Justeena	DGS/34	2
Ch. Lofthouse Golden	DGS/80	2
Oudenarde Blue Moon	DGS/84	2
Ch. Pledwick Drusilla	DGS/9	2
Redletter Maura	DGS/59	2
Ch. Redletter Miss Splinters	DGS/4	2
Redstacks Lobelia	I/3	2
Sadie of Mistyfell	GR/63	2
Thistleclose Rosette	DGS/59	2
Drusilla of Rossarden	DGS/109	2
Duntiblae Top Score of Toptwig	DGS/4	2

APPENDIX D

AMERICAN STANDARD OF THE BREED

(Reproduced by kind permission of the American Kennel Club)

GENERAL APPEARANCE – That of an active, game hardy, small working terrier of the short-legged class; very free in its movements, strongly but not heavily built, standing well forward on its forelegs, deep in the ribs, well coupled with strong hindquarters and presenting a well proportioned build with a medium length of back, having a hard, weather-resisting coat; head shorter and wider than any other terrier and well furnished with hair giving a general foxy expression.

HEAD – *Skull* Broad in proportion to length with a decided stop and well furnished with hair on the top of the head, which may be somewhat softer than the body coat. *Muzzle* Strong but not too long or heavy. Teeth large – mouth neither over nor undershot. Nose back. *Eyes* Set wide apart, rather sunken, with shaggy eyebrows, medium in size, hazel or dark hazel in color depending on body color, with a keen terrier expression. *Ears* Small, pointed, well carried erectly, set wide apart on the side of the head. Free from long hairs.

TAIL – In proportion to head, well furnished with hair but not feathery. Carried gaily but must not curl over back. Set on at back level.

BODY – Well muscled, strong, active body with well-sprung, deep ribs, coupled to strong hindquarters, with a level back of medium length, giving an impression of strength and activity without heaviness.

SHOULDERS, LEGS AND FEET – A sloping shoulder, medium length of leg, good but not too heavy bone; forelegs should not be out at elbows, and be perfectly straight, but forefeet may be slightly turned out. Forefeet larger than hind feet. Legs must be covered with hard hair. Pads should be thick and strong and dog should stand well up on its feet.

COAT – Hard and weather resistant. Must be double-coated with profuse harsh outer coat and short, soft, close furry undercoat.

COLOR — May be of any color except white. Dark ears, muzzle and tail tip are desirable.

IDEAL SIZE – Involves the weight, the height at the withers and the length of the body. Weight for bitches 13 lbs, for dogs 14 lbs. Height at withers – bitches 9½", dogs 10". Length of body from 14¼" to 15", from the front of the chest to back of hindquarters. The dog must be of balanced proportions and appear neither leggy nor too low to ground and neither too short nor too long in body. Weight and measurements are for matured dogs at two years of age. Older dogs may weigh slightly in excess and growing dogs under these weights and measurements.

CONDITION – Dogs should be shown in good hard flesh, well muscled and neither too fat nor thin. Should be in full good coat with plenty of head furnishings, be clean, combed, brushed and tidied up on ears, tail, feet and general outline. Should move freely and earily on a loose lead, should not cringe on being handled. Should stand up on their toes and show with marked terrier characteristics.

Faults

1. SKULL – Too narrow in skull.
2. MUZZLE – Too long and heavy a foreface; mouth overshot or undershot.
3. EYES – Too large, prominent, yellow and ringed are all objectionable.
4. EARS – Too large, round at points, set too close together, set too high on the head; heavily covered with hair.
5. LEGS AND FEET – Too light or too heavy bone. Crooked forelegs or out at elbow. Thin, ferrety feet; feet let down on the heel or too open and spread. Too high or too low on the leg.
6. BODY – Too short back and compact a body, hampering quickness of movement and turning ability. Too long, weedy and snaky a body, giving an impression of weakness. Tail set on too low. Back not level.
7. COAT – Open coats, blousy coats, too short or dead coats, lack of sufficient undercoat, lack of head furnishings, lack of hard hair on legs. Silkiness or curliness. A slight wave permissible.
8. NOSE – Flesh or light colored nose.
9. COLOR – White on chest, feet or other parts of body.

ADDENDUM TO FOURTH EDITION

Between December 1960 and December 1968 eighty-four champions were added to the records; an examination of the pedigrees of these new champions discloses a further decline in the influence of nearly all the lines referred to on page 58. Of these eighty-four champions no fewer than sixty stem from the male DGS line and nineteen from the I line; the other five being one from line DR and four from line GB.

While the number of families has risen to 106, only four have added materially to the number of champions previously produced. Family No. 3 has added sixteen. Family No. 9, which traces back through a mixture of Gunthorpe and Hyver blood to Diana of Harris, has emerged from oblivion with the production of seven champions, and Family No. 11 has also been responsible for seven champions, the background of this family being, in the main, Mrs Dixon's Gunthorpes. The other family to add to the number of champions it has produced is No. 59 which has added nine to its total.

From an examination of the pedigrees of the most successful of the Cairns currently being shown it is obvious that the influence of what has been designated as the DGS line is submerging all other male influences. While the letters DGS indicate Duan (D) the most remote known male ancestor Ch. Gillie of Hyver (G) and Ch. Splinters of Twobees (S) it must be remembered that these three letters indicate not only the three dogs (the two most outstanding of the male descendants in the upper line of the pedigree) but also the combination of the influences of their ancestors both male and female; further, these letters indicate the continued association of the influences transmitted through their descendants.

The same applies to the bitches bearing the number of a family.

During the period 1961 to 1968, there has emerged a number of influential dogs of which the outstanding sire is Ch. Redletter

McBryan (line DGS) which, in addition to winning seventeen Challenge Certificates, has sired no fewer than eleven Champions and five certificate winners which did not reach championship rank. It would be difficult to find such an impressive male ancestry as has McBryan: sire Ch. Redletter McMurran (twenty-six certificates), grandsire Ch. Redletter McJoe (ten certificates), great-grand sire Ch. Bonfire of Twobees (five certificates), g.g.grandsire Ch. Splinters of Twobees (eight certificates). Including his own, a total of sixty-six certificates in five generations.

Ch. Lofthouse Geryon of Mistyfell has sired seven champions; Ch. Blencathra Brochter five champions; Ch. Blencathra Elford Badger four champions; Ch. Blencathra Milord, Ch. Blencathra Reynard, Ch. Dorseydale Tammy, Ch. Gerolf of Mistyfell, Ch. Merrymeet Marlin, Ch. Oudenarde Special Edition and Ch. Ronaldshay of Rossarden have each sired three champions.

Thus out of the eighty-four champions winning the title during the years under review a large proportion (forty-eight) have been sired by eleven sires which seems to indicate a greater concentration of influences than formerly.

No bitch has the same opportunities to produce a number of pups as has the average popular stud dog; Felshott Araminta whelped two champions in one litter (sired by Ch. Redletter Maestro); Elford Spratt, two by Ch. Blencathra Reynard; Dorseydale Justeena, two by Ch. Lofthouse Geryon of Mistyfell; Ch. Felshott Bryany, two by Ch. Redletter Master Mac; Ch. Glenmacdhui Mohra, one by Ch. Redletter McBryan and one by Hillston Bracken of Lapdown; Ch. Merrymeet Tathwell Therese two by Ch. Cairntop Nicholas and Ch. Blencathra Milord respectively; Ch. Redletter Miss Muffit, two by Ch. Redletter McBryan; Redstacks Lobelia, one by Blencathra Chataboy and one by Blencathra Rudolph; and Doonrae Elfin Gay, one by Ch. Blencathra Elford Badger and one by Ch. Blencathra Reynard.

The whole picture seems to indicate that, with the passing of years, the streams of influence which lead to the production of outstanding Cairns are being concentrated into a limited number.

1969   A.F.

Peggy Wilson's Addenda to Fifth and Sixth editions: Since Mr Fisher wrote his addendum, many more Champions have been added to the records. These are set out in Appendix B. Appendix C has now been added, listing in order of achievement all the influential stud dogs and brood bitches covering the period 1946–1973.

Following on from the end of 1968, forty-eight Champions have been added to the records up to the end of 1973. Full details are given in Appendix B, but may be summarised here by saying that forty were sired by line DGS dogs, five by dogs of line I, two by dogs of line DR, and one from line GR.

The dominant families in this five-year period have proved to be Family 11 which has produced twelve Champions, Family 90 (six), Family 59 (three), and the recently emerged Family 108 which has added four.

It is interesting to note that the top stud dog is Ch. Redletter McBryan, who sired thirteen Champions, and that one of his daughters – Ch. Felshott Bryany – is the only Champion bitch to become the dam of four Champions, and shares top place in bitches with Foundation Sylvia.

Turning now to personalities, pride of place must go to Walter Bradshaw who has recently passed the marks of 250 C.C.s in the breed. With one exception, the Redletter Cairns which have contributed to this score have either a Redletter sire or dam or both – a remarkable achievement. Mr Bradshaw is not only a Cairn man, but is well known and respected throughout dogdom. He is Chairman of the Kennel Club Liaison Area Council, to which Council he was elected at its formation as the area representative for Lancashire, and is the only original member still serving. As Chairman of this Council he is their representative on the Show Regulations Committee, and he is also their elected representative on the newly formed Kennel Club Administrative Committee. He is President of the C.T.A. and a Committee member of the C.T.C. In addition he is a well known Judge of many breeds, and has judged Groups and Best In Show at Championship shows in Great Britain and overseas.

Mrs Drummond's Blencathra affix has still been very much to the fore, but unfortunately she is now unable to travel to many shows as her sight no longer allows her to drive her car. This is particularly sad since she has always been an ardent motorist and she drove the first Austin 7 in the R.A.C. Rallies of the 1920s. The Cairndainia Salver for the stud dog siring the highest number of individual certificate winners has been won by Blencathra dogs twice in the past four years.

The Oudenarde affix has also made a big contribution. Miss Helen Hamilton was the original founder of this kennel in the 1920s, later to be joined by her sister, the late Mrs Temple, and later still by her sister-in-law, Mrs Diana Hamilton. Although Miss Hamilton is not seen in the Cairn ring, she is, nevertheless, one of our most senior exhibitors. Mrs Diana Hamilton was the Hon. Secretary of the Cairn Terrier Association for twenty-five years where she was most ably supported by the meticulous work of her husband, the late Lt Col. G. F. Hamilton, M.C. She continues to serve the breed as President of the Southern C.T.C., and as a committee member of both the C.T.C. and C.T.A. She is also our breed representative on the Kennel Club Liaison Breed Council. Her daughter, Ferelith Hamilton, is the well known editor of *Dog World* and both rank among our well known Championship Show Judges of many breeds and Groups.

In Scotland the Craiglyn affix of Miss E. Campbell has proved to be a great influence producing four Champions in the five-year period.

In the north of England, the Felshott strain – owned by Madge and Dorothy Hall and myself – has added a further eight Champions to our Family 11 strain.

Mrs Marsh and Jack Danks have been consistent winners in the Midlands, with Ch. Toptwig Tilden (fourteen C.C.'s) and with Ch. Wandering Willie of Toptwig with seven C.C.'s in 1973.

Mrs Harding's Brucairns Strain Family 108 has emerged in the past five years to produce four Champions.

The Avenal House affix is new but old! Belonging to Major and Mrs Small it is really based on the two affixes previously held by Mrs Small as Hazel Longmore – Uniquecottage and Jollee. The Uniquecottage affix is now owned solely by Mrs Parker-Tucker (*née* Marshall).

Following the death of Miss Betty Dixon, Miss 'Charlie' Dixon has carried on the Rossarden strain which has added two Champions.

One really pleasing feature of the Cairn breed is that it is dominated by breeders who have each maintained a top winning strain for generation after generation. The regular top winners all have either a sire or a dam which was bred by the owners. Although competition is keen, it is always the long term wellbeing of the Cairn that is all important to the people who seek to serve the breed.

Occasionally, however, circumstances may arise where a Cairn may be in distress, perhaps through the death or illness of the owner, and needs a new home. To cover such eventualities a Cairn Rescue Fund has been founded and anyone requiring help should contact the Hon. Secretary and Treasurer of the fund.

In November 1973 Miss Bengough died. The plain historical facts alone pay tribute to her memory; but they exist because she had the strength of character, charm, and ability to pass on her knowledge to breeders willing and able to accept her guidance. The historical record of her service to the breed lies in Appendices A, B and C.

Remembering that Ch. Splinters of Twobees was the 'S' in Line DGS and that every Cairn bearing this annotation is descended in direct tail male line from him, her personal pride in Splinters was truly justified. 108 DGS Champions are listed in Appendix B, and a careful look at the outstanding sires and dams listed in Appendix C quickly reveals the enormous influence of DGS. Splinters, through his son Ch. Bonfire of Twobees (born 1943), linked the pre-war Cairn with the post-war Cairn, as Bonfire emerged to be the dominant sire, who, through his sons Ch. Redletter McJoe and Ch. Blencathra Elford Chiefton ensured the continuity of the quality of this line.

Miss Bengough and Alex Fisher linked the past with the present. Miss Bengough gave the linking dogs, and Mr Fisher's meticulous work with his records and written word made possible the interpretation of the trends in the breed. This is their legacy to the Cairn they both loved so much and served so well.

December 1973   M.D.W.

The main purpose of this addendum is to emphasize the significance of the contribution made to the breed by the breeders and owners of the forebears of the dogs which breeders have retained, in contrast to the dogs which are being discarded to the point of rarity. To avoid unnecessary repetition, I would ask that my comments be read in conjunction with the index, and particularly with Chapters two to five in the main text.

In the revisions for this sixth edition to the end of 1976, every male champion which had to be added to Appendix B was Line DGS. Every entry or promotion in the lists of influential stud dogs and brood bitches was sired by a Line DGE dog. Moreover, they are all descended in direct tail male from one dog: Ch. Bonfire of Twobees. This emphasises the continuation and acceleration of the trend mentioned by Mr Fisher in the third paragraph of his addendum to the fourth edition (1969).

Viewed from the mid-1970s the most important breeders of the past were Messrs Ross and Markland, who owned Ch. Firring Frolic– the first champion of Line D, and the sire of Raeburn Conas, owned by Mr Donald McLennan of the Carngowan affix. From here on, the forbears of all the present winning Line DGS dogs can be found on the top line of the pedigree of Ch. Splinters of Twobees in Appendix A. Notes on most of these dogs will be found in the main chapters. However, Mr Fisher's notes on Ch. Trashurst Chip (page 43) are somewhat brief. Breeders who knew and greatly admired Chip feel that he has been given insufficient credit for the undoubted excellence of the great Splinters. Therefore I have searched the records and found a wholly independent contemporary description written by Major Townley when awarding Chip's first CC in 1932. This reads:

'When last I saw him I considered that his magnificent head was too good for his body; he has now bodied up and matured, and is a beautifully balanced dog; his head and expression are perfect; he has the best of legs and feet; stands and moves beautifully; he is absolutely sound and is full of terrier-like qualities; he stood right out by himself and was the easiest of winners; in my opinion he is the best young dog of his breed on the bench today.'

The most significant mating in the history of the modern Cairn took place early in 1943, when Mrs E. L. Hazell mated her bitch, Mitzie of Zellah, to Ch. Splinters of Twobees. Splinters was then ten years old, and at that period of the war very few Cairns were being bred. This produced a litter in which a dog was registered as Sport of Zellah. This dog was later acquired by Miss Bengough and Mrs Butterworth; at that time the Kennel Club allowed the holders of a registered affix to change a name completely. Hence, Sport of Zellah's name was changed to Bonfire of Twobees.

Now to what I think can be claimed to be the second most important mating in the history of the modern Cairn. This occurred in 1948. Round about 1947 and 1948, Mr Bradshaw was on the show circuit making up his first Cairn champion. At the same time, Miss Bengough and Mrs Butterworth were campaigning Ch. McJoe of Twobees and Bonfire of Twobees, the latter being made up when he was five years old in 1948. Mr Bradshaw looked long and hard at both of the Twobees dogs, then eventually went to Miss Bengough and told her that he wished to send one of his bitches to be mated to Bonfire. Miss Bengough tried to persuade him to use McJoe of Twobees as McJoe had such a magnificent head. But McJoe was Line SD, and Mr Bradshaw, with true North Country determination, insisted that it was the Bonfire Line that he wanted. After the debate and argument, Mr Bradshaw declared that 'If there is a good dog in the litter I will call him McJoe just to please you!'

The influence of Ch. Redletter McJoe, the eldest of Bonfire's three most influential sons, is the most important because it has spread throughout the breed most widely. In addition to being the founder sire of the entire string of all the Redletter champions, he sired Ch. Redletter Fincairn Frolic. From Frolic came Ch. Uniquecottage Sir Frolic, sire of Riskin of Rossarden who sired Ch. Ronaldshay of Rossarden, who in turn sired Ch. Uniquecottage Gold Goblet and

Ch. Uniquecottage Gold Rouble, and Reactor of Rossarden who sired Ch. Star Turn of Rossarden, while Gold Goblet sired Ch. Felshott Wine Taster.

The influence of Ch. Redletter McJoe can also be seen in the Yeendsdale strain, as the sire of Ch. Yeendsdale Masterpiece, the sire of Ch. Yeendsdale Merry Fiddler, who in turn, was the sire of Ch. Yeendsdale Inspiration.

McJoe was also the sire of Oudenarde Herald, who became the sire of Oudenarde Game Bird, the sire of Ch. Oudenarde Special Edition, the sire of Ch. Oudenarde Carefree Pete.

Through McJoe's son Ch. Redletter McMurran, himself the sire of six champions, came Ch. Redletter McBryan, the top sire in the history of the breed as the sire of thirteen champions. Apart from the continuation of the Redletter strain, his influence too has spread throughout the breed, particularly through his son Ch. Cairncrag Caesar; who sired Ch. Blencathra Brochter: Brochter became the foundation sire of all the more recent Blencathra champions. Here it might be mentioned that Brochter was a direct descendent in tail female from Speedalong of Zellah-family 3, and a sister to Bonfire of Twobees. Brochter sired Ch. Blencathra Elford Badger, who sired Ch. Craiglyn Stornoway, and Ch. Craiglyn Commodore and Blencathra Derryvale Tara. Tara sired five Champions, including Chs Blencathra Brat, Buchaneer, and Barrie. Brat became the sire of Ch. Heshe Donovan and Ch. Avenel House Golden Oriole, while Barrie sired Ch. Blencathra Barrett.

The earlier Line DGS Blencathra dogs came down from Bonfire direct. Through Bonfire's son Ch. Blencathra Elford Chiefton, came Ch. Blencathra Milord, the sire of Ch. Oudenarde Fellemelad the sire of Ch. Campanologia Pricket. Milord also sired Ch. Merrymeet Marlin, who was the sire of Ch. Rossarden McDougal of Wimpas.

Bonfire was also the founder sire of the influential Oudenarde variation. He sired Oudenarde Firelight, the sire of Ch. Oudenarde Sandboy, the sire of Ch. Oudenarde Midnight Chimes, the sire of Ch. Oudenarde Midnight Magic and Ch. Oudenarde Midnight Marauder. Marauder sired Ch. Oudenarde Raiding Light, Ch. Oudenarde Bold and Free and Ch. Toptwig Fly by Night of Oudenarde, the latter being from the last litter bred by the late Mrs Gay Marsh.

In the foregoing paragraphs I have only mentioned the male *dogs* sired in direct tail male line. Reference to Appendices B and C will show in detail the achievements of each dog more fully. If the present trend continues, it is probable that in ten years time every male line in every five generation pedigree could go back to Bonfire, and no variation or outcross would be available from dogs who have attained the status of a stud book entry. If this happened it could be claimed that our Cairns had lost the influence of all our early founders other than Messrs Ross and Markland, Mr McLennan, Mrs Stephens, Mrs Prichard, Miss Crossman and the partnership of Miss Bengough and Mrs Butterworth.

The fact remains that since 1961, Judges have made up only sixteen male champions of any line other than Line DGS. Twelve of these were Line I, all of whom were direct descendents of Ch. Blencathra Redstart; three were of Line GB, and one DR. Perhaps the implications of this can best be seen from a list of these sixteen dogs, showing the most recent champions first, then working backwards through the years.

Line I first. The most recent champion was Ch. Avenelhouse Cloth of Gold, who was made up in 1972. Prior to that the champions were: Lofthouse Geryon 1971 (exported); Brucairn Crackerjack 1971 (exported); Brucairn Red Robin 1970; Lofthouse Rough Tweed 1968; Uniquecottage Powder Monkey 1966; Lofthouse Davey 1965 (exported); Glenmacdhui Gillie Gold 1964; Vinovium Pledwick Tiger 1962; Blencathra Reynard; 1962.

The last of the three male Line GB dogs to be made up was Ch. Glenmacdhui Tearlach, owned and campaigned by Miss Jean Husdon, who was made up in 1965. The other two were Redstacks Kelly, made up in 1964, and Merrymeet Marksman made up in 1962 (exported). Both Tearlach and Kelly were direct tail male descendents of Ch. Blencathra Sandpiper.

The only Line DR champion dog was Ch. Vinovium Graham, made up in 1966 (exported).

Now to the bitches. From Appendices B and C the immense impact of Families 3, 11 and 59 can readily be seen. So too, can the influence of Families 80, 90 and 100. Two new Families have emerged in recent years. Family 108 has produced all the Brucairn champions; Family 109 has produced two bearing the Heshe affix, and one Rossarden.

Colonel Whitehead was the first Judge to make the observation that the quality of the bitches exhibited before him was far better than that of the dogs. This appeared in his report of the 1924 Caledonian Championship Show. Throughout the subsequent years, Judges have often made similar comment; but in the 1970s with ever increasing frequency. The real strength of the breed lies in the undoubted quality of the bitches.

October 1977   M.D.W.

Doreen Proudlock's Addendum to Seventh Edition: I begin the addendum on a sad note. During the last ten years we have lost several notable breeders who have contributed so much to the breed during the years. First Peggy Wilson who, after Mr Fisher's death, took on the arduous task of Breed Historian carrying on his wonderful records – every Cairn winning a challenge certificate from 1912 when the first certificates were awarded is entered in the pedigree book. We have an unbroken record continuing right through to the present day. It has been my task to continue this work since taking over from Peggy in 1980. Peggy Wilson joined the Felshott Kennels of Madge and Dorothy Hall eventually becoming a partner, and her tremendous knowledge of lines and families contributed to the great success of this well-known kennel. For a considerable number of years she wrote the weekly Breed notes for *Dog World*. They were always interesting and at times controversial, giving breeders a talking point. Peggy judged the American Cairn Speciality Shows (this is equivalent to our breed club championship shows). Her last judging appointment was Crufts 1985.

In 1979 we recorded the death of Mrs Diana Hamilton who owned the Oudenarde Kennels in partnership with her sisters-in-law, a successful kennel making up twenty-nine British Champions; a number of Oudenarde Cairns gained their overseas titles. She was a keen exhibitor and was to be seen at most championship shows with a team of Cairns.

Diana Hamilton was a lady with many interests; for twenty-five years she was secretary to the Cairn Terrier Association, running a successful, happy club. She ran the first joint show held by the Cairn Terrier Club, Southern Cairn Terrier Club and the Cairn Terrier Association. She was a much sought after judge both in this country and overseas awarding CCs in many other breeds as well as Cairns. She was a BIS judge and judged the Terrier group at Crufts. All these appointments were carried out with quiet efficiency and charm. The Oudenardes are now in the very capable hands of her daughter Ferelith Somerfield.

Mrs Mabel Drummond died in 1980. She made up twenty-five Blencathra Champions. The Blencathra Cairns were renowned the world over for their outstanding heads, a feature breeders would do well to emulate today. As a championship show judge, Mrs Drummond's opinion was always valued. The Blencathra success story was a team effort between Mrs Drummond and Mary Elliot, her friend and kennel maid over a considerable number of years.

Walter Bradshaw died in 1982. His world famous Redletter Cairns held a number of records, many of which still stand today. The Redletters won 243 CCs and forty-three champions gained their title. Redletter McBryan, winner of seventeen CCs sired thirteen champions, a record he held from 1967 to 1984. The only Cairns ever to get the top honour of going Best in Show at a General Championship show were Walter Bradshaw's Ch. Redletter McMurran at Paignton and Ch. Redletter Twinlaw Seaspirit at Manchester. Twinlaw Seaspirit was bred by Mrs Alice Henderson but he was sired by Ch. Redletter Maestro. His grandsire on the dam's side was Ch. Redletter Master Mac. He was owned and campaigned by Mr Bradshaw.

Walter Bradshaw was a well-known judge both in this country and overseas. He was qualified to award CCs in twenty-six breeds. One of his last appointments was to judge the Terrier group at Crufts. Peggy Wilson in her 1973 addendum also paid tribute to Walter Bradshaw listing many of his activities and achievements.

Madge Hall died in 1984. She founded the famous Felshott kennels with her sister Dorothy in 1925. There were sixteen Felshott champions; fifteen were home bred and the sixteenth was sired by Felshott Lordling. Three were owned by Mrs Hamilton, Miss C. Dixon and Messrs Camish and Williams respectively. Madge was a committee member of the Cairn Terrier Club and also a championship show judge.

Bessie Shea was one of the stalwarts of the breed and made up three Redstack champions. She was deeply interested in the welfare of the Cairn and was a hard working committee member of the Cairn Terrier Club. A popular championship show judge, she judged Crufts in 1976.

Alick Hogg died in 1984. He was secretary of the Cairn Terrier Club from 1966–1975 and his knowledge of club administration was par excellence. He was President of the Scottish Breeders Club, a committee member of the Border Union Championship show and a member of the Kennel Club where he served as one of the three Scottish representatives on a liaison council. He was also a prominent figure at the LKH Championship show at which he ran the award room. It was through Alick Hogg's encouragement that the North of Ireland Cairn Terrier Club reached championship show status in 1982. He was a championship show judge both in this country and overseas.

Ch. Robinson Crusoe of Courtrai, winner of 5 CCs, now holds the record as top stud dog behind the seventeen Cairn champions to date. Bred by Mrs Robinson and owned and campaigned by the

Courtrai partnership of Miss D. Howes and Miss C. Clark, Crusoe was sired by Ch. Heshe Donovan of Courtrai Nimble Nell, line DGS family 80. In 1983 and again in 1984 Ch. Robinson Crusoe of Courtrai gained the honour of being awarded the top terrier stud dog of the terrier group.

In 1981 Mrs Sally Ogle's home-bred Ch. Pinetop Montana was awarded Reserve Best in show at Darlington Championship Show. Ch. Dear Gabriella won the terrier group at both W.E.K.S. and the Birmingham National in 1986. Ch. Ugdale Leadall won the terrier group at the Border Union Championship Show in 1977.

DGS continues to be the dominant line. Hamish of Seltirk is the only GB Champion during the last ten years. The GR line produced Ch. Lindcoly Miss Simply Super and Ch. Courtrai Sally Ann. The I line has four champions to its credit in Ch. Glenbrae Avena, Ch. Rough Cut of Kinkim, Ch. Kinkim Lotina Lady Can and Ch. Rustlebury Tarragon of Ramslow. Family 90 is very much the dominant family with twenty-eight champions, followed by family 11 with fourteen and family 2 with eleven. Mrs Parker-Tucker's Uniquecottage is the top winning kennel. She made up eleven champions between 1977 and 1986.

During the past ten years three new families have been established. A family is founded on the bitch line, the very bottom line of the pedigree. Family 112 is founded on Miss Hudson's Clanranald strain, Ch. Sine of Clanranald being the foundation bitch. The tap root for family 113 is Velora Prim and Proper belonging to Mrs Morrison. Last comes family 114 based largely on David Wright's Ljekarnas. Jim Wilson's Foxgroves also had an influence on this family. Foxgrove Venus is the foundation bitch.

The Cairn Relief Trust continues to do valiant work rehoming unwanted Cairns; each of the six British Cairn Terrier Clubs have appointed two trustees to help with rehoming and caring for unwanted Cairns in the area. They are always ready with help and advice when needed. Anyone with a problem should contact Harry Price the hard-working and dedicated secretary who will put them in touch with a trustee in their area.

Mr H. Price (Hon. Secretary)
Rustlings
1A Winterhill Way
GUILDFORD
Surrey
Tel: 0483 66643

I received a letter one day from a Miss Jane Beynon who wrote telling me she had been browsing in a book shop and had picked up an earlier edition of this book. As she owned a Cairn she bought it, and was interested to see that the original author was John Beynon. As Beynon is an unusual name she asked her father if he could have been a relation. 'Oh yes,' came the reply, 'that was great uncle John.' When she chose a Cairn as her companion Jane Beynon had no idea she had inherited, through great uncle John, the love for Cairn Terriers.

This small terrier from Scotland has many devotees and dedicated breeders the world over; he is equally at home in castle or cottage and has been companion and friend to Kings and commoners. How apt is our slogan 'The best little pal in the world' or, as the Scots would say, 'The best little pal in aw the airts'. For those who don't wear the kilt, 'aw the airts' means 'all points of the compass'.

1988　　　　　　　　　　　　　　　　　Doreen (Bunty) Proudlock

Index

Aberdeen, Countess of 29–30
Aberdeen Beauty 27
Aberdeen Lassie 27
Aberdeenshire terriers 23–4
accommodation 111ff.
  dogroom
    preparing 111
    sleeping arrangements 111
  kennels
    choosing 111–12
    positioning 112
  for puppies 112–13
  runs
    construction of 112
    grass 112
    gravel 112, 113
    for whelping bitch 112
Alexander, Sir Claud 30
appearance
  American standard 199
  breed standard 124
  judging 138
Ardsheal kennel 35
aspirin 152
Avenelhouse kennel 49, 204

badgers, terriers for hunting 19, 20
Banshee Donan 60
Basset, Mrs 38
Beansith Dhu of the Shieling (Ch.) 42
Beechacre prefix 41, 76
Bell, Miss 43
Bengough, Miss 45, 204, 206
Benylin 151
Benyon, John 79–80
  The Popular Cairn Terrier 19, 20
Binney, Mr C.A. 26
bitches
  coat-casting 108

and heredity 52
  shows for 118
bitches brood 83ff., 205
  accommodation for 111
  'breeding terms' 81–2, 84
buying 80–1
  'payment' for 82
  as puppies 83
  checking season 84–5
  dieting 84
  exercise for pregnant 86
  gestation period 85
  influential 197ff.
  kennels for 112
  maiden 94–5
  mating 85, 95–6
    confirming 85–6
    free 86
    failure of 86, 94
    readiness for 85
    timing 83
  preparing 84–5
  studying pedigree 81, 84
  visiting 93–4
    checking 94
  whelping
    accommodation for 112
    care after 98
  worming 99
Blencathra prefix 46, 203
Blencathra Brochter (Ch.)
  influence of 207
Blencathra Crackerlad 46
body
  breed standard 122, 125–6
  judging 137
  'pouter-chested' 137
  'short' back 129
Bogton kennel 40–1

Bogton Ballach (Ch.) 41
Bogton Breda (Ch.) 41
Bogton Brindie (Ch.) 40
Bon Accord 23
bone meal, sterilized 100
bones 152
  for puppies 100
Bonfire of Twobees (Ch.) 205
  influence of 206–7
Bradshaw, Mr Walter 47, 203, 206,
    209–10
Brassy 26
Bride 28, 61
Brigit 61
Brilliant O' the Braes (Ch.) 45, 59
Breed Club Championship Shows 118
Breed Clubs 141–5
breed standard 122ff.
  American 199ff.
    faults 200
  'entire' dogs 137
  'Anatomy and its influence' 138
breeders
  most important historical 205
  see also individual names
Breeders' Code 89–91
breeding
  ancestors 51
  bans on crosses 128
  booking a service 84
  early history 19ff., 59
  Families *see* Families
  'finger-posts' 51, 54, 56
  genetics 51–3
  line *see* Lines
  object of 53–4, 56
  outcrossing 84
  production of champions 54
  scientific 51
  and show record 64
  stud fees 84
  see also interbreeding;
    'Telegony'
Broc O' the Braes 45
Brocaire prefix 36, 67, 68–9
  and Harviestoun line 76
  physical properties 68
Brocaire Donan of Gesto (Ch.) 68, 69
Brocaire MacRose of Carse (Ch.) 68
Brocaire Speireag (Ch.) 68
Brogach Out of the West 40
'broken-haired terrier' 24

Brown Owl of Barassie 63
Brucairns strain 204
Bruin of Keycol 26–7, 42
Bubbles of Barassie 63
Bunbury, Miss 42
Burton, Baroness 35, 36
Bussels of Hyver (Ch.) 72
Butterworth, Mrs 45, 206

Cairn Reich 37
Cairn Rescue Fund 204
Cairncross Caesar (Ch.) 207
Caius, Dr 19
Calla-mhor 26
Callum of Frimley (Ch.) 39
Campbell, Miss E. 204
Campbell Mrs Alastair 26, 27, 28, 65,
    66, 67–8, 120–1
Canovel 100
Carngowan kennel 34, 69–71
  pedigrees 71
Carngowan Clarice (Ch.) 71
Carngowan Manus (Ch.) 37
  influence of 70
Carngowan Murran (Ch.) 57
  influence of 71
Carysfort kennel 43–4
Caspersz, Mr and Mrs 37, 51, 55, 57,
    72
Castlehill Tang 36
Ceoach 61
certificates
  allocation of 188–91
champions 201, 203, 208
  alphabetical listing 156ff.
  first bitch *see* Firring Flora (Ch.)
  first dog *see* Gesto (Ch.)
  pedigrees of 55, 56
  qualification for 118
  see also Families; Lines and branches;
      individual kennels/prefixes,
      names
championship status 27
character 120 ff.
characteristics
  breed standard 123
Childwick prefix 34
Cinders O' the Braes (Ch.) 45
Cionas 41
Clanranald strain 210
class
  origin of 29–30

Clifton, Miss A. K. 28
Cloughton kennel 35
Cloughton Bunty 35
Cloughton Drumochter (Ch.) 35
Cloughton Kyle 35
  see also Kyley Out of the West
Cloughton Lorna 35
coat 121, 128–9
  breed standard 123, 126
    American 199
  brood bitch 84
  casting 108–9, 110
  condition of 138
  cutting 110
Codis 152
colour 20, 73
  breed standard 123, 126
    American 200
Complete Balanced Dog Food 100
Completely Balanced Expanded Dry
    Food 100
condition
  American standard 200
Corrie-Ba of Fair City 43
Craiglyn prefix 204
Crantock prefix 48
Crossman, Miss 34
  see also Rudland, Mrs
Crossman, Mrs 43
Crufts
  first appearance at 27–8
  first challenge certificates 31
  1910 classes 28
cryptorchidism 96–7, 137
Cuag 70
Cuillean Bhan 26, 28
Culaig 62

Dandy Dinmont 22
Danks, Jack 204
Derelict Out of the West (Ch.) 74
Dettol 151
Diana of Harris 201
diet
  additives 152
  adult dog 100
  dried food 100
  for mild tummy upset 100
  for pancreatic deficiency 152
  fresh/frozen meat 100
  pregnant bitch 86
  puppies 98–100

high-protein 99–100
  mineral supplements 100
  tinned foods 100
  varying 152
  water in 100
  vegetarian 152
  see also feeding
Dinkie 63
Disprin 152
Dixon, Misses 48
  'Charlie' 204
Dixon, Mrs 39, 76
Dochfour kennel 35–6
Dochfour Kyle (Ch.) 42
Dochfour Molly 36
Dochfour Vennach (Ch.) 36
Dochfour Vuiach Vorchard (Ch.) 36
dogs
  breeding from champion 65
  first mating 92
  'entire' 96–7
    checking 137
  and heredity 52
  influential 64ff.
  top 207, 210
dogs, stud 53, 91ff., 205
  acquisition of 91, 92
  champion 91–2
  choosing 83, 84
  condition of 93
  effective life of 93
  frequency of mating 93
  ideal 91
  influential 195ff.
  mating 92–3, 95–6
    first 92
  proving capability 92
  shows for 118
  success of 91
Donnington prefix 37
Donnington Cheeky (Ch.) 38
Donnington Badger (Ch.) 38
Donnington Surprise 38
Doonrae Elfin Gay 202
Doran Bhan 28, 65
Dorseydale Justeena 202
Doughall Out of the West 58
  influence of 72–4
Drummond, Mrs Mable 46, 203, 209
Drungewick prefix 44–5
Drungewick Jacob (Ch.) 45
Drungewick Jade 45

Drungewick Jeanetta (Ch.) 45
Drungewick Junk (Ch.) 45
Duan 57, 65

ears
  'Bat' 131, *132*
  breed standard 122, 125
  checking before grooming 108
  felted hair 109
  parasites in 151
  Scottie *132*
  trimming for showing 116
'earth dogs' 19
Elford Spratt 202
Ewing, Major 35
eyes
  breed standard 122, 125
    American 199
  checking before grooming 108
  faults 128
Eyes prefix 37

Fair City kennel 43, 61
Families 54
  champions in 56, 59
  numbers of 55
    in 1960 201
  No. 2 59—60, 210
  No. 3 60, 201
  No. 4 60
    champions 60
  No. 5 61
    champions 61
  No. 6 61
    champions 61
  No. 8 78
  No. 9 201
  No. 11 201, 203, 210
  No. 17 40, 61–2
    Scottish Terriers in 61
  No. 20 66
  No. 21 67
  No. 59 45, 62–3, 201, 203
    basis of 37
    champions 62–3
  No. 80 63
    champions 63
  No. 90 203, 210
  No. 109 208
  No. 112 210
  No. 113 210
  No. 114 210–11

faults 123, 126–7
  common 127ff.
Fear Nil of Carysfort (Ch.) 43–4
Fearg 26
Fearnaught of Carysfort (Ch.) 43, 44
feeding
  adults 100–1
  after mating 95
  cleanliness and 101
  puppies
    individually 99
  see also diet
feet *see* legs/feet
Felshott strain 204
Felshott Araminta 202
Felshott Bryany (Ch.) 202, 203
Ferrier, Mr 30
Fifinella of Carysfort 44
Fincairn kennel 48
Fincairn Gillian (Ch.) 48
Fincairn Silver Charm 48
Finlay, Mrs 48
Firring prefix
  champions 66
Firring Fionn (Ch.)
  influence of 66
Firring Fling 35, 65
  description of 65
  influence of 65–6
Firring Flora 27, 66
Firring Frolic (Ch.) 31, 39, 57, 65, 66
  description of 65
  influence of 65–6
first-aid/medicine kit 151–2
Fisher, Mr Alex 205
Fisherman Out of the West 74
Fleming, Mr 72–3
Fleming, Mrs Noney 81
Flett, Baillie 23–4
'flyer' 53
Foxgrove Venus 211
foxes, terriers for hunting 19, 20
'foxy outlook' 120
Forbes, Mrs 38
Foundation Sylvia 63, 203
Foster, Miss 48
Frimley kennel 34, 38–9

Garbutt, Mrs 47
General Championship Shows 118
Gesto (Ch.) 31, 37, 121
  description of 67

influence of 66–8
Geum Woffington (Ch.) 39
Gillie of Hyver (Ch.) 37, 41–2, 57
  influence of 71–2
Glasein 33
Glencairn Gillian (Ch.) 41
Glencairn Kirstie 41
Glenmacdhui Mohra (Ch.) 202
Glenmhor prefix 36, 42
Glenmhor Pride 76
Glenmhor Rascal 42
Gooch, Lady 44, 45
Granite 23
Gray-Buchanan, Misses 45
grooming 107ff.
  equipment 107
    cleanliness of 109
    for showing 116
  inspection before 108
  sequence for 108
    for showing 116
  washing 109
Group Championship Shows 118
Gunthorpe kennel 39–40, 62, 76
Guynach kennel 38
Guynach Eachunn (Ch.) 38

Hall, Madge and Dorothy 204
Hamilton, Ferelith 204
Hamilton, Miss Helen 203
Hamilton, Mrs Diana 46, 203–4, 209
Hamish of Seltirk 210
'Happidog' 152
Hard-haired Highland Terrier 22–3
  see also Skye Terrier
Harding, Mrs 204
Harris, Mr 26
Harris Kennel 33–4
Harviestoun prefix 34, 36, 37, 38, 61–
  2, 75–6
Harviestoun Brigand (Ch.) 39, 57, 75
Harviestoun Chieftain (Ch.) 57, 75
Harviestoun Forgie 39, 57, 76
Harviestoun Raider 39, 42, 57
  description of 76
  influence of 75–6
Hawke, Hon Miss M. 26, 28, 31, 34,
  61, 68, 121
Haywood Kennel 45
Haywood Dilly 45
Hazell, Mrs E. L. 206
head/skull 128, 129, 131

breed standard 122, 124–5
  American 199
  judging 136
heredity, laws of 52
Heyworth Rascal (Ch.) 23
Hillston kennel 47
Hispid of Hardings see Doughall Out
  of the West
history, early 19ff.
Hoyle, Mrs 44
Hubrich, Rosemary
  Lament of a Stud 92
Hunter, Mr Donald 35
Hyver kennel 34, 37, 38, 39, 72
  and Harviestoun line 76

Ian of Frimley (Ch.) 39
illnesses 150ff.
  Bordetella 150
  canine distemper 150
  canine parvovirus infection 150
  constipation 152
  dehydration 152–3
  diarrhoea 152–3
  ear trouble 108, 151
  from cats 151
  hard pad disease 150
  hepatitis 150
  kennel cough 150–1
    antibiotics for 151
    vaccines 150
  leptospirosis 150
  liver virus infection see hepatitis
  pancreatic deficiency 152
  parasites 94
    ear 151
    fleas 151
    internal 151
    worms 151
  skin diseases 151
    contagious 94
  temperature rise 152
  tummy upset 100
inoculation 105
  intra-nasal 150
interbreeding 25–6
  in Inverness kennel 36
  ruling on 25, 31–2
  with West Highland Whites 25–6
Intrac 150
Inverness kennel 36–7

Inverness Doran 36
Inverness Glenorlie 36
Irving, Miss 41

James VI and I 19
Jaquet, Mr E. W. 25
Johnson, Mr and Mrs 42
Jollee prefix 49
Jollee Gay Memory 49, 60
Jollee Gay Sprite 49
judges
    qualifications 139
    treatment of 117
judging 136ff.
    basis of sound 138
    checking dogs 137
    coat 138
    general appearance 138
    movement 137–8
    picking out 138
    procedure 136–8
    table examination 137

Keay, Mr J. 46
Kelly, Farquhar 21
Kennel Club
    American
        registration 149
    British 83
        and interbreeding 25, 31–2
        registration 148
        registration form 85–6
    Scottish 84
    selection of judges 139
    shows
        details 145, 148
        exemption 119
        types of 117–19
kennels starting 79ff.
    accommodation 79
        for visiting bitch 93
    buying/selecting stock 80, 81
        adult bitch 80, 81–2, 83
        guidelines for 80
    considerations 79
Kerr, Mr 75
Keycol kennel 42
Knipton kennel 37
Knipton Bundle 37
Knipton Buntylow 37
Knipton Careless 37
Knipton Gillie *see* Gillie of Hyver

Knipton Tibbie 37
Kyley Out of the West 72, 73, 81

Lady Gay of Frimley (Ch.) 39
Laughing Eyes (Ch.) 37
Lectade 153
legs/feet 128, *134*
    breed standard 123, 126
        American 199
    checking before grooming 108
    judging 137
    pads *135*
    trimming for showing 116
Leigh, Mrs 45
Leighton, Mr Robert 30, 31
    The Complete Book of the Dog 23, 27
Leslie, John 19
Leverton, Mrs 48
Lines and branches 54, 84, 108, 208
    B line 67
    champions 58
    D line 57, 65, 72
        champions 57
        subdivisions 57
    DGE 205
    DGS 201, 205, 210
    DR champion 208
    dominant *see* DGS
    G line 57, 76
        champions 76–7
        feminine equivalent 61–2
        root of 76
        subdivisions 57, 76–7
    GB champions 208, 210
    GR champions 210
    I line 58
        champions 58, 208, 210
    main male 56–8
    number of 55
    of post 1960 champions 201
    SD line 57–8, 74
        influence of 74
Ljekarnas 211
Lockwood, Miss L. 35, 73
Lockyers kennel 61
Lockyers Ian (Ch.) 34
Lofthouse Geryon of Mistyfell (Ch.)
    offspring 202
Longmore, Miss 49
Lottie of Frimley (Ch.) 39
Lowe, Mr Bruce 50, 51, 59
Lynwil Lady MacIan (Ch.) 48

Macdonald, A. 20–1
MacDonald, Mr John 20
Macdonalds of Waternish 20
Mackinnon of Kilbride 20
MacLeod, Captain M. 20, 21
MacLeod, Mr Simon 33
MacLeods of Drynoch 20
MacPherson, Mr Brester 71–2
MacSporran (Ch.) 70
  description of 70
  influence of 70
Maid of the Mist 33
Maisie of Harris (Ch.) 33
Markland, Mr 65, 66, 205
Marsh, Mrs Gay 204, 207
Marshall, Miss 49
mating
  best place for 95
  experienced bitch 94
  first 94–5
  free 94
  most important 206
  restraining the bitch 95
  the 'tie' 95–6
McCandlish, W. L. 138
McDonald, Mr J. 65
McJoe of Twobees (Ch.) 206
McKenzie, Mr Alex 40
McLennan, Mr D. 69–70, 71, 205
McLeod, Mrs Simon 69
McLeod of McLeod 28
McNeill, Mr C. 31
McRob of Frimley (Ch.) 39
measurements, comparative 140
'Mendalism' 51
Merrymeet Tathwell Therese (Ch.) 202
Michelcombe prefix 47
Michelcombe Fearless 47
Minx of D'Ornum 40
Mirrlees, Mrs 40, 60
Miss Rogue of Mercia (Ch.) 34
Mitzie of Zellah 206
Moccasin kennel 40
Moccasin Betsy (Ch.) 40
Moccasin Linda (Ch.) 40
Moccasin Mercy 40
monorchidism 96–7, 137
Moody Miss 49
Morgan, Miss 45
Morghan 26
mouth
  breed standard 122, 125

movement 123
Moyes, Mr 40

nails
  over-long 109–10
  trimming
    for showing 116
    puppies' 98
neck
  breed standard 122, 125–6
Nichols, Miss 47
Nicholson, Mr N. 26
Nisbet prefix 35
Nuzzle of Mercia (Ch.) 34

O' the Braes kennel 45
of the Shieling kennel 42–3
Offley Brimon 39
Open Show 118–19
Otford kennel 38, 43
Oudenarde prefix 46, 203–4
  founder sire 207
Out of the West kennel 40, 47, 72–4
  champions 73–4
  colour 73

Parker-Tucker, Mrs 204
  see also Longmore, Mrs
Payne Gallwey, Mrs 37
pedigrees
  of Carngowan kennel 71
  extended 56
  family side 58–9
  Scottish terriers in 75
  and starting a kennel 81
  studying for breeding 84
  system of 50–1
Pigott, Sir Paynton 23
Piuthara of Fair City 43
Pledwick kennel 48
points 120ff.
  breed standard 122, 125
    forequarters 131, *132*
    hindquarters 122, *134*
  comparison with West Highland
    White 128
  scale of 127
  size 120
  weight 120–1
    American standard 200
Poltalloch Terrier *see* West Highland
  White Terrier

popularity of breed 148–9
Porritt, Mr James 30
Prestbury Silverfyord (Ch.) 38
Price, Mr Harry 211
Prick-eared Skye Terrier 26
    first registered 67
Pritchard, Mrs 37–8
Puithara of Fair City 43
puppies
    accommodation for 112–13
    bones for 100
    buying for breeding 80
    dew claws 98
    handling 88–9
    indoor cleanliness 103
    inoculation 105, 150
    management 102–7
    nail trimming 98
    newborn 88
    number in litter 53
    regularity 103–4
    selling 149
    sex of 96
    sleeping arrangements 102, 103
        box 102
        wire cage 102–3
        bedding 103
    timing of birth 83
    training 102–7
        aggressive 107
        approaches to 104
        collar and lead 105–6
        purpose of 104–5
        shy 107
        vocabulary for 105
    weaning 99–100
        first stage 99
    worming 98–9

Raeburn Conas 57
Raitts Rannaich 60
Redstacks Lobelia 202
Redletter prefix 47, 203
Redletter Fincairn Frolic (Ch.) 48
Redletter Marjose (Ch.) 48
Redletter McBryan (Ch.) 201–2, 203,
        210
    influence of 207
Redletter McJoe (Ch.) 47
    influence of 206–7
Redletter McMurran (Ch.) 47, 210
Redletter Miss Muffet (Ch.) 49, 202

Redletter Twinlaw Seaspirit (Ch.) 210
registration
    conditions for 31
    of crosses 31–2
    early history 28–30
    first 26–7
    in 1910 27
    of litter 85–6
    separate 27
    of Short-haired Skyes 30
Relief Trust 211
Reoch, Miss 44, 76
Rhoda of Rossarden 48
Rhodes, Mrs 45
Rhosbridge kennel 49
Rhu kennel 46
Riskin of Rossarden 48
Robinson Crusoe of Courtrai (Ch.)
        210
Roger Rough 23
Rogie of Rossarden (Ch.) 48
Rogue of Mercia (Ch.) 34
Rona (Ch.) 35, 36
Ross, Mr Errington 42, 65, 66, 75, 205
Ross, Mr G. J. 31
Rossarden strain 204
Ross-shire kennel 38, 48
Ross-shire Glenara 38, 58
Ross-shire Old Gold 38
Ross-shire Warrior (Ch.) 36, 38, 58
'roughterrier' 24
Roy Mhor 26, 28
Rudland, Mrs 43
Ruffie of the Shieling (Ch.) 43
Rufus of Rhu (Ch.) 46, 48

Sammy of Keycol 42
Sanction Shows 119
Sandwith, Mr E. R. 30
'sandy' terrier 24
Saunders, Mrs 38, 43
Savlon 151
Scott, Lady Sophie 33, 65
Scottish Terrier 19, 22–3, 61
    Family No. 1 27
    measurements 24
        comparative 140
Sheila of Harris 31
Shinnel prefix 40, 60
Shinnel Simon (Ch.) 40
Shinnel Wistful (Ch.) 40
showing

equipment for 116
in the ring 117
main object of 114
preparation for 114ff.
    physical condition 116
    for table examination 114
responsibility of handler 117
stewards 117
shows
    championship 118
    exemption 119
    matches 119
    types of 118–19
    see also individual names
Silver Hawk Out of the West (Ch.) 34
Sine of Clanranald (Ch.) 210
skull *see* head/skull
Skye, Island of
    early kennels in 20–1
Skye Coffar 33
Skye Crofter (Ch.) 33, 34, 37, 69
    description of 69
    influence of 69
Skye Terrier 19, 22, 23
    registration of 28–9
Skye Terrier, Short-haired 21, 27–8
    in early shows 30
    measurements 24
        comparative 140
Small, Major and Mrs 204
Smallburn, Daisy 61
Splinter II 23, 27
Splinters of Twobees (Ch.) 34, 45, 47,
        57, 77–8, 205, 206
    direct descendants 77–8
    influence of 77–8
    pedigree 154–5
    sire of 43
Sporran (Ch.) 70
Sport of Zellah *see* Bonfire of Twobees
Spuch 59
Stephens, Mrs 39, 72
strains, oldest known 20
stress 100
'stripping' 109, 110
Summers, Mrs 48

tail 131, 133, *133*
    breed standard 123
        American 199
    'Gay' 133 *133*
    'Hound' 133, *133*

trimming 109
    for showing 116
teeth
    checking for tartar 109
    judging 136
'Telegony' 85
temperament 122
temperature, normal 151
Temple, Mrs 46
The Digger *see* Doughall Out of the
        West
Thistleclose prefix 45, 62–3
Thistleclose Rosette 62–3
Thompson, Mr Charles 36
Thomson, Mr P. C. 23
Thomson Gray, Mr D. J.
    The Dogs of Scotland 22
Tibbie of Harris (Ch.) 31, 33, 61
Tighru Fiona 31
Toptwig Tilden (Ch.) 204
Townley, Major 43–4, 206
toys 101
training
    for show ring 114ff.
        difficulties 115
    see also puppies
Trashurst kennel 43
Trashurst Chip (Ch.) 43, 45, 205–6
    description of 206
Trashurst Fan (Ch.) 43
Treblig prefix 41–2
Treblig Janet (Ch.) 41, 42, 47, 62
Turberville 19
Turfield Mystic Eyes (Ch.) 37
Turfield Smiling Eyes 37
Twobees kennel 45, 77–8
types 127ff.
    correct 129, *130*
    'Weed' 130, *131*
    wrong 129, *130*

Uiseag O' the Braes 45
Una of Keycol 42
Uniquecottage kennel 49, 204
Uniquecottage Blackgold (Ch.) 49
Uniquecottage Goldigger 49
Uniquecottage Sir Frolic (Ch.) 49

vaccination
    brood bitches 84
Valiant kennel 44, 76
Valiant Leaflet of Beechacre 41, 44

Valiant Rab (Ch.) 49, 59
Valiant Rob Roy of Rhosbridge (Ch.)
    44, 49, 59
Velora Prim and Proper 210
vermin, terriers for hunting 20
Viccar, Miss 34–5

Wales, Prince of 36
Wandering Willie of Toptwig (Ch.) 204
Warberry kennel 44
Warberry Frederick of Dalry (Ch.) 44
Ward, Miss 34
Weetabix 99
West Highland White Terrier 24–5
    'Chadwick' 34
    interbreeding with Cairn 25–6
    white puppies as 31
whelping

bedding for 88
box 86–7, *87*
place for 79, 86–8
'Whinstone' *see* Thomson Gray,
    Mr D. J.
Whinyon of Rossarden (Ch.) 48
Whitehead, Lieutenant-Colonel 38, 46,
    208
Wilson, Peggy 81, 209
Woodthorpe kennel 45–6
Woodthorpe Clansman (Ch.) 46
Woodthorpe Madcap (Ch.) 45
worming 98–9
    brood bitch 84

Yeend, Mrs 47
Yeendsdale strain 47–8, 207
Young, Colonel 34